Counter-Guerrilla
Operations

COUNTER-GUERRILLA OPERATIONS

The Philippine Experience

Napolean D. Valeriano
and
Charles T.R. Bohannan

Foreword by Kalev Sepp

PSI Classics of the Counterinsurgency Era

Praeger Security International
Westport, Connecticut • London

Library of Congress Cataloging-in-Publication Data

Valeriano, Napoleon D.
   Counter-guerrilla operations : the Philippine experience / Napolean D. Valeriano and
Charles T.R. Bohannan; Foreword by Kalev Sepp.
      p. cm. — (PSI Classics of the Counterinsurgency Era)
   Includes bibliographical references and index.
   ISBN 0–275–99265–9 (alk. paper)—ISBN 0–275–99266–7 (pbk : alk. paper)
1. Guerrilla warfare 2. Hukbong Mapagpalaya ng Bayan (Philippines).   I. Title   II. Series
U240.V3 1962   62022024

British Library Cataloguing in Publication Data is available.

Library of Congress Catalog Card Number: 62022024
ISBN: 0–275–99265–9
       0–275–99266–7 (pbk.)

First published in 1962

Praeger Security International, 88 Post Road West, Westport, CT 06881
An imprint of Greenwood Publishing Group, Inc.
www.praeger.com

Printed in the United States of America

The paper used in this book complies with the
Permanent Paper Standard issued by the National
Information Standards Organization (Z39.48–1984).

10 9 8 7 6 5 4 3 2 1

CONTENTS

CONTENTS

FOREWORD

It was the start of the age of the guerrilla, but almost no one realized it. The year was 1946 and crises loomed on the world stage. George Kennan dispatched his "long telegram" from Moscow that shaped thinking about the Cold War. Civil war resumed in China, after simmering while the Japanese interrupted the contest between communists and nationalists.

The Greek civil war also intensified in 1946, and President Harry Truman conferred with his cabinet on the consequences of abandoning that country to the communists. Turkey and Iran were threatened by the Soviet Union. And Prime Minister Winston Churchill grimly warned of an "iron curtain" descending in Europe between the forces of democracy and communism.

The events of 1946 also included atomic tests on Bikini Atoll that raised the possibility of conflicts that could bring an end to the human race. And the threat of World War III, which was expected to be similar to World War II with the added horror of nuclear weaponry, dominated military strategy. Yet another form of warfare was being widely practiced, insidious and subtle but just as threatening to the fragile post-war governments of the Free World.

Guerrilla warfare was not a novelty to those who studied World War II and the conflicts that led up to it. But with the end of the global conflict between armies and navies of sovereign nations, irregular forces—partisans, insurgents, and guerrillas—stood out in stark relief.

On the island of Luzon in 1946 one of the armed bands that had been formed deep in the mountains to resist the Japanese turned against the Filipino government. Almost eight years of civil war would follow before Manila put down the rebellion. It took the first half of the war to discover how to effectively fight the guerrillas and the remainder of the time to implement hard-learned political, military, economic, and social lessons needed to convince the local population to cast their lot with the legitimate government and forsake the Huk rebels.

The Huks formed one of the long-standing insurrectionist gangs that had coalesced into guerrilla units after the Japanese invasion of the Philippines in 1941. Luis Taruc, a Filipino of peasant stock, helped lead this mixed band of communists, socialists, intellectuals, politicians, and soldiers. They assumed a Tagalog name, *Hukbo Na Bayan Laban Sa Hapon* (literally, the People's Army [To Fight] Against Japan) and were popularly known as *Hukbalahap*.

General Douglas MacArthur, commander of Far Eastern Forces and son of the military governor of the Philippines at the time of the 1899-1901 insurrection, refused to arm the Huks during the Japanese occupation because of their communist sympathies. In turn, the Huks refused to cooperate with Allies or their sponsored guerrilla units. By mid-1944, U.S. advisors reported renegade Huks were fighting the Japanese as well as other Filipino resistance groups, and were robbing and killing their countrymen. At the end of World War II, Manila's relations with the Huks deteriorated even further. At demobilization negotiations, officials shunned the Huks and denied them the occupation-period "back pay" given to other Filipino guerrillas.

The post-war leadership of Philippine might have staved off the insurrection in 1946 by integrating representatives of the Huk minority into the newly established legislature. Instead, the new government jailed Taruc and his deputy on trumped-up war-crime charges, after their legitimate election to the national congress.

Taruc was eventually released, and he and other Huks literally fled to the hills, armed with weapons cached after the Japanese defeat. They reverted to their wartime organization, established an underground politburo in Manila, and reactivated their potent auxiliary force, renamed *Pambansang Kaisahan Ng Mga Magbubuked* or the National Peasant Union (PKM). It soon claimed half a million members, supporting some 10,000 to 20,000 armed Huks.

The National Peasant Union posed a serious threat to the traditional landowners who had exploited the tenured peasantry since before the Spanish colonization. The Huks seized on this deep-seated peasant grievance that had been the cause of their dissent before World War II, and held as their chief aim "land for the landless."

Manila's reaction was the "mailed fist" policy of President Manuel Roxas. The peasant population was caught between government ineptitude and brutal repression reminiscent of the Japanese occupation and Huk intimidation-through-terror, which generally benefited the Huks. The guerrillas changed their name to Hukbong Mapagpalaya Ng Bayan or People's Liberation Army. Between 1946 and 1950 most of central Luzon fell under their control, even becoming known as *Huklandia*.

The ineffective level of support being provided by the United States improved after the invasion of South Korea, when communist threats in Asia suddenly appeared real and powerful. Washington tripled aid to the Philippines and strengthened the U.S. military advisory group. In addition, the Central Intelligence Agency also dispatched an Air Force officer, Colonel Edward Lansdale, to advise the new Philippine Secretary of Defense, Ramon Magsaysay, who had been appointed at the insistence of the U.S. ambassador.

Magsaysay and Lansdale made an excellent team. In consultations on the poor socio-economic situation of the Filipino peasantry that fostered support of the Huk movement, they developed programs to redress injustices that fueled peasant support of the rebels. These were primarily keyed to a sophisticated psychological warfare campaign that identified various target audiences, particularly part-time or soft-core Huk supporters who could be proselytized to join the government side.

There were many facets of the overall counterinsurgency effort. Magsaysay reformed and professionalized the army. The government placed bounties on the heads of Huk leaders, gave rewards for surrendering firearms, and eliminated free-fire zones that often caused civilian casualties. The Ministry of Defense assigned judge advocate general lawyers as free counsels for peasants in filing court cases against wealthy landlords. Manila subsidized "ten-centavo telegrams" that could be sent by any citizen to report grievances directly to the government.

Another indirect action program designed to undermine Huk political objectives was the economic development corps (EDCOR), which was named for an element of the pre-war army corps of engineers. In contrast to British efforts in Malaya to resettle segments of the populace away from communists, the economic development corps resettled former guerrillas away from their base of support. Rather than punishing Huks, the Philippine government rehabilitated them. To redress grievances about inequality in land distribution, EDCOR usurped the Huk slogan of "land for the landless" to compete with the guerrilla's political agenda.

The civil affairs office of the Philippine army carefully managed national and local media as well as psychological warfare activities. As a result, the perception of the success of EDCOR exceeded the actual commitment of government resources and the number of people resettled. In a dramatic move in 1953, a resettlement camp was established in Taruc's home town of San Luis on Luzon. At this point, the Huks acknowledged the loss of their mass base. Dispirited, Taruc surrendered one year later, effectively ending the rebellion, and Magsaysay resigned as Secretary of Defense to devote himself land reform.

Korea eclipsed the success of the campaign against the Huks. Some analysis of the war appeared, such as *Lessons from the Huk Campaign in the Philippines* by Uldarico Baclagon in 1956, which focused on army operations and was only published locally in Manila. An article entitled "The Philippine Anti-Communist Campaign" by Tomas Tirona in 1954 appeared in the United States in the *Air University Quarterly Review,* not in an Army or Marine Corps journal. But it was not until eight years after the defeat of the Huks that two veterans of the conflict, one Filipino and the other American, would produce a definitive study of the conflict.

First published in 1962, the now-classic *Counter-Guerrilla Operations: The Philippine Experience* is the result of collaboration by Colonel Napoleon D. Valeriano, Philippine Army, and Lieutenant Colonel Charles T. R. Bohannan, U.S. Army. Their first-hand knowledge gained in fighting against the Huks in the *bundocs* (that is, the "boondocks" or mountains of Luzon) is evident in the tone and detail of their book. As soldiers, their language is practical, direct, and unambiguous. Their credibility is enhanced by the candor with which they admit mistakes and failed efforts as well as reveal proven, viable procedures. Throughout, they connect the tactical to the strategic, the conceptual to the practical, and never let the reader lose sight of the central characters in a civil war, especially the guerrilla.

Counter-Guerrilla Operations might have had more impact on U.S. counterinsurgency doctrine, and on the military and political strategy coalescing in Vietnam, if it were not for the timing of its publication. As the Korean War masked the Filipino victory over the Huks in 1953, the British success against the communists in Malaya in 1960 and intensifying conflict in South Vietnam drew attention from other events. This work by Valeriano and Bohannan seemed dated and less relevant, which was unfortunate. In a time of global turmoil, in the age of the guerrilla, what could have been more useful than analysis of how a nascent democracy reformed its army and police, rallied its people, and changed its policies to defeat an insurgency.

In the 21st century these lessons remain important. And they always will be.

Kalev I. Sepp
May 2006

Dr. Kalev I. Sepp is an assistant professor in the Graduate School of Operational and Information Sciences at the Naval Postgraduate School and the coauthor of *Weapon of Choice: U.S. Army Special Operations in Afghanistan.*

PROLOGUE

Minamahal kong Magbabasa:

Many thousands of men, and not a few women, have fought in the Philippines, often on both sides in the same war, for what they have believed to be the cause of freedom and democracy. We seek here to present some of their experiences and some of the conclusions that can be drawn from them. The result is neither scholarly history of the Philippine experience nor doctrine on how to fight guerrillas, but may, we hope, assist in achieving an understanding of both.

Guerrilla warfare in the Philippines extends far back into the dim mists of prehistory. In the last sixty-five years, out of guerrilla and counterguerrilla war, and out of the wise and the unwise acts of civil and military administrations, have come situations unique in modern history:

a. Only in the Philippines have conquerors of another race succeeded in quelling a nationwide indigenous rebellion while so winning the trust and respect of the conquered that, in less than forty years,

b. Only in the Philippines, of all the "new" nations, did the Japanese in World War II find themselves opposed by a massive popular guerrilla movement (and one that loudly proclaimed its allegiance to the former "colonial" power); and

c. Only in the Philippines has an elected indigenous government using only indigenous troops succeeded in liquidating a major Communist guerrilla movement. More remarkable, this was accomplished without massive external assistance and without suspension of elections.

These accomplishments were not accidents. Neither were they the result of careful planning. Least of all, we believe, were they the result of any unique inherent characteristics of the countries or the peoples involved. They were the result of the sometimes thoughtful, sometimes unthinking, manifestations of a creed of human relations, of a concept of the proper relationship between government and governed—a concept on the whole effectively expressed in civil and military action.

Where guerrilla or counterguerrilla action succeeded in eliminating more than the gross outward manifestations of opposition, it succeeded because it was an effective implementation of acceptable concepts of government-to-people relations. Failures in such action can be attributed to failures to equal the opponent in establishing or implementing acceptable concepts of the proper relationship between government and governed. Is this not true everywhere?

The importance of successful guerrilla and counterguerrilla action is steadily increasing. The forces unleashed by the splitting atom and the forces of Communist imperialism alike proclaim it. In contacts with the military and civilian circles that have recently developed interest in counterguerrilla operations, we have been surprised to learn how little is known about the Philippine experience. We have been appalled by the misunderstanding of the reasons for successes, and of the causes of failures.

The free world urgently needs to achieve a better understanding of the principles and practices of successful counterguerrilla operations. We have tried to set down here matters that will assist in achieving such understanding. We have selected incidents that we believe illustrate basic principles, and we have discussed conclusions drawn from many others. We have relied largely on our memories, so we cannot guarantee complete accuracy in all details. We regret our inability to give adequate representation to many fine units and gallant soldiers who have participated in military actions or to many public-spirited organizations and devoted civilians who have participated in equally important civic actions. To do so would require many volumes and many years.

We have sought objectivity, but we cannot claim to have achieved it. The views of every man are inevitably colored by his experience, his background, his personal frame of reference. Our views owe as much to Kentucky hill farms where the liquefied corn crop was hauled away on dry-land sleds, and to Philippine *Kaingins* where a scanty crop is made among the tree stumps, as they do to the sanitized, deodorized, chrome-and-enamel culture some Americans and some Filipinos think should be the goal of human effort. They owe more, perhaps, to discussions around guerrilla campfires and the tales of old soldiers than to the bull sessions or the formal lectures at military and civilian educational institutions.

Above all, our views are an outgrowth of, are our heritage from, the extraordinary Fil-American relationship begun in a Hong Kong consular office, forged into an unforgettable partnership after an ill-starred fratricidal strife of sixty years ago that proved to each protagonist the worth of the other, and finally tempered on Bataan and a thousand guerrilla battlefields. It was those years that made clear the necessity for demonstrating to the governed the good intentions and effectiveness of the government and its representatives, made clear the basic strategy of counterguerrilla success. So strongly does this relationship between Filipino and American hold that it contributed greatly to the success of operations against the Hukbalahap; so strongly does it bind both the writers that each has chosen to spend his retirement in the birth land of the other.

It is fitting that we sign this letter on 12 June, the date that has been chosen for celebration of Philippine independence. On this date, the Philippines declared their intention to follow the path of individual freedom and government for the governed, a path in which they were faithfully guided until the much less significant date of 4 July 1946, when they accepted titular as well as actual responsibility for their own destiny.

NAPOLEON D. VALERIANO
CHARLES T. R. BOHANNAN
Washington, D.C.
12 June 1962

Chapter 1

WHAT AND WHY IS A GUERRILLA?

YOU MAY be killed by a guerrilla. You may die fighting as a guerrilla. A guerrilla is a man who will fight without the backing of an organized society, who will risk death for his beliefs or his comrades. If the guerrilla does not meet an enemy who has an equally firm commitment to victory, who has equal dedication, equal will to persevere in a sustained, relentless, and usually very unpleasant effort against seemingly insuperable odds, the guerrilla will win.

The guerrilla must be thoroughly understood if he is to be defeated. His reasons for being, his goals, his ways of seeking to achieve his goals must be understood. The guerrilla goes by devious routes, part civil, part military, all political in the broadest sense of the term. He must be met by men and by a government equally determined and equally skilled in the use of civil and military means, if the cause they represent is not to be irreparably damaged or destroyed by the guerrilla.

Guerrilla and counterguerrilla warfare are "irregular warfare." Perhaps a better term would be "irregular political activity," since they represent a contest, a relationship between individuals that touches on every sphere, every form of human relations. There is an infinity of seemingly applicable terms.

Probably no areas of military thought and practice are so plagued with semantic and definitional difficulties (and misconceptions) as are the two closely allied fields of irregular and psychological warfare. It is natural that this should be so, for of all the ways of acting against an enemy, these two fields of warfare appear most properly to belong to the social sciences. More often than not, the practitioner in these fields has never formally studied the social sciences, indeed he is probably fortunate if he has not, since he is neither tempted to apply the highly stylized jargon of the student, nor unduly concerned with finespun theories imperfectly understood. Student or not, in these two fields of the military art, the practitioner and theoretician alike find extreme difficulty in communicating intelligibly and precisely with others unless each individual first defines what he means by the terms he employs.

Guerrilla literally means "small war"; the man who participates in waging such a war is properly called a *guerrillero.* The terms first came to English from the exploits of the Spanish irregulars and civilians who so fearsomely harassed the troops of Napoleon while he was trying to expel the English from Spain. The ferocity of this harassment, and the gruesome retaliatory measures taken by the French, were powerfully illustrated by Goya in a series of etchings entitled "The Disasters of War" (*"Los Desastres de la Guerra").* The impact of these pictures is enough to explain why the term "guerrilla" was adopted to describe particularly the acts and actors of a people's resistance to an invading enemy.

"Small war" is perhaps a better term; it does not have the connotations either of the Spanish term "guerrilla" or of the same term as most recently used for the current fighting in Vietnam. Nevertheless, the term "small war" seems to have fallen into desuetude and the term "guerrilla warfare" has taken its place.

By contemporary usage, too, the term "guerrilla" has come to refer to the man who makes the small war, the protagonist on whose account the war is small and unconventional rather than large and orthodox. Say "guerrilla" today, and you conjure up the picture of the little man with the ragged clothes, carrying his simple, perhaps homemade, weapons, the people's hero whom much larger forces of well-trained, well-equipped "regular" soldiery seek almost in vain to run down, capture, or kill.

He is the essence of individuality, in a state-ridden, automation threatened world; the hunted man whose lonely courage appeals deeply to the outsider— particularly to the nostalgic sophisticate in his armchair, denied physical challenge and the romantic ideal of "the frontier." This small Robinson Crusoe with his homemade weapons becomes even more appealing when he evades the juggernaut, the trained army supported by the legitimate government.

It is not a picture arrived at accidentally. For thirty years, the Communists have been painting this canvas: the "agrarian reformer" nobly fighting for the "people's rights" against corrupt officials supported by evil property owners. It has saved the Communists untold millions of dollars, it has cost untold millions dead, this Communist picture of the guerrilla.

The term "guerrilla" is loosely used in almost all the literature on the subject. Sometimes it is used to refer to untrained, disorganized, indigenous forces; sometimes to identify members of regular military establishments operating without the benefits of regular supply lines or conventional tactics. Again, it has been applied to bandit gangs, just as the term "bandit" is sometimes applied to idealistic guerrillas by their detractors.

Accordingly, it appears appropriate to open a work on counterguerrilla operations by defining what is meant by "guerrilla"—although no definition can possibly cover all the connotations of the word or be in agreement with all the points of view held by participants in guerrilla or counterguerrilla operations. (The term "insurgent," recently adopted for official U.S. use, is even more confusing in its connotations.)

A guerrilla may be defined as an individual or a movement relying on the support of the people, fighting the government administering his (their) country for an ideal believed not otherwise attainable; and avoiding combat except under circumstances of his (their) own choosing. Guerrilla warfare is characterized by maximum employment of deception, concealment, intelligence, and improvisation; by surprise attacks and quick withdrawals; above all, by the avoidance of open tests of strength with the enemy unless success is assured. The guerrilla usually lacks the logistic capability, the training, and the time for unhindered preparation, for so-called conventional or regular war.

Mao Tse-tung has said that "the guerrilla must move among the people as a fish moves in the sea." Add to this that the fish draws his support largely from the voluntary contributions of the sea and is without the support of an organized government in his country, and one has a fair understanding of the guerrilla.

Quasi guerrillas may be defined as members of a regularly established military force of a substantive government, assigned, volunteered, or required by force of circumstances to take up a guerrilla-like role. History is replete with examples of quasi guerrillas. Perhaps the earliest quasi guerrillas in American history were men of the early Virginia colonials who used guerrilla tactics while engaged in actions against the Indians. The Civil War produced many examples: Mosby and John Morgan were both typical quasi guerrillas.

Probably such forces of World War II as Wingate's Chindits and Merrill's Marauders should be included in this category, perhaps as a subclass. Certainly the quasi guerrilla plays an important role in modem warfare, a role that seems destined to become even more important. Quasi guerrillas, with civilian auxiliaries, may well be the "conventional" ground combat forces of the future, once the devastating impact nuclear weapons can have on the conventional forces of today is understood.

To continue Mao's analogy, the quasi guerrilla might be likened to a submarine, moving freely in the sea, but drawing motive power, and much, if not most, logistic support, from an outside force—most often the government of a country other than that in which he operates.

Bandits are persons or groups, usually in a rural setting, who seek their livelihood by theft and extortion. Some, with more or less justification, claim political philosophy or desperation as a motive. They fight only when it is essential for personal gain or for survival; they look for popular support from the impressionable, or they demand it by bribery and/or intimidation.

In some of the bandit plagues that exist today, as in Colombia, small gangs (many of them ex-guerrillas) still seek shelter under the honored term guerrilla. Actually they are little more than "protection squads," which exist primarily to further the unlawful commercial interests that were established by politicians and businessmen at the time of the major (and true) guerrilla troubles. (The situation in Colombia is, of course, complicated by the existence of Communist guerrilla forces, temporarily quiescent.)

There is some dispute between the romantically minded and the practically minded as to whether such persons as Robin Hood and his Merry Men should be called guerrillas or bandits. Certainly, such Robin Hoods—if one examines the long history of banditry in Italy or in China—become in retrospect the outward indications of deep national disturbances. Similar national disturbances have been, and will be, exploited by Communists or other skilled technicians and made the bases for substantial guerrilla movements. But bandits are not guerrillas.

To carry on Mao's analogy, bandits might be likened to sharks preying on their fellow denizens of the sea, sometimes allowing small fish to snap up the unconsidered morsels.

There is a fourth category that should be considered: the mob and its members. Mobs are by no means solely an urban institution. The *Jacqueries* against individual "lords of the manor" by which villeins and serfs sought redress of wrongs in post-Renaissance France typify the rural mobs. Conan Doyle in "The White Company" gives a description of a mob that is as unforgettable as the photographs in *Life* magazine showing Communist-led urban mobs assailing Vice President Nixon.

In some parts of the world, mob actions are almost an accepted means of forcing the redress of wrongs that, for one reason or another, cannot be requited by legal means. In the past, mobs were often born on the spur of the moment, because of a single, final provocation (the last straw that broke the camel's back) and had a single objective—the death of a particular individual, the destruction of the Bastille. More recently, they have often been manipulated into instruments of mass destruction over a period of limited duration (as the Nazis were, or Mussolini's Fascists). The mobs that raged in Bogotá after the assassination of Jorge Eliécer Gaitáin, the famous Bogotazo, are an example.

Mao's analogy can scarcely be stretched to cover the mob unless it be likened to a tidal wave, a sudden upsurge of a portion of the ocean, wreaking destruction and quickly subsiding. But as a tidal wave may alter the shoreline it strikes, so the mob can effect an irreversible change in the body politic as enormous as that which followed the fall of the Bastille.

All these forces have some things in common. All, except the mob, operate primarily in rural areas. All, except the mob, require a high proportion of self-reliant individuals among their personnel. Often, they are deficient in organized support and in equipment—at least as compared with the forces opposing them. Finally, all, except the mob, are usually numerically inferior to the forces that seek to oppose and eliminate them.

Why then attempt to classify or define the various kinds of protest by violence? The immediate answer is that only by determining the true character of the opponent can one arrive at certain general conclusions as to his strength and weaknesses. There is some validity to this answer, particularly if one expands it by saying that classification may indicate where the movement in question will be most vulnerable to attack, or where the attack must be aimed if the movement is to be extirpated.

This answer is substantially correct, but it is dangerously deceptive. It may lead to the same disastrous self-confidence as that felt by the military man who knows nothing of guerrilla warfare when he hears that his splendidly trained and equipped troops are facing a guerrilla force one-quarter their number, poorly armed, short of ammunition, rations, field equipment, communications, and without a single motor vehicle.

Determining the character of the enemy as guerrilla, quasi guerrilla, bandit, or mob is only the first step, and determining the generic weakness of his class is only the second. More important is identifying the weaknesses in the government he opposes. The existence of a viable guerrilla movement indicates a serious weakness in the political base of government—or the lack of a political base in the country. Identification of a guerrilla movement not confined to an ethnic minority is a major signal that something is seriously wrong, especially when the government attacked rests on a political base within the country.

Identification of a quasi guerrilla movement today signals the desire of an external power to overthrow the government. This may or may not be a surprise, or significant, but any continued existence of the quasi guerrilla indicates a weakness in internal defenses. It also suggests that all is not well with the political base of government.

The bandit and the mob indicate weaknesses in internal defenses and somewhere in the economic, legal, or social structures. How significant these weaknesses may be is not a matter susceptible to a prior determination. Their identification and possible correction should be given early attention, since such weaknesses may well result in erosion of the political base—or signal its lack of breadth and stability.

There is almost as much theoretical discussion about the causes of guerrilla movements as there is about the causes of crime. The search for first causes often seems likely to be of little immediate value to the people concerned with quelling a rebellion. The substance of current theory appears to be that guerrilla movements may arise wherever there are social tensions, strong individual anxieties and/or frustrations, and unsatisfactory or inept government leadership.

Given an ideal and a spokesman who can relate this ideal to the ambitions, the needs, or the frustrations of the people; given agitators who urge that the ideal cannot be attained without fighting for it; given provocateurs who create incidents generating repressive measures; given a sufficient number of believers, and the prerequisites for a guerrilla movement have been met.

Whether or not the guerrilla movement will be viable—or successful— depends largely on the art with which proponents and opponents will act. Skill in the tactics of counterguerrilla warfare and in exploitation of the physical and cultural environment may temporarily defeat the movement, but can never eliminate it so long as a substantial number believe in the validity of their cause and feel that it can be achieved only by fighting.

The motives of all members of a guerrilla movement, or of its leaders, need not be wholly idealistic or even socially desirable. The once-thriving guerrilla movement of a certain Papa Rios in the province of Batangas, on Luzon, well illustrates this. It sprang up in the first years of this century, when memories of the unsuccessful bid for independence still smoldered among many Filipinos. Rios, with motives readily to be deduced from his propaganda line, "discovered" a black box in which, he said, independence was locked away.

Papa Rios appointed himself "pope" of an armed pseudo-guerrilla movement which he described as a crusade to drive the Americans away from the islands in order that independence might be released from the box. Of course, "independence" had to be related to the expectations and grievances of his prospective recruits and supporters.

"When independence comes out, there will be no more taxes, no more work, and no more jails," he told his supporters. Truly a cause worth fighting for! Eventually, men of the Constabulary captured the box, publicly opened it, and showed that it held no independence.

Having lost the confidence of his supporters, Papa Rios was soon captured, tried for murders committed during the course of his operations, and eventually hanged.

At heart, of course, Papa Rios was hardly more than a bandit—but he was a bandit with an effective sales pitch; so are many guerrillas and so are many of their followers. Note, however, that Papa Rios had called on men to fight not for their personal gain but for an ideal. True, it was an ideal by which they would profit and it was an ideal reduced to its simplest terms—but it was expressed in terms of ambitions and hopes readily aroused in the only class of persons whose support he could hope to win. The Communist appeal not infrequently is expressed in just such terms to just such an audience.

At almost the opposite end of the scale of guerrilla movements was the Philippine national resistance to the Japanese occupation. This began even before the occupation was completed—in fact, before most Filipinos had seen a Japanese soldier, and while most Filipinos still believed that the defenders of Bataan and Corregidor would be reinforced and take the offensive.

Most of the leaders of the Philippine resistance had either military or government service and training; most sought to form at least semiregular military and civilian institutions. On Leyte, when the Americans came in, schools had been reopened and a newspaper was again being published. Nevertheless, it was a true guerrilla movement. There was some encouragement—and eventually a small trickle of supplies—from outside; but the movement was basically indigenous, as was the vast majority of its support.

The motive of the anti-Japanese guerrilla was overwhelmingly idealistic: Loyalty to country and loyalty to the concept of democracy were inextricably intertwined. This loyalty was reinforced in many ways, ranging from fear of death at the hands of a playful or annoyed Japanese soldier to desire to regain a former position of authority. Some leaders and some men were bandits at heart, just as others were impractical Utopians, but the basic motivations of the movement, its members and supporters, were well expressed in the chorus of a favorite song of the Leyte guerrillas:

Come and fight for the Philippines,
Come and fight for Uncle Sam,
Come and fight for Democracy . . .
Come and fi—i—ight!

What of the motivations of the individual guerrilla? Are they necessarily purely idealistic or purely selfish? By no means; they vary as widely as human motivations ever can; they may be so complex that an analysis would peel away layer after layer, until there would seem to be no recognizable basic motivation.

Field evaluations in such an "iffy" topic as the search for motives vary with the attitudes, biases, and perceptiveness of the evaluator. There does seem, however, to be a definite utility in classification of motivation as: personal devotion to, or hatred for, a cause; social pressure; compulsion (conscription by guerrillas); fear of an established authority; adventurousness; ambition—hope of personal gain. Frequently, perhaps most often among leaders, these motivations may have grown out of a feeling of frustration, which may or may not be a dominant characteristic of the individual. One driven principally by his frustrations, however, is not likely to last long as a guerrilla.

An individual will initially join the guerrillas because of any one or any combination of these motives. Continuance may result from the same motives or may—and perhaps most often does—result from a modification of the original reason. The adventurer will usually get a bellyful of hardships, but may remain in the field because he fears punishment from the authorities. The would-be looter may find the pickings too slim—but like the adventurer, he may fear the constituted authorities. Ideals of patriotism or service to mankind may fade when the belly is growling for food and the back shivering in the rain, but the idealist continues because he cannot show himself less enduring, less determined, than his comrades. The conscript may catch fire with ideals of service, or with lust for loot, or he may remain a guerrilla only so long as he sees no way out. And for some, the very routine of comradely outlawry can become a habit and a way of life.

It is important for the counterguerrilla operator to understand the motivations of his opponents—to seek to determine their proportionate representation and weight. The proper appeal to a conscript may result in his eliminating a leader, followed by his own surrender; a similar appeal to a patriot or a conformist may bring only increased contempt for the forces and motivations of the government.

Understanding of motivations and how they may be modified, aroused, or suppressed is as important as understanding that all other motivations tend to pale when the basic drives for food, rest, and shelter are too long denied satisfaction. It is even more important to understand that these more basic drives seldom take lasting control of a certain percentage of people, but may contribute to the acceptance by this group of less than complete satisfaction of all the demands which impelled them at the outset.

An ideal attainable only by fighting the existing government—and one that seems worth such a fight—is the essential requirement and the distinguishing characteristic of that war of the weak against the strong which is called guerrilla. Usually the ideal is one of government (whether in form, in practices, or in individuals), an ideal that is set in sharp contrast, by real or fancied grievances, against the existing government. The movement may be strengthened by external sympathizers and support; it may be weakened by too much reliance on external support.

The quasi guerrilla, on the other hand, counts largely on external support; is, in fact, often a manifestation of the interests of forces outside the area of operations. The quasi-guerrilla movement may take on the characteristics of a true guerrilla movement as it generates local support. Until it does, the channels of external support will usually remain its weakest point. Cut off this support and the movement is likely to die. This may well be the easiest way to end the quasi-guerrilla menace—if it has been accurately characterized. However, it is dangerous to rely solely on this method, for the quasi guerrilla, if he has begun to win significant popular support, may thrive and multiply even while his external roots are being attenuated.

As an individual, the quasi guerrilla will be motivated by very much the same forces as the true guerrilla, but the forces will be represented in different proportions in a group. The pressure of the military society to which he belongs may well be his major motivation at the time the group goes "underground." The nature, sanctions, and effects of this social pressure will change rapidly after the soldier has become a "guerrilla," and new pressures will be added.

One of the more significant of these new pressures will be his evaluation of his place in the plans of his sponsors. If he feels that he is a cheap and expendable tool, his effectiveness and value will be small. If, on the other hand, he feels that he represents a laudable conservation of energy and resources, that he personally has been honored with an opportunity to be of far greater service than most other soldiers, his determination and effectiveness may be as great as those of any true guerrilla, and greater than those of his opponents.

The shifts in pressures, the often greater frustration of basic drives, and the changes in values that occur when the soldier becomes a guerrilla may make proffered, or selfish, substitute motivations more effective. It is at this point that the great importance of careful selection of individuals for the quasi-guerrilla role becomes apparent. Dedicated volunteers with positive motivations will withstand these pressures better than most guerrillas, who are often moved by their frustrations. If selected at random, or lacking positive motivation, a quasi guerrilla under continuing physical and psychological pressures is far more likely to surrender, or to die unprofitably, than is the true guerrilla.

Bandits who behave like guerrillas offer an interestingly different problem. As individuals, they can be said to act from substantially the same motivations as a guerrilla or quasi guerrilla—but with bandits, practically all alleged motivations can be distilled down to a search for the easiest way out. In other words, their motivations are in general much closer to their basic drives, hence the individuals are much more readily accessible in terms of those drives.

The key to the banditry problem, often, perhaps usually, lies in identifying and/or neutralizing those apparently law-abiding citizens who profit by the banditry. Make banditry unprofitable for the solid citizens, the paragons of respectability whose pockets it so often lines; offer the bandits a better route to satisfaction of their basic drives; and the problem can be solved.

Essentially, a guerrilla is one of a group of men of varying motivations and desires, bound together to achieve objectives, to realize an ideal, using force against great odds and collectively exhibiting a determination to achieve at least a measure of success against these odds. Usually they operate in remote rural areas, but sometimes they are exclusively in big cities. By any realistic standards, by any evaluation of motivation in terms of basic drives, by any assessment of material resources, facilities, organization, or training, the guerrillas have no chance of victory and scarcely any chance of survival. They do survive, quite illogically and quite irrationally; and frequently they attain at least qualified success.

Chapter 2

CHARACTERISTICS OF GUERRILLA MOVEMENTS AND OPERATIONS

"THE RELATIONSHIP that should exist between the people and the troops. . . . The former may be likened to water, and the latter to the fish who inhabit it. How may it be said that these two cannot exist together?"

—*Mao Tse-tung on Guerrilla Warfare*

"The people are to the army [the guerrillas] what water is to fish."

—VO NGUYÊN GIAP, *People's War, People's Army*

This is the central, the essential, the ineluctable characteristic of guerrilla warfare. If it may be said that "without vision the people perish," it may equally be said that without people the guerrillas perish.

All guerrilla movements have many characteristics in common—just as each has its virtually unique features. The similarities and the dissimilarities owe far more to human similarities and differences than to the physical environment. It is difficult to determine which is the more dangerous and expensive error for the counterguerrilla operator—failure to recognize the characteristics common to most or all guerrilla movements, or failure to recognize those that are virtually unique to the movement it is his duty to oppose.

There is always a tendency to treat each guerrilla problem as though it were a new phenomenon—a *lusus naturae*. This is especially tempting to the well-trained, knowledgeable staff officer or senior commander without prior experience in guerrilla warfare. He knows that his forces are so much better equipped, better trained, better fed, better treated, and better paid that at first glance it seems utter folly for the guerrilla to challenge him. Since he is unwilling to fall into the obvious trap of thinking his enemy a fool, this orthodox soldier will believe that there must be, and will seek, the apparently missing factor, the secret weapon, the new tactic, the concealed support, which makes this operation new and different. While searching for it, he may well irrevocably lose the initiative to the audacious, not to say impudent, guerrilla who does not believe that victory is necessarily to the heaviest artillery.

The numerous similarities that may exist among guerrilla movements must be appreciated if the basic routes of attack on guerrilla movements are to be readily apparent. Movements based on a common ideology, whether it be Communism or Hamiltonian democracy, will certainly have many features in common. Similarities will be particularly striking among movements based on aggressively evangelical ideologies, especially if they actively seek to encourage and propagate guerrilla warfare. The lessons learned from one Communist guerrilla movement will have many applications to other Communist movements, especially in strategy and tactics.

Too much reliance on these similarities, too much reliance on a particular Communist movement adhering to accepted Communist doctrine can be fatal, however. Had Castro followed the doctrines of Mao Tse-tung and Vo Nguyên Giap, he would still have been a guerrilla rebel on April 17, 1961, busily converting his forces into conventional armies that could eventually fight a conventional battle against the conventional forces of the Batista government. Instead, he bypassed the stages of conventional warfare, effecting a national revolution by erosion of the political base and by political rather than military defeat of the armed forces opposing him.

Similarities in climate, terrain, religion, culture can produce similarities in guerrilla tactics and strategy. So can the attitudes of external powers, whether favorable to or opposing the guerrilla. Assumptions based on similarities or dissimilarities are often most appealing but they can be most treacherous. The similarities between Laos and Vietnam, for example, are so great that one may be forgiven for having concluded in 1955 that Laos, having the advantage of an indubitably securely ensconced chief of state, was much more safe from Communist attack than Vietnam.

Despite the dangers of possible misinterpretation, an appreciation of the problems and characteristics all guerrilla movements share is essential to understanding the problem of counterguerrilla operations. Some characteristics of a guerrilla movement are so closely linked to its success or failure that they may properly be called imperatives, which must be met or the movement is foredoomed. Recognizing these imperatives will reveal profitable targets to the counterguerrilla forces, targets often far more profitable and far less costly than the physical target presented by the guerrilla himself.

Viable guerrilla movements usually arise in one of two ways:

1. Remnants of a defeated national army ally themselves with indignant civilians to carry on the war against the occupying power;

2. Organizations whose ideologies oppose the existing government, deliberately or under pressure from the government, adopt the "armed struggle."

Like any human effort, a guerrilla movement requires organization if it is to live and win more than transient success. Guerrilla movements of the first category (spontaneous resistance to an occupying power) frequently lack effective organization at their beginning. Conceivably, prompt action in isolating groups, picking up leaders, etc., can prevent or long delay their effective organization.

Even more vulnerable are those organizations that are formed before the adoption of the armed struggle. These organizations, typically Communist dominated, work long and arduously to prepare the ground for revolution. An alert government should be able to recognize this preparation and to take the necessary measures to eliminate the organization. Governments often fail to act at this stage, fearing political repercussions, and being unwilling or unable to take the necessary political actions to preclude effective political reactions. These other actions may include parliamentary logrolling and similar maneuvers, as well as careful election assistance.

Organization may be regarded as the first imperative of a guerrilla movement, since it is essential for the success of any but a mob-type revolution, even though it may not precede guerrilla actions.

The second imperative for a viable guerrilla movement is a cause. The more closely this cause is allied to the religious, social, political, and personal aspirations of the society from which the movement seeks support, the more support the movement can muster. Paradoxically, in many instances, the more concrete the objectives of the guerrilla, the more easily he can be defeated. So long as the cause remains an ideal, a not too sharply defined concept, it may be difficult to rally support, but even more difficult to engender opposition to it. Who can oppose the ideals of home, country, and early motherhood?

A cause, the achievement of which is easily and factually discernible, is a two-edged sword; its proponents lose or win, with little chance to obscure the actuality. If the goal is one the opposition cannot effectively pretend to support (by removing its forces, ending its occupation) it is one the counterguerrilla forces will be forced to meet by indirection. If the cause of the guerrilla is one the counterguerrilla can seem to adopt, or make more readily obtainable to the citizens by their cooperation with the government, it is not a good one for the guerrilla. If the government can, and does, give what the guerrilla only promises, the guerrilla loses his announced reason for being.

The third imperative for a viable guerrilla movement is obtaining minimum essential food and shelter without devoting full time to this occupation. Guerrillas *can* live in uninhabited areas if they can grow their own food, but they can be effective only if they can simultaneously have time left over for operations against their enemy.

Normally, fighting forces of a guerrilla movement must rely on civilian supporters for their food. Sometimes the food is voluntarily given; sometimes payment is expected. Often much, if not most, is obtained through a form of taxation implemented by the "shadow government" composed of active civilian supporters of the guerrilla movement. (In turn, for this to be effective, the guerrillas must appear to support the shadow government whose service gives their actions at least a pretext of legality.)

The fourth imperative for a viable guerrilla movement—and it is really the most important of all—is to gain and maintain either active support or passive toleration from a majority of the people in the area of operations. Excluding those grass-fire *(niñgas cogon)* movements where an entire area or community is swept for a brief period by a sort of mass hysteria (really extended mob action), residents of an area of guerrilla operations usually fall into three categories: (1) those actively supporting the guerrillas; (2) those actively opposing the guerrillas; and (3) those neither supporting nor opposing the guerrillas (often by far the largest group). Unless Group 1 is as large as Group 2, and unless Groups 1 and 3 together heavily outnumber Group 2, it is doubtful if the guerrilla movement can long continue to exist. Certainly it cannot be effective, cannot offer an active threat to established government if it does not have approximately this degree of popular support—or at least benevolent neutrality.

The fifth imperative of a viable guerrilla movement is visible action against the enemy. This action need not be significant in terms of over-all defeat or victory; it may well result in greater hardships for the supporters of the movement and for "innocent bystanders"; but it must be productive of visible results, even though these be no more than one or two enemy dead. Something tangible must be done from time to time to convince supporters and individual guerrillas alike that the movement is effective, is contributing to the achievement of the goal. These actions may be, often are, defensive reactions to fights forced by the counterguerrilla, but they must show enemy casualties; they cannot always be silent retreats to avoid actual combat.

The sixth basic imperative is hope. Characteristically and typically, it is hope for ultimate achievement of the long-range objective of the movement. Occasionally (atypically for a true guerrilla movement, much more often true for quasi guerrillas or bandits), it is hope for a short-range, essentially selfish accomplishment, such as living for a while longer. Hope must be sustained, no matter how, or the movement dies.

These six imperatives, plus the conditions that dictate a resort to guerrilla rather than political or conventional military action, give guerrilla movements their distinctive characteristics. The conditions that cause guerrilla warfare might be summarized as conditions of inferiority to the enemy in almost everything tangible, but an assumed superiority in ideals and determination. As a result, the guerrilla habitually must:

Fight only at times and places of his own choosing.

Develop comprehensive intelligence and counterintelligence screens.

Rely generally on decentralized command.

Punish his enemies among the civilian population.

Rely on primitive, often improvised, communication and transportation facilities.

Emphasize gaining popular support and good will.

Seek to overcome the enemy's will to resist more by psychological than by physical action.

Assuming that the foregoing propositions are true, it would seem that counterguerrilla operations should be easy, and so they should. As with so many human operations, it is only the pigheadedness of the humans involved, especially on our own side, that makes them difficult.

In this connection, the authors would like to adopt for their own, the statements made by the late Brigadier R. C. H. Miers in his brilliant "Both Sides of the Guerrilla Hill," in the March, 1962, issue of *Army:*

> Junior leaders must be trained to use guile rather than orthodox methods: brains before sweat. . . . Ruses as old as those in the Bible will work if not repeated too often, and ... the guerrilla has many weak points which must be exploited. . . . Other things being equal, which hat would I prefer to wear: that of a guerrilla or [that] of a government official? Personally I would go for the guerrilla's every time.

Chapter 3

APPROACHES TO COUNTER-GUERRILLA WARFARE[1]

REVIEW AND analysis of the history of counterguerrilla operations suggests that four basic approaches may be employed, singly or in combination. All have been used in the last 17, as in the last 170 years; most are being employed in one part or another of the world today. Each has repeatedly been acclaimed as a cure-all, and each has had apologists who have attributed its failure to everything from ineffectual application to a lack of hardware.

The oldest approach, perhaps, is extermination or resettlement of the guerrillas and the civilian population, which includes those who support them. The Chinese Communists seem to have employed, to their satisfaction, the exterminatory approach to their guerrilla problems, effectively clearing areas by the wholesale slaughter of everything that moves. So have the Russians, on perhaps a somewhat less drastic scale. Outside the Communist sphere or Africa, it is doubtful whether many commanders today would be either willing or allowed to use such methods.

Employment of terror, or drastic retaliatory measures against the civilians in the area of operations is essentially only a variation of this approach. The danger to the user of such measures was exemplified in the war-crime trials after World War II, and the limited success achieved by German terrorist methods suggests that the gains are not worthwhile in any case.

In Malaya, the British employed a contemporary version of the area-clearance system, which was acceptable and feasible under the social and political conditions there. They resettled some 500,000 Chinese, among whom were included most of the local supporters of the Chinese guerrillas. In this way, they succeeded in cutting off the guerrillas' sources of supply. The resettled Chinese were forcibly concentrated in "new villages" behind barbed wire. Existing villages were at times placed under curfew or under stringent food control that required whole villages to be fed from a central kitchen and that forbade individual possession of food. Some areas were placed under an absolute interdict; that is, people moving in them were subject to being shot on sight by security forces.

These measures, coupled with active patrolling, a major intelligence effort, and a psychological-warfare campaign that leaned heavily on a reward system, eventually suppressed the guerrillas, whose number probably never exceeded 5,000. Most important, perhaps, was the British promise of independence for Malaya by 1957 if the situation was under control. This brought the Malays into an action they had previously regarded as being an affair between the British and Chinese; the action succeeded and independence was granted as promised.

Success in such an operation seems possible only where the political base of the government does not include the affected elements of the population. In Malaya, for instance, the people involved had no direct ties with the indigenous government; both the guerrillas and their supporters were Chinese in a non-Chinese country under British administration. Further, success is possible only if the government determination is so great, and so well supported that it can afford to use, in the counterguerrilla effort, forty to fifty soldiers and civilians for every guerrilla in the field.

Most often, a solution to the guerrilla problem is initially sought by the military (or police) approach, which aims at arresting the guerrillas, or if necessary, destroying them in combat. Their civilian supporters are frequently ignored, or attempts are made to seal them off physically from the guerrillas by setting up highway checkpoints, curfews, etc. Military operations in this category fall into two general classes, perhaps best denominated as conventional and unconventional. Conventional actions are those taken by regularly constituted elements of the military or police force, operating in accordance with doctrine for operations against a conventional enemy.

The weakness of this approach is indicated by the experience of the Philippine Government: From 1946 through most of 1950, as many as 25,000 government troops and auxiliaries sought to destroy some 12,000 guerrillas. Perhaps 150,000 of the nearly 2 million people in the area (Central Luzon) were sympathizers and supporters of the Huk. By September, 1950, there were in the area a few more Huk, many more sympathizers, and a widespread distaste for the government and its troops.

Conventional operations against guerrillas have met with many such failures and some few successes. Success seems most often to have come from adequate and timely intelligence about the guerrilla and/or the exploitation of a guerrilla weakness. The weaknesses most commonly exploited have been either slipshod security or disregard of a basic tenet of guerrilla strategy: that guerrillas should never try to hold terrain against an enemy in possibly equivalent or greater strength.

It was the latter rule—or disregard of it—that gave the Japanese their one major success against the Huk in the Philippines, when they launched an attack on the Huk Mount Arayat "redoubt" in 1943. The attack was successful only because the Huk foolishly sought to hold their ground.

The Huk showed how well they had learned their lesson when Philippine troops undertook an almost identical encirclement of Mount Arayat in 1947, with approximately the same number of well-trained troops, but with far more popular support than the Japanese had had. Reporters, ice-cream and soft-drink vendors, and sightseers accompanied the government troops, and all the while, horse- and ox-drawn carts driven by guerrilla supporters carried away the supplies of the Huk through gaps in the troop lines. Few Huk were killed, or even seriously inconvenienced, and it appeared later that more casualties had probably been inflicted by government troops on unidentified friendly forces than on the Huk.

Conventional military operations are not infrequently successful against inexperienced quasi guerrillas, against guerrillas strange to the area of operations, or against guerrillas who have not won substantial popular sympathy or support. United Nations troops during the Korean War used substantially conventional tactics successfully against quasi guerrillas.

Conventional military operations usually require troop strength vastly greater than that of the guerrillas and are inordinately expensive in terms of time and material. If troops in such numbers must be maintained for protection against a conventional enemy, their use in conventional operations against guerrillas can be justified as a means of training. It is seldom that conventional operations destroy a guerrilla force by causing the death, capture, or surrender of a large proportion of its personnel, but conventional operations can make such a force ineffectual.

Unconventional military operations may for the present purpose be defined as operations conducted by military personnel aimed at gaining information about, making contact with, harassing, destroying, or capturing guerrillas, in ways for which there are no direct precedents in contemporary military doctrines. They range from the introduction into guerrilla channels of supplies or information designed to harm or disadvantage them, through the employment of soldiers disguised as guerrilla or civilian supporters, to the adoption of practices at variance with tactical doctrines for conventional warfare. Unconventional military operations are limited only by the ingenuity, ethical standards, and resources of those responsible for their use.

(Operations by the military to assist civilians are classed as "civic action" or civilian support, even though they may also be at variance with traditional military practices.)

Unconventional military operations against guerrillas take many pages of Philippine history. They range from the ancient Chinese practice of using fire-crackers or joints of bamboo thrown on the fire to simulate small-arms reports, to the famous Filipino cannon. These were not unlike the wooden "Quaker guns" once used on American merchant ships to give the appearance of heavy armament. The Filipino cannon, however, had the added advantage of sounding like cannon, thanks to a little kerosene poured into the breech. Its fumes were periodically detonated by a match.

Probably no campaign in Philippine history has seen such extensive use of unconventional operations as that against the Huk, especially after 1950. The use of disguised troops became almost routine—so much so, in fact, that on one occasion at least, two Huk units shot it out, each under the impression that the other was made up of "phonies." No effort was spared to make continuation as a Huk guerrilla at least decidedly risky if not fatal. One device that some might consider unsporting was to encourage civilians living in the Huk-infested marshes to go frog-hunting by torchlight. Unknown to the civilians, a small patrol would be following, ready to pick off any Huk attracted by the lights and the possibility of getting food.

At times, it was desirable to persuade the Huk that an area was heavily infested with government troops. A number of flares fired at intervals by a few men spread throughout the area was both economical and convincing. Conversely, an area might be saturated with troops who would ostentatiously pull out after a fruitless operation. Small parties left behind often succeeded in putting an end to the relaxation of Huk who came out of hiding after the departure of the troops.

Some of the unconventional operations in the Huk campaign were almost incredibly successful; others failed, often through lack of adequate advance preparation. Many of the failures, even one operation that brought in its wake the wanton destruction of food and storage facilities, eventually assisted in lowering Huk morale and weakening them by increasing their suspicion of their fellow guerrillas and creating difficulties between Huk and civilian supporters.

Dirty tricks and disguises are by no means the whole story in unconventional warfare. The habitual use of small patrols as the major combat effort, with standing orders to attack any enemy who learns of their presence, is one of the most useful practices in counterguerrilla operations. Departure from accepted doctrine, special training, and special equipment of combat personnel are often valuable and frequently should be adopted. These, if well considered, adapted to the terrain and the situation, will often be found to be simpler, less expensive, and more successful than the conventional items or practices they replace.

Certainly unconventional operations are by far the most economical of personnel and matériel. Given adequate support, communications, and—above all—information of the enemy, a small number of trained guerrilla hunters can kill, or force into permanent submergence among the civilian population, a far larger number of guerrillas. Too often, such specialized forces have been improperly used, have in fact been committed to relatively static roles in support of already static conventional troops, and their value has been lost. When well-conceived unconventional operations fail, it is almost always because of inadequate preparation or halfhearted and ineffectual support.

Surrender as the initial approach to guerrilla operations appeals only to those who sympathize with the guerrillas and their objectives and to the hopelessly woolly-witted. It will be urged from the beginning by confirmed enemies of the administration, by secret sympathizers of the guerrilla, by the guerrilla himself—and by his propagandists. As antiguerrilla operations continue and become more expensive in lives and material, with success seeming ever further away, a negotiated end to the struggle becomes appealing. As operations drag on, losses increase, and the propagandists' wiles make secondary issues loom larger while the political, economic, and moral purposes of the counterguerrilla blur, and demands for peace at any price (almost) increase.

Small nations that have enlisted the support of a major power will face increasing external pressures to either seek or refuse an accommodation. And as these pressures become apparent, they engender a resentment that tends to obscure the *casus belli,* creating a strong motive for seeking peace with those who seem at least to share a common nationality. Major powers, fearing a possible expansion of the local struggle into a world war, or fearing that their own troops may become involved, not infrequently urge a negotiated peace between government and revolutionaries.

These phenomena have been repeated time and again in the past twenty years. The latest example (at this writing) is Laos, where such negotiations, and a reluctance for resolute action by the major power assisting the government, have marked the troubled years since 1950. It has not been confined to small countries. France in effect surrendered to the Vietminh at the Geneva Conference of 1954, as she has since surrendered to the Algerians. Nor has this situation been confined to guerrilla warfare. The Korean "peace" urged and accepted by the United States is another outstanding example in recent history. Allied policies and actions amounting to surrender in China after World War II and in Russia immediately after World War I justify the old cynicism that the only thing we learn from history is that we learn nothing from history.

Because of the historical precedent as well as because of the nature of the human animal, surrender as an approach to the problems of counterguerrilla operations must be borne in mind. And if there are no successes in the counterguerrilla effort, the cry for peace will increase until the government responsible for the operation may come to believe that the only alternative to its own dissolution is an accommodation with the enemy. These are, in fact, the only choices remaining after unsuccessful counterguerrilla operations.

There is another approach to counterguerrilla operations, one that might be called "stealing their thunder." As the name implies, the idea is to beat the guerrilla at his own game, to try to attract more support from the civilians in the area of operations than can the guerrilla, while at the same time winning combat superiority.

The guerrilla claims a moral superiority over his government enemy. He claims a greater concern for the welfare of the people. To beat him at this, not only must the forces of government demonstrate their own moral superiority; they must find ways to dramatize their concern for the people.

One such drama was played out in a Huk-dominated area in 1951, after Ramón Magsaysay's advent as Secretary of National Defense. A sector commander heard that the wife of a Huk commander was in the *sitio* (hamlet) of San Agustín, awaiting the birth of her baby. Into this tiny settlement (fifteen houses, approximately fifty people), he sent a radio transmitter (and five men for surveillance, in case the commander came to visit his wife). The radio transmitter flashed the word of the baby's birth, and a doctor and nurse in a jeep ambulance were sent out to the village. Meanwhile, the sector commander flew over San Agustin, sending messages of congratulations and telling the new mother that medical help was on the way in case she needed it. As might be expected, the entire population came out to wave and cheer. Soon after, the arrival of the jeep ambulance—as promised—brought more cheers.

When she recovered, the wife sent her thanks to the sector commander, and at the same time her apologies that her husband should be a fugitive. Would it be possible for him to return to government allegiance? It may be imagined what the sector commander answered. The story of the birth circulated quickly through all the Huk area, reaching the husband, who found himself not only a father but part of a legend. When his wife sent word that it was possible for the commander to surrender with honor, and that such an act would be for the welfare of his family, he "came in," and in the days following, by twos and threes, the twenty-five armed Huk who had been under his command followed his lead by surrendering.

Once the new Secretary of National Defense made it possible for government troops to carry out such unconventional tactics, the Huk claims to superiority in trying to satisfy the people's legitimate aspirations were signally weakened.

The guerrilla's claims can only be beaten when the forces of government forcefully demonstrate their ability and determination to satisfy the legitimate aspirations of the governed, while at the same time exhibiting greater day-to-day concern for the popular welfare. Often, the guerrilla rests his claim to moral superiority on the behavior of the guerrilla to the people, on the "iron discipline" of the guerrilla soldiers as compared with abusive practices by government troops. It is virtually essential that government forces demonstrate superiority in this field.

Although it is requisite for government forces to make a greater and more convincing effort to win the support of the people (and to give justification for turning from support of the guerrilla), it is also essential to beat the guerrilla militarily. This means taking the initiative from him, forcing him to fight at places and at times not of his own choosing as well as beating him when he chooses to fight. It is not necessary, nor is it usually possible, to defeat the guerrilla decisively in combat to the point of military annihilation of his forces; it is necessary to carry the war to him. As the campaign to win popular support, augmented by a demonstrated desire to come to grips with the guerrilla, begins to carry conviction, military action becomes easier and more profitable. Usually this action will be unconventional, at least in many aspects.

Probably the first to use twentieth-century knowledge and techniques in a deliberate, rigorous exploitation of this approach to counterguerrilla warfare was Ramón Magsaysay, Secretary of National Defense of the Republic of the Philippines from September, 1950, to February, 1953. He dramatically presented his program as offering to the Huk "All-Out Friendship or All-Out Force." He drastically reoriented the campaign that had been carried on desultorily by the government for five years and achieved proof of success within fourteen months. The techniques and principles he employed seem appropriate to many, perhaps most, counterguerrilla operations.

NOTE

1. Much of the material in this chapter previously appeared in *The Annals of the American Academy of Political and Social Science,* CCCXLI (May, 1962), 19–29.

Chapter 4

THE SITUATION AND
THE TERRAIN

"IT ALL depends on the situation and the terrain"—the handiest phrase ever thought up to give a little breathing space to the military student asked for "Actions and Orders, please," this is one of those devilish half-truths too often used to cover up a lack of knowledge or unwillingness to think. In any given tactical situation, much does depend on the situation and the terrain; certainly the commander who best understands and employs both is the commander most likely to win—if he also understands the basic principles of the type of action he is preparing to fight.

The terrain of Europe has undoubtedly influenced the many wars that have been fought there, but it has not been allowed to hamper the development of principles and tactics applicable to any kind of war. The proof is that the best tactics and principles developed there have been successful wherever they have been applied properly. In consequence, military schools around the world teach principles and tactics *and* their application to the situation and terrain that may be encountered.

Too often, studies of guerrilla or counterguerrilla operations have so emphasized the situation and the terrain that the generally applicable principles have been obscured. To those on the periphery of such operations, to those whose academic disciplines could contribute greatly to the solution of the problem, the situation or the terrain has often overwhelmed everything else in their thinking. Their views often becloud the issues, sometimes create crises, sometimes end them.

This is most typical of rebels. Luis Taruc, most influential of the Huk, achieved that position because of his love for his fellow men and his distorted view of a society in which he was unable to work his way through school.

Ramón Magsaysay defeated him because of his love for his fellow men and his clear view of a political system that enabled him eventually to become his country's best-loved President, even though he, too, encountered great difficulty in working his way through school.

The campaign against the Huk for a time fumbled, not for lack of knowledge of the situation and the terrain but for want of understanding of the principles, tactics, and applications of successful counterguerrilla action. It became a snowballing success when these principles and tactics were applied on bases partly theoretical but largely pragmatic.

The Philippines is an archipelago of eleven large and some 7,000 small islands in the Western Pacific. Excluding lakes, rivers, and the many small specks of islands, the area of the Philippine land is roughly 115,000 square miles. The topography includes flat, irrigated rice lands, rolling grassy uplands, seasonally flooded swamps, and many, many miles of precipitous mountains, with forest cover ranging from great pines to the most dense tropical rain forest.

The people, of a basically Malay stock, with some admixture of Chinese and Spanish, numbered about 21 million in 1950, at the height of the Huk campaign. Their ways of life range from completely Americanized to the food-gathering culture of wandering pagan bands. The strongest reminder of their prehistoric society is the languages, about eighty-five of which are still spoken, with English being the lingua franca of the whole archipelago.

Three-fourths of the people lived on farms in 1950. The pattern is typically one of small farms; half the farms are less than five acres. Less than a fourth of the total area of the country is included in the farm lands. Social organization is family oriented and strongly colored by the years of Spanish occupation. Political attitudes and structures are patterned on those of the United States, yet retain marks of Spanish and pre-Spanish customs.

An important element, often overlooked or misunderstood, is the great stress placed on responsibility for and to members of the family, whether by blood or by choice. This constitutes a real and substantial social-security system, which goes far to ameliorate real hardship, while at the same time it can be an excuse for laziness or a compelling reason for favoritism. The practice of extending the family by the selection of godparents, the so-called *compadre* system, is the target of much criticism, yet constitutes a valuable means of ensuring vertical social mobility.

Manila, the *de facto* capital, situated on Luzon, the northernmost of the large islands, has, with its suburbs, a population of nearly 2 million, much of which is transient. A sprawling, bustling city, which has doubled in size since the war, it contains the most marked contrasts between East and West, between swank American-style suburbs, Chinese tenement slums, and sprawling shanty-towns. Its influence on the country is great, especially in ideology. As the most politically minded place in a politically minded nation, it is a natural hothouse for radical movements.

More than the plains, swamps, and mountains, the conditions in the agricultural portions of the Philippines form the terrain on which guerrilla movements operate. The attitudes of the residents of these areas are to a large extent the situation with which guerrillas and counterguerrillas must contend.

On some islands, like Leyte and Samar, and indeed in many parts of Luzon, most of the farmers till their own lands, often wresting from them barely enough for survival. Many of the children leave home to seek work in the cities as soon as they are old enough. The hand of the government rests lightly on such men, and the slogans of the Huk had little or no appeal.

On two islands, Negros and Panay, much of the agricultural land is in large sugar plantations, whose laborers are paid by the day. Agitators for higher wages have natural appeal, and radical unionists always find some followers. The Huk managed finally to make some headway in organization in Panay, under the leadership of two veteran labor racketeers, Nava and Capadocia. (The latter was a Communist leader of long standing.) Neither plantation workers nor small farmers found the appeals of the Huk compatible with their attitudes, and the Huk movement there was soon liquidated by aggressive intelligence and psychological operations. These latter leaned heavily on local defense units formed largely of ex-guerrillas and on the rewards offered for top leaders of the Huk.

Only in three areas of Central Luzon did the Huk find conditions favorable for their type of revolution. One of these was the area to the south of Manila, a region where farming is diversified, with perhaps half of the people working little farms that they think they own, and the remainder divided among laborers on large estates, sharecroppers, and workers in cottage industries. This region has been systematically victimized for 150 years by land reformers and demagogues, unscrupulous politicians and land racketeers selling what they did not own. In consequence, there is a strong tendency to banditry, which makes it easy for any revolutionary leader who promises good government and land to attract followers, if he offers them good pickings. Such groups affiliated themselves with the Huk, and for some years were a nuisance, but never a serious menace.

Manila, similarly, is an easy place in which to recruit followers, from the unemployed and the discontented, and from intellectuals and students in search of a brave new world. While the Communist Party kept up its efforts in the "legal struggle," it met considerable success in infiltrating labor unions in Manila. Had they really worked at organization there, the danger could have been acute. Even so, Manila offered a virtual safe haven for Huk headquarters and leaders until the authorities cracked down, taking advantage of the feeling of security Communist leaders in the city had long enjoyed.

It was only in Central Luzon that the Huk movement really flourished. This is an area of some 6,000 square miles, much of it rich rice land. It is bordered on the east and west by mountains, on the south by Manila Bay, swamps, and more mountains, on the north by Lingayen Gulf and yet more mountains. An extension of the bayside swamp, Candaba, runs far up into the eastern portion of this area. It has been the granary and garden for Manila for centuries.

Well over half the farmers in the rich rice lands are sharecroppers, farming large estates, often held by absentee landlords. So keen is the competition for land, and so eager are the occupants to continue to farm in the same place as their fathers, even though this means further subdividing rented lands already too small to be economical, that the average farm runs from four acres in some provinces to eight in others. Social customs, the village fiesta and the cockfight, the overwhelming desire of the farmer to send his children to school, all make heavy demands on an income barely enough for subsistence. The tendency is to borrow, often at ruinously high rates of interest, sometimes exceeding 100 per cent per annum.

As in Southern Luzon, for more than a century, demagogues and well-intentioned persons of little understanding have been telling the people in these provinces that they are abused. To some extent, they have been, but at least since the Spanish left the Islands, this abuse has always been easy to escape, or overcome, legally. Needless to say, many were inclined to believe that they were abused, that they had no salvation except through revolution, and found the Huk slogans of land reform, equal justice, and good government easy to accept. It was among these people that the Huk grew under the Japanese, from whom they organized their shadow government, their Barrio United Defense Corps, and their Pambansang Kapisananng Magbubukid, or Peasants' Union.

It was in this area that the Huk had their strength and in which they had to be destroyed. They were everywhere. They were in the *poblaciones* (county seats) of the municipalities (counties). They were in the *barrios* (villages) and in the *sitios* (hamlets). They were in the fields, the swamps, the mountains.

The cultivators of this granary seldom live on their farms. Rather they live in *sitios* and *barrios,* going into the fields in the morning and returning at night to their settlement. Since the *barrio* plays such a role in the life of the people, it is important to have a basic picture of it. The following description of a typical *barrio* in Huklandia—the nickname given to the central plain of Luzon in recognition of its long domination by the Hukbalahap—was written by a perceptive American artist in 1952:

> The ways of life among Filipinos range from one extreme to the other, with the city of Manila containing the heights of modernization. There we find the highly sophisticated internationally educated, driving imported cars, smoking imported cigarettes, eating imported foods. We find their counterpart also in provincial cities or country estates, enjoying the blend of contemporary gadgetry with the traditional gracious living of the financially solvent Filipino. Among the middle class those things Americans now take for granted as "necessities" of life are still luxuries greatly to be desired. Refrigerators, modern stoves, television sets,

vacuum cleaners are hard to come by and, once acquired, highly prized. Even schooling one's children calls for sacrifice.

In the smaller settlements in the provinces, away from Manila, we find the opposite extreme from the life of the wealthy Manilan. Here there is no electricity, no piped water, or piped sewage.

San Mateo, in Pampanga Province, is just such a small village in the heart of Huklandia, near Mount Arayat, where many encounters between Huk and government have taken place. Even now the Army is operating in this area. Many *barrios* nearby have been abandoned because of the difficulties of carrying on life in the midst of a battlefield, but the people of San Mateo have tried to hold on.

Barrio San Mateo is hidden in a small forest of trees made feathery by tall bamboos. We trudge toward it on foot over a dusty road worn by the passage of *carabao* (water-buffalo) carts and dry-land sleds. Rice fields stretch dry and golden on either side. Our road edges up abruptly from the glaring rice flats into the cool shade of mango trees, where *carabao* rest near several tall conical stacks of unthreshed rice. We are stopped by the view. Mount Arayat stands as a blue pyramid seemingly not too far across the fields, with a shimmer of the river between. Close at hand is an abandoned weathered brown-thatched nipa hut, flanked by the brilliant green of bamboo and papaya trees. It's a cloudy day. The colors are rich. Maybe someday when the fighting is done, the owner will come back to his nipa hut and lovely view.

Our road turns at right angles to become the main street of the village, three kilometers (not quite two miles) long. Children come shyly closer, ready to grin and make friends, as we turn left toward the school, the chapel, and the home of the Teniente del Barrio.

The Teniente comes to greet us. Children trail us to his home and multiply in number by the second. *Barrio* Lieutenant Anselmo Parungao is fine looking, barefooted, and wears a sparkling clean white shirt and trim broad-brimmed straw hat. Conversation switches back and forth between English and Tagalog. A companion keeps me abreast of the Tagalog with running commentaries and translations. "Parungao was appointed to his post by the Mayor of Arayat town, and although he is supposed to receive a salary, so far it has not been paid. Parungao is bitter, not because of his pay, but because he has not been given the authority that goes with his post. He cannot even issue identification passes for his people so they may move about during military operations in the area. Anselmo, like his fellow San Mateans, is a poor man, but he does own his nipa house and the lot on which it stands." He poses graciously before it for pictures, then takes us on a tour of the *barrio,* showing us points of interest.

We stroll down the main street walled on either side by a series of woven bamboo fences that surround each house to keep chickens and pigs from wandering. A few of the houses are of wood with sliding windows of shell, but most are built of thatch over a bamboo frame-work—thatched walls, thatched roof, thatched shutters to close down over window openings, thatched box standing high off the ground on stilts. Pigs and chickens find shade under the house.

We climb over a stile at a gateway to visit in one of the typical nipa huts. We climb the almost vertical bamboo ladder up to a tiny platform, or outside porch, floored with large half-bamboos spaced slightly apart so water can drip through to the ground. Here Lola (Grandmother) squats doing her washing; here the men will bathe when they come from the fields. Here sits a clay jug keeping the drinking water cool, and beside it a topless kerosene can holding water for general use. The earthen cookstove is located here also during the dry season so that it doesn't smoke up the house so badly.

We step inside into the one room of the house, about twelve feet square and void of furniture, but orchids hang in coconut-shell pots in the window openings. A small platform in one corner is the rainy-season cook spot, with an opening in the wall above it so smoke may be persuaded outside. (Sometimes this cook spot is a specially built balcony.) One corner of the room is screened off with *sawali* (woven matting) as a dressing-changing-room. The possessions of the household are meager, consisting of the jugs for water, clay pots for cooking, spoons and dippers contrived from gourds or coconut shells, a few metal spoons, perhaps a metal pot, basin, and frying pan. Knives are the handmade bolos, so important for chopping food or chopping wood. A canister of matting several feet in diameter holds the rice supply, where it will be dry.

Across a corner of the room is slung a hammock where baby can be rocked to sleep. Woven mats stand neatly against the wall, to be unrolled at night onto the bamboo floor for beds. A few candles and an improvised beer-bottle kerosene lamp provide needed light at night. Clothes are at a minimum; those not being worn are being washed. A woven *buri* box holds extra items like blankets, which are so scarce and so desirable when the nights get cold. Later in the day we spread banana leaves on the floor and shared the lunch we had brought along.

Strolling on through the *barrio,* we stop to talk to people as they work to learn their thoughts, to let them know we care what they are thinking. We stop to watch an elderly couple turning rice spread on mats. "This is their share in the recent harvest. For three days, they must dry it in the sun and gather it in when the sun gets low," the Teniente explains.

Here life depends on rice, as it does in most parts of the Philippines, wherever rice will grow. Rice is so basic that without it, a person does not feel that he has eaten. Rice is served for breakfast, for dinner, for supper, with fish, vegetables, meat, or sauces on the side to vary the flavor, but always rice in as great a quantity as can be afforded. There are more varieties of rice than we have kinds of potatoes. Between meals, you reach for a leaf-wrapped pillow of gluey "sticky rice" instead of a candy bar.

And rice farming is a very personal thing. It is not a mechanized industry. Every blade in the fields was placed there by hand, by bent figures standing knee-deep in water all day long, thrusting shoots firmly down into the mud, as the folk song so truly says:

Planting rice is never fun.

Bend from morn till set of sun,

Cannot stand and cannot sit,

Cannot rest for a little bit.

The hand work does not end there. The rice is harvested by hand, stacked to dry, threshed and winnowed, spread in the sun to dry again, turned, sacked, and carried to market by *carabao* cart or stored for personal use in a dry spot in the home. Husks must still be pounded off and grains winnowed clean before cooking. All by hand, and by sweat. Being a farmer means all this—to raise rice. Any other crops are incidental, grown only in small patches, tended in spare time, and not really counted as farming.

"Farmers here are sharecroppers," one tells us, "splitting expenses with the landowners 50–50 and getting 55 per cent of the crop. Without irrigation, only one crop of rice a year is possible, and attempts at irrigation are poor and inefficient. Fertilizers are seldom used and not understood, so the crop is meager. A tenant farmer may make around 250 pesos a year (in 1952, approximately $125), and a very few make a maximum of 300 pesos a year from the harvest. There is not enough land available to be worked in this area."

The Teniente del Barrio estimates that a family of five needs at least 120 pesos a month to get by on, so farming alone cannot support a tenant family. (Official estimates are about half this amount.) Fishing can net an income of 50 pesos in a good month. Early in the morning, men leave for fishponds and streams, some near, some many kilometers away, to return about five o'clock with the day's catch. When there is fighting in this area, their movements are restricted, and at times, many are prevented altogether from fishing, so that source of food and income is cut off.

Some San Mateo men can make a few extra pesos a month cutting bamboo and gathering *buri,* the leaves of a swamp palm from which the women make strong shopping bags. This is the chief gainful occupation of the women in San Mateo. The *buri* is spread in the sun to dry, then stripped into ribbons from which the bags are woven. Working hard, one woman in one week can make 100 bags, which she takes to town and sells for 4 centavos each. It is possible to earn 16 pesos a month making *buri* bags. With the husband making 30 pesos a month from fishing, their joint income may not come to more than 45 or 50 pesos a month. Each grown son and daughter adds to the total income, helping to fish, farm, and make *buri* bags.

To provide for the schooling of the 200 children in the *barrio,* the villagers skimped and sacrificed to accumulate 2,500 pesos from their tiny incomes, with which they purchased a half hectare (slightly more than one acre) of land, on which they erected a long bamboo-and-nipa shedlike affair which is The School. It is timeworn and outgrown, but still a monument to the quiet courage and concern of these good people in the interests of their children, manifested not by loud complainings but by sacrificing and laboring to build this school on their own initiative. The government cooperated to the extent of providing a few wooden desks, small blackboards, maps and charts, and five teachers at salaries of 120 pesos a month.

A flag now flies over this little schoolhouse. Although it is traditional for every school in the country to fly the Philippine national flag, this little school obtained its first flag only this year. An army unit stationed near San Mateo noticed they lacked a flag, obtained a flag for them, and presented it to the school. On the day it was given, the schoolchildren gathered around it in admiration. It was the first time they had actually seen the flag of their country.

The original building is not large enough now to accommodate all of the children of the *barrio*. The overflow is being taken care of in two small buildings adjacent to the school. The Chapel, not often used as a chapel since the nearest priest in Arayat town does not often visit the *barrio,* is filled with makeshift seats and desks and makes a fairly substantial school building. The other annex is a split-bamboo, nipa-thatched shed. A bamboo screen divides the one room into two, each about 10 by 20 feet. Blackboards, the small portable kind, are attached to either side of the dividing partition. Desks filled to capacity crowd the room. Unlighted, the interior seems far too dark for small eyes to attempt to read. The two tiny windows are almost closed in an effort to keep out the heavy clouds of dust being whipped up by the strong wind. The floor is packed earth, dusty in summer, muddy in the rainy season.

It is a geography class we intrude upon, taking our flash pictures. The children and teacher carry on like troupers. The children are taking turns reading aloud in English from the teacher's book, while the rest of the class follows the reading from books they share at their desks. The teacher clarifies in Pampango from time to time, or corrects pronunciation. Books are dog-eared and aged. There are not enough to go around. Paper and pencils are luxuries. Crayons are unknown. The children are quiet, well behaved, eager and anxious to learn, valuing the opportunity to receive education and doing their utmost to absorb as much as possible. One boy quietly replenishes the water supply, a kerosene can he filled from the pump across the street. No paper cups here, but a single gourd dipper from which everyone could drink. There are no balls or bats or sports equipment for these children, either.

Classes end at the fifth grade here in San Mateo. The nearest school for advanced classes is in the town of Arayat, nine kilometers (about five and a half miles), or two hours' walk, away, where enrollment fees are prohibitive for the small wages of San Mateans. Older boys, therefore, spend their days not in school but in caring for the *carabaos,* transporting rice, fishing, and similar jobs.

Little twelve-year-old Filomena, carrying her year-old baby brother, follows us throughout our visit. She cannot go to school because there is no one to look after her baby brother, with Mother busy making *buri* bags all day long and Father either in the fields or fishing. Her one dress has already lasted many months and will continue to be worn until it falls to pieces in spite of the mending. "But," she says, "I wash it once a week." Baby brother has a shirt (pants are too much of a luxury) and a sardine can for a toy. He also has a bad cold. There is no doctor nearer than Arayat, where there is only one to care for its 15,000 people. There is no clinic available, and the nearest hospital is at San Fernando, a ten-hour trip by bull cart from San Mateo.

There are two privately owned pumps in San Mateo, but in a town of this size, this water supply is neither adequate nor convenient, so the families near the river obtain their water from the river. After all, the pump water may be no better for drinking. No one knows. It has never been tested.

The river is an integral part of the daily life in a *barrio.* In San Mateo, the women gather there on bamboo rafts to wash their clothes, while men bathe and children frolic, and *carabaos* are rejuvenated with many daily dips and soaks.

When the *carabaos* enter the cool water, nature takes its customary course, and they promptly relieve themselves, the waste matter dropping unnoticed and forgotten, polluting the water above it, where soon someone may be filling containers with drinking water. It is so common an occurrence and health awareness so lacking that no attention or thought is given to this dangerous situation. Even dead animals are brought to the river to be disposed of.

"Across the river and extending on to Mount Arayat is no man's land," we are told. "Once this was a thriving fertile land, with healthy *barrios* and farming. Now the Huk situation, the constant fighting, has made it a dead land."

As we watch one man drive his *carabao* up the shady lane from the river bank, the stillness is suddenly broken by the wild clamor of a bell from the other end of the *barrio*. All is sudden motion as the cry of "Fire!" is taken up!

The Teniente leaves us on a dead run down the road, his white shirttail flying. We hurry after him. There is a strong wind blowing, and the whole *barrio* may be threatened. Women are already emerging with bundles of possessions. Unless the fire can be brought under control quickly, it may spread too far to be stopped. Bucket by slow bucketful, water must be carried or passed to the fire, no matter how far, and it takes a minimum of forty seconds to fill one bucket at the pump.

We reach the fire. A stack of precious *palay* (rice) representing many days of labor, and food supply for months, is going up in smoke. It is one of two stacks in a bamboo grove shading thatched sheds and houses. There is no hope of actually putting the fire out, only of confining it to the one stack. Men have already cleared a firebreak of sorts and are doling out the scarce water to soak the ground and quench the flames that try to spread across this break.

The bucket brigade is already in action. Fortunately, the pump is not far from the fire but the pump, like the houses, is up on stilts and climbing the six-foot ladder—up with the empty, down with the full, nearly a minute between to fill the bucket—rather slows operations. Meanwhile, men positioned on the adjacent stack of *palay* pour their rations of water carefully to quench the flames licking at its base. Nearby, inflammable sheds of nipa are lifted bodily from their bamboo frames and carried out of spark range; animals are led away to safety. Fortunately, the wind fanning the flames suddenly dies down, so that after about thirty minutes, it is possible to get the fire under control. "Someone was very careless," said one tired man reprovingly.

This is *barrio* life. No television, no refrigerators, no electricity, for that matter. We talked to many people during our visit about their problems and their thoughts. Here are a few of the comments made by residents of San Mateo, in a Huk-ravaged area, where fighting goes on around them as they live and try to work.

F. G., farmer, says: "There is a big piece of land near our *barrio* that belongs to the Catholic Church. It has been left idle for so many years and is now covered with tall grasses. The government could buy or lease this property and turn it over to us for cultivation. There are more than 200 men among us who are jobless."

J. K., fisherman: "I don't know what to do. Many times I cannot fish because the army has operations and they might shoot thinking I'm a Huk. I keep borrowing money to support my family and I already owe so much because I have to pay 10 per cent interest every month. Soon I may lose my house, even my fishing equipment."

L. K., farmer: "The Huks are even better treated than we by the government. When a Huk surrenders, he is given a house and a piece of farm land in Mindanao. And when he is captured, he is fed and given shelter and does not have to work and worry about his next meal. I might as well become a Huk and then surrender."

P. K., basket-maker: "Why is it that in Manila, where our government stays, the people have hospitals with free wards and free medical attention, while we here who cannot afford to buy medicine, much less pay for a doctor, do not get anything free at all for our sick? Even a small clinic could help us very much."

L. P., farmer-fisherman: "I suppose leadership is what we need here. Someone who can show us how to get up. But is not the government supposed to be our leader? How can they expect us to see their guiding hand when they are always in Manila, which is just as far as one can be? To tell you the truth, I wouldn't even know our own President if I met him face to face!"

The *barrio* Lieutenant: "We do not know much about governments. We have been told that under the Sobiyet the people are like slaves; that if you raise pigs, the Sobiyet gets the pigs; if you raise chickens, the Sobiyet gets all the chickens. If that is true, we don't want the Sobiyet. What we want is a government that lets us have what is really ours, and lets us be kings in our own home as long as we do not do anything bad."

F. P., farmer-fisherman: "The government never comes here to see how we live. The only man who comes to these parts is Magsaysay. Maybe he should be President. At least he knows how badly we need help, and seems to be the only one interested in the welfare of the *barrios*."

The life of the residents of San Mateo is not too different from the way of life of some three-quarters of the population of the Philippines. It is a better way of life than many, perhaps the majority, in the world enjoy. Almost all in the Philippines are keenly aware of how life could be better for them, keenly want it to be better, but understand that it can be made better only through patient work, and the implementation of democratic processes, fair to all.

This is their strength, a strength that is shown most clearly when they feel that due democratic process is denied them for the unreasonable personal benefit of an individual or a group. The people of the Philippines have often been the target of unscrupulous demagogues, just as have the people of the United States, or of any other free country. They have also had the benefits of having among them perhaps a higher percentage of practicing idealists than has existed in any other country in modern history. Since it is often difficult, at even a very little distance, to distinguish between demagogue and idealist, the people of the Philippines listen readily, but are slow to believe. When they do believe, they act.

There seems to be only one factor, significant to successful guerrilla or counterguerrilla action, in which the Philippines differs from other countries that may be faced with the necessity for such operations. Some such countries have, perhaps more do not, a comparable degree of political awareness among their people, a comparable broadly based structure of cherished democratic institutions. To the extent that countries lack this structure, that their people lack political awareness, guerrilla and counterguerrilla operations will be slowed by the necessity for educating the people in order that they may form a political base, the *sine qua non* of success.

Chapter 5

KNOW THINE ENEMY: ESTIMATE OF THE ENEMY SITUATION

"KNOW THINE ENEMY" IS so ancient and basic an axiom of war that it would seem to need no elaboration. The fact is, however, that lack of knowledge and understanding of the enemy—of who he is and how he operates, of his true objectives and his announced goals, of his actual and supposed capabilities, of his plans and of his intentions, and above all, of the reasons he gains support from the people—has repeatedly hampered, and not infrequently hamstrung, antiguerrilla operations. Sometimes (especially at combat levels) this lack is the result of poor intelligence work. More often (especially at national levels) it arises from misconceptions, unwarranted assumptions, or, often unwitting acceptance of propaganda.

"Agrarian reformers," a label applied to Communist insurgents by their own propagandists, and adopted by well-meaning but uncritical individuals, has become a byword for, as well as a classic illustration of, refusal to know an enemy. Its concealment of the true motives and objectives of Communist-led guerrilla movements contributed greatly to their success in China and elsewhere. The French assumption that Communist indoctrination and ideology (rather than the desire for an end to foreign, i.e., French, domination) was the mainspring of the Vietminh movement contributed substantially to the disaster in Indochina.

Many antiguerrilla operations have failed because of lack of pertinent data; some have succeeded despite lack of knowledge of the enemy. These successes may in general be attributed to the guerrilla's ignorance of his trade, or to the literally overwhelming strength of the antiguerrilla forces.

The counterguerrilla at every echelon from squad leader to chief executive of the nation, needs to know the answers to two compound, complex (and not infrequently confusing) questions, one offensive, the other defensive in its application. First, he needs to know "What can the enemy do to me, what does he intend to do, and when will he try it?" Second, he must find out "Where is the enemy, in what numbers? What are his strengths that I must avoid, and what are his weaknesses that I can exploit?"

To answer those questions, many others must be asked and data from many sources must be analyzed. Securing the needed information requires detailed planning and devoted effort, which is far from ended when the information is obtained; it must then be placed in the hands of the users. This never-ending "intelligence effort" is, in the tripartite counterguerrilla operation, an equal partner with combat operations and psychological operations.

When insurgency flares into open guerrilla warfare (or when planning for a specific counterguerrilla operation is first begun), the counterguerrilla must have certain information immediately. How strong are the guerrilla forces? Do they seek combat with government forces, and if so, in what strength, on what terrain, under what conditions? If not, why not? What is the basic motivation of the guerrilla leaders and what are the appeals they use to get support from guerrillas and from civilians? What is the basic plan of the guerrilla leadership? Is it to build strength in order to engage government forces in open combat; or is it to weaken government forces and fan popular discontent until the guerrillas can seize power in a short, sudden national revolution? How and where do the guerrillas get their supplies—especially food? Do they have any reserve stocks of supplies? To what extent do civilians in the guerrilla areas actively sympathize with, passively tolerate, or fear to oppose the guerrillas? What is the nature of the area of operations?

Answers to these questions will often be found in the daily newspapers, in troop reports, in enemy propaganda, and in intelligence information. How accurate the answers are—how much is fact, how much rumor, and how much surmise—is another matter. Continuous verification, cross-checks, and healthy skepticism are always desirable. The answers immediately available can usually serve as a lead in deciding on immediate actions—or inactions—and little more.

Traditionally, intelligence (knowledge about the enemy) is broken down into categories of strategic and tactical, based on its presumptive ultimate use. There are, of course, nearly as many ways of categorizing intelligence as there are categorizers. In the intelligence field, as in others, counterguerrilla operations tend to make conventional classifications less meaningful. Perhaps the most useful classification of intelligence applicable to counterguerrilla operations is that which divides it into basic and tactical.

Basic intelligence can be considered as information concerning the things the guerrilla must have and must do if he is not to be defeated in the initial military action against him. What is his organization, his cause? What are his sources of supply, his support (or tolerance) from civilians in the area of operations? How does he demonstrate effective action? How can he sustain hope for victory?

Basic intelligence must also be at least equally, perhaps more, concerned with the reverse of these questions, i.e., with the weaknesses in the society, the political base, and the administrative machinery of government that have allowed the guerrilla to organize in the first place. True, this is knowledge about yourself, but the enemy is an enemy only because of you.

The enemy is the best source of knowledge about himself, and often one of the best guides to information about oneself. Of all the things the enemy says and does, the most important for basic intelligence, the easiest to tap, and in some ways the most reliable (and easiest to misinterpret) is the information he gives through his propaganda. The statements of aims and objectives, claims of accomplishment, and outlines of future plans made in his propaganda give clues to the bases on which he claims the popular support he must have (but perhaps not to what he really seeks).

In the Philippines, the Hukbalahap made much use of such campaign slogans as "Land for the Landless" and "Equal Justice for All." These were not, of course, their only appeals; they used many. They decried "feudal landlordism," "government inefficiency and corruption"; they charged the highest officers of government with holding office illegally. The Huk fought, they said, for the "New Democracy," with land, food, and justice for all. Sometimes— although this did not work for very long—they charged that government officials were the "running dogs of the American imperialists." Another familiar tactic was threatening local officials and residents who "failed to cooperate with the People's forces"—threats occasionally backed up by audacious assassinations and kidnapings.

This propaganda was significant in many ways. To anyone familiar with the international Party line, to anyone familiar with Communist techniques, its phraseology, no less than its themes, clearly showed that the Hukbalahap movement was under Communist direction.

Of course, propaganda lines were not the only source of such identification. Since 1943, intelligence services in the Philippines had been reporting the Communist inspiration and domination of the Huk movement; great masses of documentation and firsthand testimony had been gathered and sent on to all who would listen. Even so, when an American correspondent, Jim Halsema, interviewed the popularly proclaimed *"Supremo"* of the Hukbalahap, it was a shock to many—in fact the authenticity of the whole interview was denied in many quarters—because he quoted the *Supremo,* Luis Taruc, as saying, "I am now and long have been a member of the Communist Party of the Philippines." Even after that statement, many continued to consider the Huk movement as striving primarily for agrarian reform.

The most important knowledge obtained from Huk propaganda came from an assessment of which themes were successful (as shown by their continuing use) and which themes were dropped because they were not acceptable to the people from whom the Hukbalahap drew their support. Perhaps the most startling was the contrast between the two themes embodied in the slogans: "Land for the Landless" and "Yankee, Go Home." "Land for the Landless" was a continuing slogan always successful, so long as it went unopposed, because it touched a universal and fundamental desire of the Filipino. "Yankee, Go Home," on the other hand, flopped with a dull thud every time it was introduced. It was simply impossible to persuade the people of rural areas in the Philippines that the Americans were other than their friends. No counterpropaganda was ever launched or ever needed. To the ordinary Filipino, this appeal was so patently spurious that it discredited those who sponsored it. Again and again, politicians have used the basic theme to gain political notoriety but they have never succeeded in getting it accepted by the common man in the Philippines.

It was significant that the lasting and successful themes (the basic concepts, either negative or positive, to which their slogans related) were "land for the landless," "equal justice for all," and "inefficiency and corruption in government." That these themes were effective in rallying popular support was early recognized by the Philippine Government. The widespread and deep entrenchment of the attitudes to which these themes appealed was less well appreciated. Worst of all, superficial analysis of the conditions that gave rise to these attitudes often led to actions that served only to reinforce doubt of the government's effectiveness and intentions.

Thus, when Huk propaganda called for a "fair share" of the rice harvest for tenant farmers, the government sought to prove its concern for the governed by passing a crop-sharing law. Traditionally, the rice harvests in the Philippines had been shared by tenant and landlord on a 50–50 basis. Legislation before World War II had set the landlord's share at a maximum of 40 per cent. In 1947, President Roxas, seeking political support, and hoping to alleviate the Huk menace by meeting their demands, obtained enactment of a law restricting the landlord's share of the rice crop to 30 per cent. This law totally failed to have the desired effect.

There were two reasons for its failure, both significant. First of all, it was an unworkable and unenforceable attempt to solve a problem that has no single or simple solution. The reason that sharing the harvest is an anguishing problem in the Philippines (and in many other places) is not that the landlord's share (as rent) under the contract is exorbitant; it is because the tenant has so little rice left after the harvest settlement. This is partly because the average tenant farm is small and partly because small rice farmers are chronically in debt, often to their landlords, and often at high interest rates. Small tenant farms, and indebtedness partly due to the small crops, reflect cultural patterns whose change would be most fiercely opposed by the small farmer. Not realizing his own contribution to his troubles, he tends to attribute exclusively to the malice of the *ricos,* or the bias of the government, the fact that often he does not have enough rice left to feed his family until the next harvest.

The new law, dividing the rice crop 70–30 in the tenant's favor, only alienated the landlords without contributing to the basic solution. It was a fatuous and obvious effort at political appeasement. The tenant farmer cared little about his rent. He merely wanted enough rice left over to feed his family and provide a few of the "nice-to-have" things of life as well. Lacking this satisfaction, he was an easy prey to guerrilla propagandists.

Secondly, the law was an attempt to placate those who would not be placated—the leaders of the Huk. They demanded the law as the price for their political support. They half-promised to give up their rebellion if the law—which they could hold up as proof of their power and influence—was passed. Of course, they had no intention of settling for anything less than total victory. Passing a law because guerrilla leaders demand it is like any other means of paying blackmail, an expensive and foreordained failure. Taking an effective action to demonstrate to the people who support or tolerate the guerrilla that their problems are recognized and that the government is trying to meet them—this is a far different matter.

For the government to adopt the slogans of the guerrilla is neither a sufficient nor a desirable response. What the government must do is make the slogans ineffective for the purposes of the guerrilla.

The primary propaganda target of the guerrilla is the civilian population that feeds and shelters him and gives him information about the antiguerrilla forces, yet denies information about him to his enemy. Identifying successful guerrilla themes enables one to discern deeply rooted and significant attitudes of the civilian population; attitudes to which the counterguerrilla operator must appeal successfully, must modify, or replace, if he is to win support away from the guerrilla. The campaign against the guerrilla can scarcely succeed until this is accomplished.

Also useful, even in the early planning stages, is the information about guerrilla leaders and heroes that may be obtained from their direct or indirect propaganda. What public images of them does the guerrilla seek to create? It must be an image that symbolizes one or more of the appeals of the movement. Obviously, the principal value of this knowledge is its application in psychological operations designed to destroy or discredit the leader. However, a man proclaimed to be a hero may feel that he must maintain this image of bravery—and it may be possible to use that feeling to lure him into suicidal or at least tactically unwise combat.

At least one Huk, Commander Rollin, was lured out of a strong defensive position, into the open, by taunts. "Come out and show that you are as brave as you claim to be!" He did, and he died. The value to guerrilla and counterguerrilla alike of an intimate linking of psychological and combat operations can scarcely be overestimated, and must never be overlooked.

Does terror—and the threat of terror—appear to constitute a major portion of the guerrilla effort in a particular area? If so, the guerrilla is obviously having difficulty obtaining support in that region and is particularly vulnerable to attack there. These and many other facts that can be put to use against him may be readily deduced from the guerrilla's employment of the terror themes.

Whom does the guerrilla threaten? How often does he carry out his threats? Is he aiming primarily at local officials who presumably are duty-bound to cooperate with antiguerrilla forces? If so, any officials in the area of operations who do not take strong precautions against being kidnapped or murdered must be suspected at least of having established a modus vivendi with the guerrilla, if not of being his active supporter.

There is the story of the Mayor of a little agricultural community situated in the very heart of Huklandia and the Colonel who finally solved the problem the Mayor presented. The Mayor was an influential politician, and also a notorious supporter of the Communist guerrillas. For four years, the Colonel had been struggling to find a solution, some way to neutralize this Mayor, who made this town a safe haven for the enemy. He finally evolved a plan and one day in early June, 1950, made a ceremonious visit to the Mayor's office.

"Oh no, Colonel," the Mayor responded to the Colonel's opening question. "There are no guerrillas hiding in our town. Those Communists who call themselves Hukbalahap have not dared to come into our town since you became military commander of the area. It is true that some of them have relatives here but they never bother us. I cannot permit you to make any investigations or searches here. I will go to the Governor and the President if you do! Everybody knows we do not permit guerrillas to come into our town."

The Colonel knew that wounded Huks were being cared for in that town at that very moment, even though the Mayor denied it. He also knew the Mayor was not lying about the political repercussions he would precipitate if action was taken. So he bowed himself out, but first, before leaving, he made it a point to have a very private talk with the Mayor, noticeably distant from all other ears. Actually nothing was said that had not already been said, but who was to know that?

Two mornings later, the Colonel's jeep, with siren screaming to attract a crowd, sped into the busy plaza of the town. It was followed by an open truck bearing the bodies of four dead guerrillas and by a truckload of soldiers armed to the teeth.

"Bring the Mayor here at once," shouted the Colonel as the townfolk rapidly gathered. "I want to talk to the Mayor." Soldiers rushed to the Mayor's office before he could leave in a different direction, and led the bewildered man to the plaza.

The citizens were terrified. They knew the Colonel's reputation for ruthlessness. They knew the Mayor to be an ardent Huk supporter. But the Colonel met the Mayor with a broad smile and shook his hand enthusiastically.

So that all could hear, the Colonel spoke loud and clear. "I want to thank you very much, Mr. Mayor. On behalf of the army, I thank you for your wonderful cooperation and for the fine information you gave me two mornings ago. Here are the results. I am going to leave these bodies here in the plaza so everyone can see that Huk are no longer welcome in your town."

Before the Mayor could answer, the jeep siren started to scream again as the Colonel jumped in with a wave of his hand, and the convoy minus corpses took off, leaving the Mayor expostulating in vain.

Shortly after dark, a truck loaded with the Mayor, his family, and household belongings pulled up in front of the Colonel's tent. The Mayor was miserable. "Please, Colonel, you have to take me in. You must protect me. I will tell everything I know and do anything you want. After what you did this morning, the Huk will never believe I am not a traitor."

The conclusions as to enemy motivations, capabilities, strengths, and weaknesses that can be drawn from this propaganda are almost limitless. There are difficulties and dangers in such deductions. It will be found that there are a host of self-appointed propaganda analysts both in and out of government service. For example, it is obvious that the enemy's propaganda line is an important aid to assessing the number, influence, and identity of sympathizers. Each repetition, each "replay" of enemy propaganda is significant, but its meaning may well be misinterpreted. The repetition may signify sympathy, or it may identify an enemy supporter. On the other hand, repetition may indicate no more than that the theme appeals to the attitudes of a certain individual or segment of the population.

Thus there were many in the Philippines who echoed the Huk cry for land reform, for equal justice, for an end to inefficiency and corruption in government. Many who echoed the Huk line were far from being Communists. Some representatives of the United States Government in the Philippines were accused of Communist sympathies because they repeated publicly or privately these demands of the Huk as being desirable, if not essential, objectives. They are still desirable in the Philippines as in the United States, or in any other country. Nowhere have they been fully achieved to the satisfaction of all, nor will they ever be.

The fascinating business of propaganda analysis must not be allowed to divert attention from basic intelligence needs. Of these, perhaps the most important is knowledge of enemy capabilities. The size and composition of the forces the enemy can muster and what he can do with these forces is obviously essential information. The significance of enemy capabilities is much more than a knowledge of what points he can attack or what strength he can muster for an operation at a specific location.

Estimation of enemy capabilities is an important and highly sophisticated intelligence activity in conventional warfare. Many types of information, ranging from the nature and amount of road and radio traffic to the number of desertions and the type of rations last issued, can be collated and combined to yield surprisingly accurate deductions as to strength, capabilities, and intentions of the enemy.

There are similar possibilities for refined deductions in counterguerrilla warfare, but the criteria and their significance are often quite different. Adequate, reliable information may seem difficult or initially impossible to obtain. What is obtained may be wrongly interpreted. For example, if it is known or strongly believed that the enemy has 5,000 men in a given area, it might be assumed that he can muster a force of 3,000 and conduct an operation lasting for several days. As a matter of fact, the need for these men to spend much of their time in gathering food and their difficulties in transportation and communications may make an operation in more than company strength utterly impossible.

Enemy capabilities are as likely to be overestimated as underestimated and with almost equally serious results. If his capabilities are underestimated, unanticipated attacks may occur and severe losses be sustained. If his capabilities are overestimated, offensive measures may not be adopted, feasible and desirable operations may be abandoned. Overestimation of guerrilla capabilities will inevitably be seriously inimical to the morale of troops and civilians alike.

The situation in the Philippines in mid-1950 abundantly illustrated the adverse effects of overestimation of guerrilla capabilities. It was believed that the Huk numbered at least 15,000 (some estimates were 50,000) armed men within 85 miles of the national capital. Consequently, Manila was ringed with troops; checkpoints and barricades were emplaced on every road. Troops not in the vicinity of the city were guarding, in strength, the main arteries of transportation. The morale of civilians and troops can well be imagined. The information as to enemy strength, coupled with inadequate appreciation of his capabilities, led to an erroneous estimate (not by intelligence personnel) and consequent actions that came close to giving the guerrilla the capacity to overthrow the government.

For strategic-planning purposes, a great deal about guerrilla capabilities can be correctly deduced from information readily available. His successful operations give very fair evidence of his minimum capacity. His unsuccessful operations, although a less reliable source, may give accurate evidence of his maximum capabilities.

Essential information about his military capabilities can be deduced from the weapons captured from him or which he has been known to use. Are his weapons of the same type as those used by forces opposing him? If so, he probably has a capability for acquiring weapons from the counterguerrilla forces. Do they include a relatively high proportion of sporting arms or obsolete military weapons of diverse kinds and calibers? Are these weapons of types known to exist in reasonable numbers in the area of operations or in the country of operations? If so, his capability for procuring standard military weapons is limited. Are they standard weapons but of a kind known not to be readily available in the area of operations? If so, he obviously has an external supply capacity. Is there an appreciable percentage of nonfactory weapons? If so, an arsenal capability may be indicated. The condition of captured weapons can yield invaluable data not only on enemy logistic resources but on his military capabilities insofar as these derive from the state of training, morale, and discipline of his troops.

The enemy's own estimate of his capabilities is probably more important to strategic planning than his actual capabilities. Does the enemy believe he can hold ground? If so, what ground and where? The answer to this may be found, in part at least, in the propaganda he disseminates. Does he boast of secure base areas, of places where government troops dare not come?

Such boasting is invaluable information to the antiguerrilla forces if it is correctly appreciated and acted upon. Almost invariably, the correct action will be to hit such areas, hard. If the guerrilla does indeed stand and fight, he may be seriously crippled. At the least, the killed, wounded, captured, or permanently discouraged guerrillas resulting from the operation will no longer need to be patiently chivied from place to place.

An unsuccessful attack, properly exploited, will be better than none. It will demonstrate at least the gravity of the situation and bring home to government troops and civilians alike the necessity for choosing between effective antiguerrilla operations and surrender.

Whether the guerrilla stands to fight and is dislodged, or employs sound guerrilla strategy and fades away before the attacking forces, his actions give valuable propaganda material to the antiguerrilla forces. The guerrilla can be charged with bluffing, with cowardice, or with ineffectiveness as his moves dictate. Whatever the charge may be, he has clearly and demonstrably lost the initiative, and prestige.

The significance of guerrilla propaganda threats to indicate attitudes and possible loyalties of persons in the area of operations has already been discussed. Threats may also reflect his capabilities; if he threatens death or punishment to civilians who cooperate with counterguerrilla forces, are such civilians actually captured and punished or killed? Does he boast that small detachments or large detachments of his enemy will be attacked, and does he indeed attack them?

If the attacks are made successfully, they obviously demonstrate a capability. If not, it must be determined why the threats were made and not carried out. Was the guerrilla seeking to cause the counterguerrilla forces to overestimate his capabilities, or is he now seeking to cause their underestimation? Was he seeking to deceive others or was he deceiving himself when he made the threats?

Again, what is the enemy known to have said and done about his supplies? Do his troops approach villages and humbly request rations? Do his tax collectors levy rations? Does he take food from villagers by force and threat? Are harvest parties attacked? Can the food staple of the country move along its normal paths of transportation unmolested? If not, what is the nature and extent of the interruption of its movement? Answers to these questions indicate the enemy's own estimate of his capabilities as well as his true capabilities.

If he does not appear pressed to secure food, he obviously is securing food without such actions. If he collects food by levying taxes but without an undue show of force, he believes—and with justice—that he exercises a substantial measure of control over the population of the area. If, on the other hand, he obtains his food by threats of violence or by force, it indicates that he is not receiving adequate support from the population of the area and sees no possibility for winning adequate voluntary support there in the near future. (Or, it may mean that he is incompetent, or acting under the orders of persons either incompetent or not desirous of his success.)

All these indications can and should be supplemented to the maximum extent possible by secret intelligence. They have been enumerated here, however, because they may supply the most reliable information available in the early planning stages of an effective antiguerrilla operation.

Probably of an importance nearly equal to knowledge of enemy capabilities and his own estimate of his capabilities is knowledge of basic, long-range enemy intentions, of the kind of war this particular guerrilla intends to fight. Even though he may be a Communist, or under Communist domination, the guerrilla leader will not necessarily follow the pattern of any one specific Communist-led guerrilla movement of the past. Successful Communist seizures of power have followed many different patterns.

The necessity for seeking accurate information about the long range plans of a specific guerrilla movement is made even greater, curiously enough, by the recent wide interest in counterguerrilla warfare and the many valuable books on the subject that have recently appeared. Many of these stress what may be called the Sino-Vietnamese concept of guerrilla warfare.

Briefly, this concept envisions a war in three stages. The first is true guerrilla warfare, where small, irregular forces relying on popular support seek to organize themselves and the civilians among whom they move in order to gain support and control of the civilians. This stage, in the Sino-Vietnamese concept, should as soon as possible give way to the second stage, where semiregular troops are formed, trained, and employed to attack counterguerrilla forces wherever possible. Special emphasis is placed on establishing secure base areas to be denied to the counterguerrilla forces, resolutely defended by the semiregular troops whenever they are threatened. The third stage envisions the formation of a regular army, based in the liberated areas, which can engage and defeat the counterguerrilla forces in regular battle.

Contemporary writing seems to depict this as the probable course of an indigenous guerrilla force attacking the established indigenous—or colonial—government. This is indeed the doctrine of the Chinese and Vietnamese Communist leaders, Mao Tse-tung and Vo Nguyên Giap, and is in sharp contrast to the traditional guerrilla role of harassing the enemy, collecting intelligence, and spreading propaganda while waiting for decisive action by friendly regular forces.

There is, however, a course for guerrilla warfare, an approach to successful revolution, that closely parallels the traditional guerrilla practice. In this, the guerrilla seeks to weaken counterguerrilla forces and the government they support by petty actions and petty harassments, inducing the government to waste its strength and lower the morale of its people by futile blows at the guerrilla, who is not there to receive them. Meanwhile, the guerrilla and his political leaders concentrate on building up popular support, organized and unorganized. At an opportune time, a quick blow, a quick "national revolution" spearheaded by the guerrilla force or, as in Russia, by political leaders, can capture or seduce the key officials of government, leaving the armed forces leaderless and the instrumentalities of government open to guerrilla control.

Because of the wide dissemination of the Sino-Vietnamese concept, it appears especially important that the intentions of the guerrilla forces be quickly and correctly recognized. It is critically important that counterguerrilla forces not be lulled by misconceptions, that an intended national revolution not be mistaken for the early stage of the Sino-Vietnamese pattern. If this mistake is made, a successful revolution can occur while counterguerrilla forces rest secure in the belief that an attempt at overthrow of the government is yet far away.

The consequences of a mistake in the other direction seem far less dangerous. A mistake in appreciation of the ability or intention of the enemy to hold ground or to attack government forces may cost extra casualties and embarrassment to the military. It is not likely to cause the overthrow of the government.

The guerrillas themselves may not be too clear or united on the course their efforts should pursue. In the Philippines, in 1950, the Hukbalahap and their political allies probably had the capability to seize the seat of power and capture the President and chief officers of the government. The principal field commanders might have been tempted to essay the adventure had the controlling Party organ, the Politburo, concurred and been prepared, through organization, to exploit such a *coup de main.*

The Politburo, however, was obsessed with following the Chinese pattern of expanding and "regularizing" military and civilian forces. It had been singularly unsuccessful and neglectful of building up a covert organization capable of operating the instruments of power that it and the guerrilla forces might have seized. As a result, a *coup de main* by the guerrilla might have wreaked havoc on the national government but would not have brought Communists or Huk to positions of lasting power or influence. Those responsible for planning effective counterguerrilla operations in the Philippines were profoundly relieved when they learned, authoritatively (late in 1950), that the Politburo was irrevocably committed to the Chinese concept of a build-up of massive force.

Knowledge of enemy intentions has many benefits. If it is known that the enemy plans to expand, or to attack, or not to attack, tactical and strategic decisions may be made accordingly. There are many facets, too, to the knowledge of enemy intentions. If known enemy intentions and plans far outrun his known capability, it may mean his capabilities have been erroneously assessed either by himself or by friendly forces. Rigorous scrutiny is in order and if it is discovered that his estimate of his capabilities is erroneous, numerous opportunities may be found to exploit his errors or to gauge correctly his future capabilities.

The wide overlapping of basic and tactical intelligence must be obvious—in fact, more obvious than the reason for any distinction between them—for there is scarcely a conceivable item of basic intelligence that will not lend itself to tactical exploitation someplace or sometime. Perhaps the distinction might be more clear if it were said that basic intelligence is concerned properly with ideas and ideals; tactical intelligence with actual persons, places, and things. (The believer in the scientific nature of war will object to "enemy capabilities" being considered an idea; the believer that war is an art will insist that capabilities are far more than statistics on personnel and supplies, more than march tables, are in fact more idea and ideal than enumeration. He will cite guerrilla victories as proof.)

Tactical intelligence helps the counterguerrilla hit the enemy and his possessions. The first requirement in tactical intelligence is knowledge about the physical environment in which the guerrilla operates. This means knowledge about the topography and terrain, the road and river networks, the vegetation and population patterns of the guerrilla area. If the guerrilla is operating in open country, that means he is susceptible to aerial observation if he moves by day in large force. It means further that if he moves at night in large force, the traces of his movements can be detected by aerial observation, both visual and photographic, and, possibly, by more sophisticated means.

What facilities of food, communications, and travel does his physical environment afford the guerrilla? What limitations of movement or communications, of strategy and tactics does it impose on the counterguerrilla forces? All these represent minimal essential knowledge for planning and conducting antiguerrilla operations.

If the guerrilla is operating in an inhabited open area, the frequency and reliability of reports of enemy movements are extremely significant. If such reports are few and/or unreliable, either the enemy is not moving in large groups or the inhabitants of the area are not reporting enemy sightings to government forces. Determination of the reason reports are few or unreliable is a priority requirement. Is it because the residents are motivated by sympathy for the guerrilla, or are afraid of him? Are the residents hostile toward the government, toward specific government representatives, or are they merely apathetic? Are government representatives not receptive to reports of the enemy? If government personnel do not want reports, is it because they do not want to take sides or do not want to be bothered?

Knowledge of the enemy's intelligence and communication capabilities is important. Some idea of his tactical intelligence capabilities may usually be gained from past experience. Have parties sent out to contact the enemy actually been able to contact him or has the guerrilla received early warning of their coming and either retreated or set up an ambush?

To gain critically needed information about the enemy's intelligence and counterintelligence system, it will frequently be necessary to mount special operations. Radio monitoring may be necessary to find out if the enemy has radio transmitters. Messages offering apparently attractive opportunities for enemy exploitation of the activities of friendly troops can be planted to determine if the enemy is monitoring the communications of friendly forces. Possible enemy penetration of friendly headquarters must be tested by starting rumors or loose talk of opportunities for exploitation by the enemy, and determining if he has indeed sought to exploit these seeming opportunities.

Accurate information on the nature of enemy propaganda media is imperative. It is particularly necessary to determine to what extent those who operate the public mass-communications media are actually sympathetic to, dupes of, or willing agents of the enemy. A test of the sympathies of mass-communications-media personnel and of guerrilla communications facilities may be incorporated in the test of guerrilla intelligence capabilities.

A message planted to test guerrilla intelligence capabilities can be so worded as to tempt the guerrilla into making a recognizable propaganda play. If such propaganda promptly appears in press or radio—particularly if it appears without prior check as to its truth—it is justifiable to suspect sympathy with the guerrilla. The time that elapses between planting the message/rumor and its reappearance in the public media can give a good idea of guerrilla communications capabilities.

The foregoing suggests the scope of information needed in order to plan and act most effectively against the guerrilla. Literally, there is nothing—his motivation; his capability; his intentions; his supporters; his knowledge; his training; his beliefs, superstitions, customs, dress, songs; or even his dreams—that cannot be used by the counterguerrilla forces.

This is true on the national level, and it is equally true on the local scene. No commander can ever know enough about his enemy. Take, for example, this story by Major Vicente Z. Opilas:

> *"Tapahan"* is a Tagalog term for kilns used in drying coprax in copraxproducing provinces. These are excavated and provided with earthen tunnels. They are aplenty in II MA (AFP)[1] and can be seen wherever coconut plantations are located. These the HMBs[2] (Huk) use to advantage as refuge during patrols or mopping-up operations of forces.
>
> *"Tapahan* warfare"* is apparently an everyday mystery to our troops, although very commonplace and simple. Huks are encountered in a certain *sitio* [hamlet] or *barrio* [village]. They are seen by our patrols. Token encounter takes place.

Our troops advance and start chasing the Huks. They are no longer where they were when the encounter began. The Huks vanished into thin air, because, unobserved during the brief encounter, they have left by twos or threes at a time, and sought refuge in the *tapahans* scattered all around the locality. The careless troops, meantime, are chasing the wind and by-passing the Huks, crouching, perhaps sweating, but smiling inside one of these kilns. Not only *tapahans* are availed to but also bushes or boulders or anything, for that matter, which can afford cover and concealment. The only risk here on the HMBs is when the troops are seasoned, well trained, and discreet in scouring areas of operation— which by the way, is wanting among the troops today who instead prefer to take it easy, as if they were under a beautiful silvery moon.

This is what might be called local intelligence. It can profitably include any minutiae, from the date the wife of a guerrilla leader is expected to give birth (and whether or not the true father is the presumptive one) to knowledge of an abandoned homestead in a remote area where fruit will be ripe at a certain date (and, therefore, signal a probable guerrilla rendezvous).

For tactical, and local, intelligence, knowledge of enemy organizations and order of battle (OB, identification of units and personnel belonging to them) is a primary objective. Guerrillas developing according to the Mao-Giap pattern normally seek to establish three strata of military organization (which often are paralleled by civilian support or "shadow government" levels of organization).

The basic stratum, and this is true of most sound guerrilla efforts, is composed of home-guard units (BUDC, Barrio United Defense Corps, in Huk terminology), the famous "farmers by day, guerrillas by night." These units ordinarily operate almost entirely in their own locality, attacking targets of opportunity, assisting or reinforcing forces from the higher strata, or simply maintaining the "guerrilla presence," their domination of the local citizens. In some guerrilla operations, these units have habitually drawn off to pull night surprise attacks in another area, allowing the local unit to establish individual or collective alibis.

The next higher stratum is that of the area forces, nominally full-time guerrillas who are training, attacking targets that require forces larger, better trained, or better equipped than the homeguard units, or traveling. Ordinarily these units—squadrons, the Huk called them—of the area forces will have their own subareas in which they are based and normally operate. They may, of course, move to other portions of the area or to other areas, as the exigencies of the situation require. Activities of these squadrons in the Philippines varied according to the situation, the seasons, and the commander. Some concentrated on looking for trouble, others on avoiding it; still others emphasized training. Some practiced leave policies so liberal that their personnel could scarcely be called full-time guerrillas.

In the Philippines, the Huk divided their theater of operations into Regional Commands (Recos), each a virtually autonomous unit responsible in practice to the Politburo, the "steering committee" of the Communist Party of the

Philippines. These area commands, with their full-time troops, were the principal combatant force of the Huk. In practice, the full strength of a well-developed area force was seldom concentrated for an operation—probably not more than three or four times in the entire campaign.

The highest stratum under the Mao-Giap doctrine is composed of the regular forces, the national-liberation army, directly under the supreme commander, to be utilized wherever needed. This element was only rudimentarily developed by the Huk for many reasons. There were no "safe" areas where substantial forces could be maintained securely for extended periods. The relatively good road nets in the cultivated areas made any large forces stationed there vulnerable to attack. Each of the top leaders, especially the nonmilitary ones, was unwilling to allow anyone (other than himself) to have full command. Taruc, popularly known as the *Supremo,* was such for only brief periods and never exercised effective over-all command. Probably the most important reason was that the experienced guerrilla leaders felt instinctively that they did not need such a force for the type of revolution they were attempting.

Since these are recurrent problems in guerrilla warfare, the tactical importance of knowing units and leaders, and their place—both geographically and in the guerrilla scheme—becomes apparent. Really good OB—and ideally, the counterguerrilla forces should be able to develop more complete rosters of guerrilla units and their members than the guerrillas themselves have—will make each prisoner, even each recovered enemy dead, a gold mine of information on the locations and probable intentions of one or more unit.

Continuing relentless command emphasis at all echelons on the production, dissemination, and utilization of adequate timely intelligence is probably more important in guerrilla and counterguerrilla operations than in any other form of warfare. Not infrequently dissemination is the weakest link in the intelligence chain. This is unforgivable, because it is the aspect of the intelligence process in which the technologically superior counterguerrilla can most easily excel his enemy. This was repeatedly demonstrated in the Philippines.

"Sergeant, why the devil did you bring these three men in as prisoners? They say they were walking home from working in their fields when you picked them up and brought them in without even giving them a chance to tell you who they were. Now get them out of here, apologize to them, and let them go before 'the man' [i.e., Magsaysay] hears about this and gives me a 'shampoo.'" The speaker might be almost any newly joined officer in the Huk campaign, 1951–54.

"Sir, if the Lieutenant pleases, these men are Huk. See the red fingernail polish on the little finger of the left hand. Report received from MIS [Military Intelligence Service] in Manila yesterday, sir. Battalion standard operating procedure, sir, that all men carrying Huk identification who see a patrol before we identify them are to be brought in and not given a chance to talk until each has been interrogated separately by the MIS team, sir." The speaker—old Sergeant Tigulang.

NOTES

1. Second Military Area, Armed Forces of the Philippines.
2. Hukbong Mapagpalaya ng Bayan (People's Liberation Army), name adopted in 1950 by the Huk.

Chapter 6

KNOW THYSELF:
ANALYSIS OF FRIENDLY FORCES

"DAMN IT, Sergeant! Why did you bring in those three guerrilla prisoners? We'll have to turn them over to the Fiscal, and then tomorrow, or the next day, or whenever they get rested, they'll be right back shooting at us again. Now, take them out of here without any nosy civilians seeing you and when you find someplace where they won't stink up the area too badly, shoot them."

Time: 1946–50; place: the Philippines; operation: the campaign against the Hukbalahap, with all civilian law on the side of the guerrilla.

Does the order "Shoot them!" mean that these officers and their men were, as one columnist charged, pithecoid savages or pseudoNazi gangsters? Were they "Filipino storm troopers making war with pitiless ferocity against the civilian population of Luzon"? Did the officers and men of the Philippine Armed Forces deserve the epithets applied to them by many elements of the Philippine press and radio? By no means. They were soldiers, good soldiers for the most part, fighting a clever and pitiless enemy who had no regard for the rules of war, but an enemy entitled to the same legal safeguards as a housebreaker, bigamist, or other petty criminal. Legally, they were supposed to arrest him and were to shoot him only if they could not otherwise effect arrest or were forced to fire in self-defense. This enemy, if arrested, was only a lawbreaker, entitled to full protection from the legal system he was endeavoring to destroy. Consequently, a Huk captured in the field or a Huk supporter picked up by the army enjoyed the same legal status as any other civilian. That legal status? He must be taken before a judge within six hours after arrest, if physically possible; within twenty-four hours a prima facie case for common crime must be made against him. If it were not, he would automatically be released. If he were formally charged and the crime were anything short of murder, he would have a right to demand release on bail. It was literally true that a Huk, captured in a fire fight, could be free and back with his unit within seventy-two hours or less.

This anomalous situation arose from a realistic appraisal by high civilian authorities of a political problem that appeared insoluble. The legal system of the country was designed to protect the public from the criminal activities of single individuals and, at the same time, to afford its citizens the fullest protection against arbitrary or unjust treatment. By principle and training, the civil authorities were bound to the strict application of those laws. The press, perhaps the most free in the world, was fiercely protective of the deeply ingrained principles of a free society and was largely hostile to the administration.

The only legal action that could stop the virtually automatic release of captured guerrillas and their supporters was suspension of the writ of habeas corpus. This was clearly, and correctly, seen as political suicide under the conditions then prevailing. This new breed of criminal lived within the law, as well as outside it. Unless and until convicted of a crime under the existing code, the guerrilla remained a voter, a full member of the body politic. His family and his friends were also voters.

Members of the legally elected government, which held office only by a small majority, were naturally and properly concerned about the next elections—never more than two years away. Political opponents, always virulently critical, certainly would capitalize successfully on any admission that sporadic raids by a few thousand armed men—whose votes they wanted and who claimed to be seeking only their just rights—constituted a state of civil war and a critical national emergency.

Similar dilemmas have faced, and will in the future face, many governments. Few legal systems can effectively protect the social body from organized attack by large groups whose members individually can only be charged with common crimes, and even the measures provided in their codes can usually be implemented only when the government has the overwhelming support of the effective members of the body politic.

The politicians' dilemma became the soldier's. If he took prisoners and treated them according to law, he was failing to accomplish his mission, which was to suppress the rebellion. If he shot his prisoners or took other measures to convince them of their wrongdoing, he was called a brute and a savage; he might find himself facing a charge of murder before a hostile civilian judge. Whichever course he took, he played into the hands of the enemy. Liquidation or even intimidation of prisoners supplied political ammunition for attacks on the government. It also made the Huk guerrilla fight better, knowing that to be captured was almost surely to be executed.

There were, then, two interrelated problems: first, the government's problem of providing a means by which troops could deal with prisoners and suspects in an acceptable, civilized way without releasing them. Politically speaking, this problem could not be solved unless the government enjoyed substantial public confidence. Second, the troops' inability to put down the rebellion effectively without the authority to hold prisoners. Neither military nor civilian authorities actually recognized the gravity of their predicament, but they did recognize that it was an apparently insoluble one, so, humanly, they sought to ignore it.

This problem was by no means unique to the Philippines. It is one that has repeatedly faced the British, from South Africa in the Boer War to Malaya and back to Kenya. Wherever there is articulate political opposition to the government in power, wherever rebels and their supporters (real or suspected) are genuinely believed to be entitled to the rights of citizens, this difficulty over treatment of captives will arise.

The impasse in the Philippines was broken by a spectacular development that emphasizes the effectiveness of a government spokesman who can be the guarantor of the government's good intentions. A minor Huk leader, one Taciano Rizal, was ordered to assassinate the newly appointed Secretary of National Defense, Ramón Magsaysay, who, by his past exploits and early actions in office, seemed to the Huk command to afford them a substantial threat. Rizal took advantage of Magsaysay's public statement that he was willing to meet with anyone who wanted to contribute to the campaign against the Huk. Rizal arranged for a secret rendezvous with Magsaysay at which he intended to assassinate him. But out of curiosity, he talked to Magsaysay. He was persuaded that Magsaysay meant what he said, meant to deal honestly with the Huk, meant to do all in his power to ensure good government.

Rizal, an idealist, became convinced that the best thing he could do to help his country would be to help Magsaysay. He gave information that led to identifying and locating the members of the Politburo, the directing organ of the Communist Party in the Philippines. A surprise raid resulted in the capture of about 150 Party members, their families, their assistants, informers, couriers, etc., together with virtually complete records of the Communist Party of the Philippines, including minutes of the meeting in which the Hukbalahap were originally organized, in March, 1942.

This dramatic event, the favorable public reaction to it, and the seizure of so many prisoners who obviously had to be detained pending complete interrogation—and review of the truckload and a half of documents—gave Secretary of National Defense Magsaysay the chance to request, and obtain, suspension of the writ of habeas corpus. For the first time, it was politically feasible to do this. Even so, the reaction would have been strongly unfavorable if Magsaysay had not set up extensive safeguards against abuse of this privilege of holding prisoners without placing charges against them. There was, indeed, a brief flurry of opposition to the request, but it soon died and could not be revived by even the most devout Huk sympathizer among members of the press.

Not every country nor every administration faced with the need to suspend the writ of habeas corpus or to declare martial law can hope for the good fortune of seizing the administrative headquarters of the guerrillas as a justification for the action. However, in planning actions against guerrillas in a country where the disposition of prisoners poses a political problem, serious consideration should be given to the early execution of a coup that will make it politically feasible to hold prisoners without formal charges.

It is often difficult to find out exactly what is being done with captured guerrillas, and what is being done with suspected guerrillas and/or guerrilla supporters. Are they being brought in, or are they being liquidated? If they are brought in, are they placed in civilian jails or in special camps? Who are the custodians? Who authorizes their detention, and who reviews the individual cases? In what ways are they interrogated, and how well? How are they exploited in psychological or military operations? This may not be the information the counterguerrilla needs most, but these answers may be most useful in evaluating the answers he receives to other, more important questions.

Possibly most critically needed are the answers to the most sensitive questions, questions concerning the status of the chief executive of the country. Clausewitz said that war is a form of political intercourse, implying that it is the final means of reaching a political decision. Guerrilla and counterguerrilla war may very properly be said to be politics submitted to the court of last resort. The political chief who is responsible for the counterguerrilla effort may well be the decisive factor in determining whether the war is to be won or lost.

What is the stature, attitude, and probable tenure in office of the chief executive? Is he determined to fight the guerrilla, to eliminate the guerrilla menace, or is he lukewarm, belittling the struggle, perhaps even secretly in sympathy with the guerrilla? Is he reasonably in control of his armed forces or are they in fact virtually autonomous? Is he likely to be ousted by a coup, by the guerrilla, by the armed forces, or by third parties? When are the next elections, and will he be a candidate? Answers at least temporarily valid, and at least reasonably accurate, to these and many similar questions are essential to realistic evaluation of counterguerrilla strength and weaknesses.

To the fervent partisan, these questions may smack of treason; to the indoctrinated soldier (especially of a stable major power), they may seem irrelevant. The chief executive and his close advisers may not know the answers themselves—worse, they may be wrong in what they think they know.

At no time during the Philippine campaign against the Huk were there serious problems about the sincerity and security of the chief executive. Each of the postwar incumbents was determined not to allow the Communists to take power, even though all offered amnesties, in fact if not in name, to Huk who would return to peaceful law-abiding lives. During the terms of office of the first three Presidents, political considerations viewed as unavoidable did, at times, affect the prosecution of campaigns against the Huk and their supporters. This was inevitable, for the Huk could influence many votes, and elections were at no time suspended.

The Huk offered the only real extralegal threat to any of the Presidents. Supporters of the defeated Presidential candidate in the 1949 elections did launch a "rebellion," in which they hoped for active support from the armed forces and the Huk. The expected Huk support fizzled, while the armed forces moved quickly against the rebels, demonstrating effectively their loyalty to constitutional government, even if many did not like the Presidential incumbent.

(There were of course many rumors of impending revolts or of virtually treasonable dealings between high government officials and the insurgents. Rumors of revolt, especially "a military revolt in the southern provinces, between Christmas and New Year's" are endemic in the Philippines, a sort of annual flying-saucer craze. Dealings between government and Huk leaders were undoubtedly sincere, if sometimes misguided, efforts to end the seemingly interminable war.)

It cannot be expected that every chief executive faced with a guerrilla problem will have a secure tenure of office. Neither can it be expected that he will have positive control of the armed forces. Further, the chief executive himself may sadly misjudge the security of his position or the extent of his control over his armed forces. Recommendations for actions directly designed to enhance the security of the President's position or to strengthen his control over the armed forces might seem outside the responsibilities (and perhaps the capabilities) of the counterguerrilla. But they should not be so considered, for the chief executive, his real status, and his own assessment of it are most important to the counterguerrilla effort. Plans for counterguerrilla operations that will not have the effect of strengthening the chief executive's position and control are unlikely to win his approval.

A parallel series of answers to equally sensitive questions about the chief executive must be secured almost simultaneously. What is the attitude of the people in the country to their chief executive? Is he regarded as a man of integrity and ability, legitimately holding office, using his power wisely? Is one or both of these qualities believed to be lacking? Is the opposition to the chief executive based on political affiliations or does it cross party lines, being based on his own record? How strong are the feelings and attitudes toward the chief executive? Do adverse opinions about him as a person—or as a political symbol—outweigh the respect the people feel is due to his office?

(Of course, in some countries these questions may be less important than the question, Do people know or care who is their chief executive? The question may even be whether they have any feeling of allegiance to a national government, or any interest in it. If the answer to these is No, the problem takes on new dimensions, especially in the fields of psychological warfare and political actions.)

If a chief executive is not respected, if significantly large segments of the public actively dislike him, sincerely disbelieve his statements, or believe that he holds office illegally, these facts must be taken into account in planning actions to build up government prestige, to win support for the government, and to establish credence for government statements. Since a government has several spokesmen, it will be advisable to select from them one with a reputation for honesty and efficiency to be the voice of government on matters of or affecting counterguerrilla operations.

Obviously, the chief executive is not the only individual whose attitudes, ability, and public image may critically influence the counterguerrilla effort. Virtually the same information is required about the other high officials of the country and the unofficial close advisers of the chief executive. Their strengths and weaknesses, their loyalties and interests are certain to affect the prosecution of the counterguerrilla effort. This is especially true of officials in the ministries of defense, interior, social welfare, and agriculture.

Almost as much attention needs to be given to the situation in the national legislature, if there is one, to determine the relative strength of political support for the administration and for its opposition. The key issues—whether political theory, national policy or action, or simply the perquisites of office—dividing the major parties and administration supporters and opponents should be identified and weighed in terms of their direct and indirect effects on the national and counterguerrilla missions.

Three questions about legislators' attitudes are of especial importance to the counterguerrilla. To what extent will administration actions be attacked on purely political grounds? What types of action (either by the government or by the guerrilla) are most likely to generate effective political opposition to the administration? How well will the legislature support the antiguerrilla effort per se, especially with appropriations for the armed forces and/or legislation supporting armed-forces efforts? This legislation may vary from such apparently minor matters as the statutory requirements for promotion (or limitations on promotion) of officers and noncommissioned officers to such major matters as instituting resettlement programs for guerrilla prisoners.

Above all, the counterguerrilla must understand the nature of political power in the country. He must understand the forms of power, and he must seek to know where power truly resides. Many students of Philippine society firmly believed that political power rested in the "*ilustrados*," the small group of wealthy, usually highly educated individuals whose names are literally household words. Two guerrilla movements, first that against the Japanese, then that against the national government, the Hukbalahap movement, failed to change the opinions of the many acknowledged and unacknowledged believers in the *ilustrado* theory. The sweeping victory of Ramón Magsaysay as a Presidential candidate shook, but failed to change, their views. Actually, in the Philippines, as in far more countries than is generally realized, political power rests in the people. They may tolerate its exercise by an elite group, but woe betide the elite that believes it owns, rather than enjoys the loan of, political power.

The way in which power, or the right to use it, is traditionally transferred in the country is especially significant to the counterguerrilla. Is this transfer authorized through elections? Is there a relatively small group of candidates who exchange positions at election time, with those in power reluctant to take action against the "outs" because of their personal relationships and their game of musical chairs? Or, is there an elite group that chooses and controls the candidates, an elite group that can and does change officeholders when it becomes displeased with them? How do the members of this group obtain their power, and how do they hold it? Do the voters take elections seriously? If not, why not? Are the symbols of power usually transferred peacefully, in accordance with legally established procedures, or are they often transferred by violence?

If the country has a democratic tradition, that is to say, is one where the members of government are traditionally elected by the governed, there are many more questions to be asked. Who is entitled to vote? How many do? Are their votes counted? What are the political parties and what is their role? Are they, as in the Philippines, primarily a grouping, with an eye to the next campaign, of individuals who through accepted practices of the country appear to control blocs of votes? If so, how significant are these individuals, and how firmly are they in control of votes? Or are the political parties virtually sacred symbolic groups, as in Colombia, where a man is "born a blue [the Conservative Party color], lives a blue, and must die a blue"? If so, all considerations of the actual or potential influence of a leader must take his party affiliation as an unalterable fact. What are the traditional ways of influencing voters, and how, if at all, may they be changed or used?

Many of these questions may seem to touch on matters far removed from the duties of the counterguerrilla, but they affect nearly every action he may take or even consider. The officer of counterguerrilla forces who does not take them into account can play only a limited role, and is likely soon to find himself unemployed, or forced to take up for himself the role of guerrilla.

The counterguerrilla, whether indigenous or a foreign adviser, must be keenly aware of the contemporary political situation, and as keenly aware that it did not develop in a vacuum. He must know its antecedents and its sources in the history, traditions, cultural facts and ideals, past and present policies of the nation. The guerrilla movement that it is his duty to combat, and the other political factors that may affect his operations are, like the government and the armed forces, the result of the societal and ideological environments. They probably owe more to them than to the physical environment.

Formulating a fully adequate appreciation of all these intangible but significant factors might well be the life work of a dozen imported social scientists; the information may or may not be available from residents of the country who have culled the people's knowledge of their heritage. Information from both sources can be of value, but neither source should be relied on exclusively. It is essential to make an objective and pragmatic analysis that seeks significant factors and evaluates them properly. Seldom can such an analysis be wholly accurate; there is some question as to which is likely to be least inaccurate—an analysis by well-informed members of the indigenous population or an analysis by foreign residents with long experience in the country. Perhaps the ultimate evaluation should be done by those familiar with similar situations in other countries.

The experience of the Philippines certainly tends to confirm this view. For five years, men with personal experience as guerrillas and as students of Communist tactics sought vainly to persuade Philippine "experts" in and out of government, indigenous and foreign, that the Communists and their guerrillas posed a serious threat; a threat that could neither be ignored nor removed by routine pacification operations. Some of those "experts" are still unconvinced. The fact remains that the danger increased until responsibility for meeting it was given to a vigorous ex-guerrilla leader who had a thorough understanding of the political base required for action, and a vivid awareness of the very real threat to the stability of government posed by the Huk movement. Within fifteen months after Raman Magsaysay's appointment as Secretary of National Defense, it was apparent that the Huk had lost their war.

If a major foreign power is assisting the threatened government in its counterguerrilla effort, an understanding of the implications of its aid is essential. An analysis similar in many ways to that made of the political situation of the threatened country is required. The attitudes of the assisting power, the kinds and amounts of aid given, and restrictions on it, may largely determine, or at least influence, adoption and implementation of counterguerrilla measures. Obviously this is a delicate and difficult task. Certain a priori guidelines may be drawn: Torture or liquidation of prisoners or accused, without trial or after summary trial, will be so strongly disapproved that it will not be feasible if further aid is to be expected. There may be strong pressure for land and social reforms based on theoretical concepts, not necessarily significant in terms of their effects either on the counterguerrilla efforts or on the conditions that brought the guerrilla into being. Major reforms in government administrative practices will be strongly recommended. The armed forces will be expected generally to follow patterns and practices of organization, doctrine, training, and equipment similar to the assisting power. A strong centralized command will be considered essential.

Aid, other than strictly military, will tend to concentrate on long-range projects enhancing the industrial or agricultural productivity of the country. Short-term local projects will be discouraged, both officially and by unofficial observers.

Money or supplies will ordinarily not be available for specific "spot" requirements outside the conventional pattern. Extensive and detailed planning will usually be required before funds are appropriated or released for major projects.

Military matériel may require a lead time of at least a year for even conventional items. Nonstandard items will be extremely difficult to obtain, especially if the request for them reflects any reluctance, however reasonable, to accept the standard. For example, an effort to get tennis shoes instead of combat boots might meet strong opposition. If there is a simultaneous request that steel helmets not be procured and not be charged against funds available for military aid, serious, if unacknowledged, repercussions are possible.

The foregoing guidelines will not be valid in all cases; some may already lack validity. To some extent, they typify United States assistance in the past; they are, accordingly, considerations that are likely to be borne in mind, and quite possibly given undue emphasis, by those seeking U.S. assistance. Some, such as the treatment of prisoners, represent immutable policy, which must be accepted; others, which may seem to pose insurmountable obstacles in some situations, can be modified.

What cannot and must not be overlooked are the political facts of life in the country faced with a guerrilla problem, and in the assisting country. Always, and for each country, the internal political situation, the national politics, the method of and speed in formulating national policies must be considered. Tacit alliances between politicians of the countries involved are by no means impossible. Two countries having a long history of close relationships are apt to find that traces of such relations enter into the apparently domestic problems of both countries. Ties between elements of international organizations—church or civic—may have significant effects. Few appreciate the amount of assistance given as a result of the ties between U.S. and Philippine organizations, or the extent of at least quasi-official Philippine interference in U.S. politics.

There is always a possibility that actions taken in one country may have serious political repercussions in the other. One field in which this is particularly common is that of nonmilitary aid, always a controversial issue. If aid funds have been spent with the blessing of the administration then in power on projects whose utility is not readily apparent or must be concealed, the whole aid program may be the object of violent partisan attacks. These may cause termination or reduction of further aid. The counterguerrilla must take these facts of life into consideration.

Operations in the Philippines were blessed by an unusual absence of critical aid problems. The traditional relationship between the Philippines and the United States and the great good will on both sides (extending not only to officeholders, but also to common citizens in both countries) largely precluded serious difficulties. In some instances, problems seemed briefly significant, but they were never a real handicap to the counterguerrilla. Indeed, the prevailing spirit of cooperation, and the aid given and used as a result, contributed decisively to the success of the counterguerrilla effort.

Analysis of the composition, strength, equipment, and state of training of the armed forces is usually not difficult. Evaluation of strong and weak points is more difficult, since it so largely depends on the evaluator's appreciation of the requirements for successful counterguerrilla warfare. Most difficult of all is using and developing strength for counterguerrilla operations—securing the cooperation of the members of the armed forces while overcoming their weaknesses.

Often problems will arise from the past training and possibly the past experience of the senior officers in the armed forces. They are almost certain to be indoctrinated to a considerable extent in military theories applicable to conventional warfare. They may or may not be equally well trained in the implementation of these theories, but any recommended action that falls outside the inculcated theoretical principles is certain to meet with strong opposition. No matter how cogent the reasons are for departing from accepted doctrine, they are likely to be unacceptable if they were not taught at the same level and with the same emphasis as was the doctrine. Worse, recommending departure from orthodox doctrine will convict the advocate of heresy, at the least, and quite possibly of ignorance and willful sabotage. Although it may be hard to persuade the U.S. military-assistance group to provide tennis shoes, it is likely to be far harder to persuade the army being helped to do away with such traditional symbols as heavy boots and steel helmets. Nor is this phenomenon by any means peculiar to the so-called military mind. It is even more marked among such professions as medicine and law, to say nothing of such academic disciplines as economics and sociology.

Matters especially to be considered in evaluating the armed forces' strengths and weaknesses, more or less in order of importance, are: (1) discipline—the speed, extent, and reliability with which orders are carried out promptly and to the best of the receivers' ability; (2) basic military attitudes, i.e., predilection for offensive or for defensive tactics; (3) morale; (4) basic training of troops; (5) effectiveness of basic logistics organization—how well and regularly troops are fed and paid; (6) appreciation at all echelons of the importance to successful counterguerrilla operations of good relations with civilians; (7) basic military matériel—shoulder-fired weapons, etc.; (8) transport, other than air; (9) field equipment and replacements; (10) air support, especially for supply purposes; (11) initiative, extent of training, morale of junior leaders; (12) medical services; (13) staff planning ability.

In some instances, political affiliations or attitudes of senior officers and of the rank and file may be of critical importance. In other situations, in other countries (as in the Philippines), this may be virtually irrelevant.

Analysis of the armed forces must take into consideration the military requirements of the nation; the size and type of armed forces it needs to repel external aggression. These requirements must be considered both in theoretical and practical terms, because planning for counterguerrilla operations must often compromise between the requirements for external defense and for internal defense, that is, counterguerrilla operations. Funds and resources will seldom seem adequate for both missions, especially if preparations for defense against external aggression rely primarily on conventional forces and doctrines. Frequently, it will be found that the importance of defense against internal aggression is so little understood that otherwise available military forces are not employed in counterguerrilla operations. This was true for a time in the Philippines; it is true today in other countries.

Consideration must also be given in this evaluation to the police forces of the country and to the nation's potential for fielding useful auxiliary forces. A country that has recently experienced a major guerrilla movement, such as that developed in the Philippines during the Japanese occupation, obviously can provide many experienced guerrillas who, if not actually in the armed forces, can be of great value in auxiliary, or so-called home-defense units. The possible dangers in the formation of auxiliary units must be carefully calculated and guarded against; however, such potential dangers will seldom outweigh the advantages to be gained from the proper organization and employment of such units.

Scarcely less important than knowledge of the abilities and weaknesses of the armed forces is knowledge about the national intelligence organization or organizations. What intelligence services are in operation? How good are they? How do they compete? To what extent have they been infiltrated by the enemy? Who gets their reports? How are they checked? What use is made of them?

These questions will be difficult to answer. Intelligence services will try to maintain maximum secrecy about everything except their triumphs and their need for funds. However, the procurement and use of intelligence cannot be delayed pending the development of the best possible national intelligence service. Planning for counterguerrilla operations must envision securing the maximum from existing services, realizing the importance of getting and using the best available information as quickly as possible. (It should also envision improving those services, but not at the cost of even a temporary loss of information.)

Popular attitudes toward the armed forces and the intelligence agencies are an essential element in the over-all strength and weakness of these critical services. What do farmers, teachers, petty government officials, reporters, businessmen think about the soldiers? Why? What type and kind of newspaper stories appear about members of the armed forces, both as a class and as individuals? What is said about intelligence agents and about the agencies they represent? Are they called Gestapo or NKVD, or are they laughed at? Why? To a very considerable extent, especially in counterguerrilla operations, a government service is only as good as it is believed to be by the people it is supposed to serve and to defend.

Analysis of the organization and effectiveness of other government departments is necessary for an adequate appraisal of strengths and weaknesses. Inadequacies in these agencies from want of funds, personnel, planning, knowledge, ability, or purposefulness have contributed to the conditions that enabled the guerrilla movement to come into being. Possibly, these conditions can be altered without changes in the departments responsible for the needed actions, but the unsatisfactory conditions can certainly be eliminated much more readily and efficiently if the appropriate departments actively participate in the effort. Particularly important in counterguerrilla operations are the departments or ministries of interior, justice, agriculture, labor, and social welfare. Inadequacies in matters under the jurisdiction of these agencies are perhaps the most common and the most serious factors predisposing the people toward guerrilla activity.

The ministries of agriculture, education, and social welfare can be especially useful in sponsoring and conducting activities to demonstrate that support of the guerrilla is no longer justified. How these ministries can and should be employed in a given situation will depend primarily on an assessment of their personnel, secondarily on their past history and the national policy, and tertiarily on their financing. Problems of personnel may or may not be susceptible of solution, but they must be recognized and reckoned with.

The more the established agencies of government enter into the counterguerrilla effort, the easier it will be to eliminate the guerrilla problem. In many instances, it may not be feasible to employ all the machinery of government. In other instances, some element of the government machinery may be so much more efficient, so much more effective, so much more able to collaborate intelligently in the counterguerrilla effort that it can and should be employed in fields properly appertaining to other government agencies.

Under Magsaysay, agencies of the Department of National Defense performed many functions properly belonging to other departments of government. Troops built schools and roads, normally functions of the Department of Education or the Bureau of Public Works. Lawyers in the military service defended civilians in civil suits over land tenure and aided in the criminal prosecution in civilian courts of military personnel accused of common crimes—both functions of the Department of Justice. The Armed Forces sponsored resettlement projects, and so on and on, until there was virtually no agency of government that did not, at one time or another, receive the often unwanted assistance of members of the military services.

This seemingly unwarranted usurpation of functions was neither a matter of empire-building nor politically inspired, although both charges were often made. These actions in question were needed actions, actions that contributed to defeating the Huk. The only way Magsaysay saw of getting action when, and how, he wanted it (yesterday, and effectively, without argument) was to have the forces under his control act. Similar situations may often occur when the individual responsible for the counterguerrilla effort is not the chief executive.

So far, the estimate of the friendly situation has considered only what might be called the existing official elements: the nation's political leadership, which is ultimately responsible for the counterguerrilla effort and the armed forces as the arm or force (primarily military) to be employed against the guerrilla, a force, also, that will either gain or lose popular support for the government. Other important elements, essentially neutral, that can be made friendly or unfriendly, depending on whether they are wisely or unwisely used, have not been considered.

The element that will first come to the mind of the soldier, perhaps, is the physical one: the terrain, the geography, the climate, the road net, the cover (vegetation cover or lack of it) in the area of operation. The effect of this complex on the enemy was discussed in the preceding chapter. Their effect on operations against the guerrilla must also be considered.

Spencer Chapman entitled his classic account of action against the Japanese in Malaya *The Jungle Is Neutral.* The jungle may be neutral, but the soldier or guerrilla who regards it as a friend will find it indeed a friend if he is dealing with an enemy who considers the jungle his enemy. The same may be said of all aspects of the physical environment in the area of operations. Terrain in general, jungle in particular, is neutral only if both contenders employ it with equal skill, knowledge, and understanding.

If practices and tactics are adopted that make the best possible use of the elements of physical environment, it may be taken as certain that the environment will seem to help. If on the other hand, the elements of the physical environment are regarded as enemies, if the flooded paddy fields or the thick rain forest are regarded as nuisances because they inhibit the use of armor, the advantage passes to the unarmored enemy. Much more than in conventional war, in guerrilla war skillful use of the physical environment marks the successful fighter.

The national economy of the country is an important consideration—particularly that portion of the national product at the disposition of the government through taxation. In the simplest possible terms, a government with an annual budget of $100 million cannot afford very many helicopters with which to chase guerrillas. It cannot afford a really elaborate communications network. In fact, the extraordinary expenses incurred in antiguerrilla operations usually must be met at least in part through outside aid, and as has already been pointed out, this aid may impose many limitations and restrictions.

Aside from the question of the funds available, there is also the question of how much of these funds should be allotted to the counterguerrilla operations and how much should be allocated to other functions of government. Take, for example, the situation in the Philippines in 1946: Four years of enemy occupation had ravaged the country; Japanese foragers and hungry guerrillas had eaten most of the livestock, including the essential farm work animals. Schoolhouses without number had been burned down, and military units occupied many of those which remained. Inflation had very nearly quadrupled the cost of living, but the salaries of government employees remained basically at prewar levels. Under such circumstances, it was indeed difficult to determine what proportion of the available funds should be put into restoring the essential services of government—desperately needed by all of the Philippines—and what proportion could be properly expended in the subjugation of a guerrilla movement that seemed to affect directly only about 5 to 10 per cent of the population of the country. American aid was sufficient to prevent utter destitution and perhaps chaos. Even so, there was little money left for action against the guerrillas (whom many Americans, like many Filipinos, did not see as constituting a clear and present danger).

The ability of the national economy to produce, or to improvise, in support of the counterguerrilla effort may be even more important than its ability to support the government with tax monies. The way in which productive support is manifested and the items which may be produced depend to a very large extent on the ingenuity and effort applied.

Napalm was not available in the quantity desired by the armed forces at one period during the Huk campaign. Thanks to the ingenuity and effort of the Research and Development Division of the Armed Forces of the Philippines, a very effective substitute, largely composed of gasoline, coconut husks, and rubber from discarded tires, was developed. During their struggle against the Japanese, some guerrillas developed an excellent field uniform made from hemp fiber woven on home looms. Match heads were substituted, not very satisfactorily, for primers in reloaded cartridges.

Civic organizations can make contributions to the counterguerrilla effort that are nothing short of awe-inspiring. They can also contribute in ways as ordinary and as valuable as supplying meat and potatoes (or fish and rice). Churches are an obvious potential source of support, but their role in the society, and popular attitudes toward them, must be carefully analyzed. Mass communications media are the most conspicuous of the civil assets or liabilities. What are they? What do they say? Why? What kinds of people, and how many, pay attention to them? What credibility is given them? Are their words for sale?

Probably more important than the personnel in government, than the training and quality of the armed forces, than the physical environment or the economic situation of the country, are the attitudes and opinions of its people and the means by which these are formed, guided, and expressed. The importance of popular attitudes and opinions about the chief executive, about the administration and about the armed forces has already been touched upon. Equally important are the popular attitudes toward government: the concepts of government, the ambitions and aspirations for it held by most citizens of the country.

Sometimes the attitudes of small groups that in one way or another are involved in the antiguerrilla operations have particular significance. One such small group were the Negritos, the pygmy blacks who inhabit the grassy uplands and rain forests of the western part of Central Luzon (then the western boundary of Huklandia). The Negritos lived in the vicinity of an American Army base set up early in the century. The Negritos always avoided contact with other Filipinos, but they knew and respected the United States Army. From 1946 to 1950, they were of little help either to the guerrillas to government forces. Since the guerrillas (the Huk) were roaming in their area and could not always be avoided, the Negritos sometimes acted as guides and couriers for them. They knew only the Huk side of the story; they had little interest in it, but they had no interest in the Philippine Government, no interest in anything but continuing their nomadic life with as little interruption as possible.

Magsaysay knew these Negritos, knew their attitude, and decided to change it. He arranged a conference at which many Negritos were present. He also arranged, unofficially, for a captain of the United States Army to address the Negritos, telling them that Secretary of National Defense Magsaysay and his soldiers now represented the government of their country and that it was their duty to assist these soldiers as they had in years gone by assisted the soldiers of the United States Army. From that time on (thanks to careful instructions Magsaysay gave on how to maintain the liaison thus begun), the Negritos proved a valuable source of intelligence and of warnings about the Huk.

Much of the success of the operations to win the people's loyalty and to eliminate the Huk was achieved by Magsaysay, owing directly to his understanding of the attitudes and opinions of the people and the ways in which their attitudes were formed, guided, and communicated. The Negrito incident is only one example.

The disposition of captured or surrendered guerrillas and their supporters has been discussed at great length, insofar as it affects attitudes toward government and the reaction of people who learn about the treatment. There are other significant aspects. Captured or surrendered guerrillas may be a valuable resource. One value is the intelligence, the information about the enemy, that can be obtained by proper handling of them. Another is that prisoners whose loyalty to the government has been won can be used to take action against their former comrades. The possibilities for such use are almost infinitely varied. Perhaps the most outstanding example comes not from the Philippines but from Kenya, where Ian Henderson organized captured and converted Mau Mau into "pseudo-gangs" that effectively cleared the die-hard remnants of the Mau Mau and their leaders from the forests of Kenya.

The most obvious and the safest use of prisoners is in psychological warfare, in the preparation of surrender leaflets and testimonials addressed to their former comrades, pointing out how well they, the prisoners, are treated and inviting their former comrades to join them. Erstwhile Huk evangelists were particularly useful in making speeches on behalf of the government in the very areas where they had once attacked and denigrated that very same government. Often, their "come to the mourners' bench" technique worked nearly as well on Huk and sympathizers as when they had been proselytizing for the guerrillas.

One particularly valuable human resource in the Philippines was the vast reservoir of experienced guerrillas who learned their trade in the widespread anti-Japanese resistance movement during World War II. In the years 1946–50, little use was made of them, although some individual ex-guerrillas made outstanding contributions during this period. Actually, this resource was little tapped for action directly against the Huk, even in the period 1950–53, when Magsaysay (himself an ex-guerrilla) was in charge. They simply were not needed.

Some units of the armed forces, it is true, were organized from ex-guerrillas. Other ex-guerrillas in the area of operations were used as intelligence agents and guides, or to serve in local defense units against the Huk. The principal service of ex-guerrillas, and it was of great value, was in generating popular support for the revitalized armed forces and for reviving faith in government.

Using the special skills of primitive peoples against guerrillas operating in uninhabited areas has long been a feature of counterguerrilla operations. This was little done in the campaign against the Huk. Operations were conducted, for the most part, in areas where special skills were not required. In some instances, and in some places outside the main areas of operation, mountain peoples did yeoman service by rounding up or eliminating Huk stragglers. Much greater use might have been made of these people had the circumstances been different. One skill (not especially developed in the Philippines) that can be of great assistance is that of trackers, who follow guerrillas who have dispersed after an action.

Copy Nr 1
National Headqtrs
FREE COUNTRY
010001 New New
U&I2

OPORD 1 (FRAGMENTARY)
References: National Constitution, Gettysburg
Address

1. SITUATION

   a. Enemy hold Obj G in strength, deny access Obj N; capable reinf from undet pos beyond PL FREEDOM; reinf fr outside natlbdry.

   b. Friendly forces

2. MISSION

   Nation atk immed; achieve, prep defend Obj N (Government of, by, for people)

3. EXECUTION

   a. Concept of operation. Main atk, Dept Natl Def reduce Obj G; as assist achievement Obj N; prevent en reinf. Other forces atk desig init obj; prep assist reduce Obj G or cont to Obj N; prevent en reinf Obj G; prevent en establishing new pos beyond PL FREEDOM.

   Accomplishment of mission dependent on:

   (1) Reduction Obj G

   (2) Prevention en establishing new pos beyond PL FREEDOM

   b. Dept Natl Def:

   (1) Reduce Obj G; prevent en reinf, new pos, beyond PL FREEDOM.

   (2) Natl Res on order.

   c. Dept Educ

   d. Dept Just

x x x x x

1. Coordinating instructions:

   (1) Effective for planning and execution on receipt.

   (2) Priority support Dept Natl Def until PL FREEDOM reached.

4. ADMINISTRATION AND LOGISTICS

5. COMMAND AND SIGNAL

Acknowledge

MAALAM
President

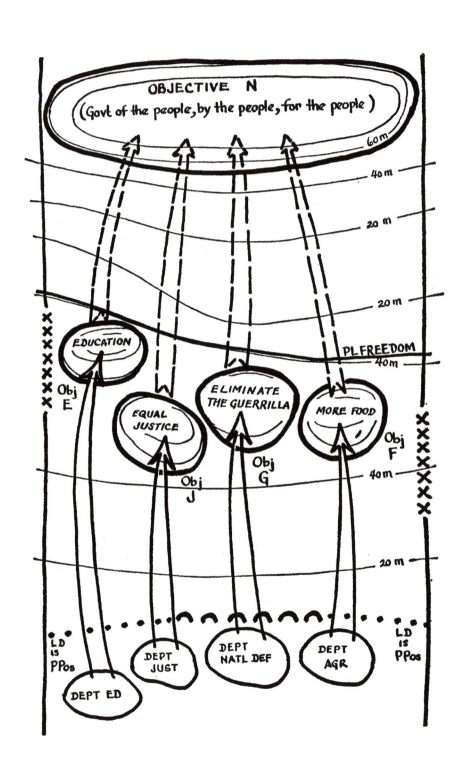

In summation, it must be realized that as guerrilla and counterguerrilla warfare are in a very real sense total warfare, the winner will be the one who best uses the totality of resources available. Note the phrase "the totality of resources." There is a difference between using all resources and using all methods. The methods chosen must be scrutinized carefully for possible undesired effects. They may achieve the immediate effect desired but have consequences harmful to the over-all effort—like a successful operation on a patient who then dies of shock. Thus, shooting prisoners, although doubtless the most effective way to dispose of them—and surely the most economical—will almost invariably produce greater hostility and strengthen the enemy forces.

What is essential is for those charged with responsibility for counterguerrilla operations to decide what must be, what should be, and what can be, done—and then to do it, by the most effective means at hand. It may be charged that this is a disorganized, even a subversive, approach; it will be said that the director of the counterguerrilla efforts (the Secretary of National Defense, for instance) has no business meddling in the affairs of other departments of government. It is entirely true that the counterguerrilla effort, broad as it must be, must not become the only object of attention; the other functions of government must be performed as well. But if the counterguerrilla operations fail, the success of other activities is of purely academic interest.

Chapter 7

THE MISSION

MISSION:

1. **The objective; the task together with the purpose, which clearly indicates the action to be taken and the reason therefor.**

2. **In common usage, especially when applied to lower military units, a duty assigned to an individual or unit; a task.**[1]

HAVING DETERMINED as well as he may the enemy and friendly situation, the counterguerrilla must next turn his attention to the mission. It has been assumed that the mission, the objective, is the elimination of the guerrilla enemy, the liquidation of the guerrilla movement.

This is indeed *a* mission; it is, in fact, probably *the* mission that the counterguerrilla is supposed to have. But it is not *the* mission of the government that is threatened by the guerrilla; it is not even *the* mission of the armed forces of that government. Their basic mission is the protection of the people of the country and/or the government.

The mission of the government is to represent its people and to defend their interests. It is this simple and reasonable purpose that is often obscured, twisted and fragmented under the assault of a guerrilla movement. Frequently, one of the first objectives of an insurrection is to draw the government into a position that makes elimination of the guerrilla seem its chief, if not its only, mission.

The man or men charged with and feeling the urgent responsibility for terminating a guerrilla movement that threatens the national existence will see very little relevance in the abstract national mission stated above. Discussion of the ultimate purpose of government—its mission—is likely to seem as ridiculous as a thoughtful consideration of "Why is a house?" when one's dwelling is on fire.

The importance of the ultimate objective of government, and its pertinence to counterguerrilla operations, becomes apparent only after analysis of the opposing forces at work in a nation under guerrilla attack. On one side is the guerrilla, who has a simple, practical program: to stay close to the people, using them at once as his support and his shield, rousing them to "self-defense" based on their known ills and the remedies he has promised—a relationship as intimate as a family council. On the other side is the government, concentrated in a national capital, obligated to provide security, economic and social health, protection for its wealthiest as well as its poorest citizen, and obligated, too, to provide a place and a voice in world affairs for the nation. What the guerrilla is promising for some distant day the government is bound—by its very existence—to provide immediately. And the rise of the guerrilla movement brings a new and heavy duty to destroy the guerrilla before his activities force a new—and untested—system on the people. That duty is further complicated by the government's obligation to maintain some measure of freedom for its individual citizens.

The guerrilla, on the other hand, is fighting for a cause. His leaders may have misstated that cause, they may have concealed their true objectives, but they have provided an ideal for the fighting man. They have provided a cause so appealing that men are willing to fight for it, to show the tenacity of purpose, the willingness to work, to endure, and to suffer that is the essential characteristic of the guerrilla. Supporters of the guerrilla must sympathize with that ideal and share in the motivation for its achievement, since they deprive themselves in order to support the guerrilla and are quite possibly risking their lives and those of their families as well.

To cope with men so motivated—unless they are to be over borne by sheer weight of numbers, which is a strategy not so easy as it might appear—the members of government, the defenders of government, and the supporters of government must muster a comparable determination, a comparable tenacity, a comparable capacity for self-sacrifice in the pursuit of victory.

For most people, liquidation of the guerrilla movement does not in itself constitute a sufficient motive to rouse them to match the efforts of the guerrilla. It may be enough for single-minded, well-indoctrinated soldiers or policemen, for alert, patriotic civilians. But even these individuals often are motivated in fact by a personal ideal—loyalty to the state, to a leader, or to their squadmates. Most people need something more than a tenuous loyalty to an abstract ideal; they need a cause they can recognize as worth struggling, working, even suffering to accomplish. They need to have that cause explained in terms they can understand. They need to understand how they, as individuals, can participate. That this cause must be an effective government seems obvious, yet, like many obvious things, it is easily overlooked. Under the pressures of a guerrilla movement, obstacles to recognition of the basic mission exist in all segments of the population.

Curiously enough, it is the military who are often the most difficult to convince of the overriding importance of the ultimate objective, the necessity for seeking always the furtherance of *the* mission of government. The better trained the military are in conventional doctrine, the greater will be the difficulty in convincing them. Curiously, because from the beginning of his military career to the end, the soldier is taught the ultimate and overriding importance of achieving the objective. Unfortunately, in contemporary Western culture, apparently through fear of the military's achieving undue dominance in civil spheres, there has been and is a continuous effort to make the members of the military think only of military objectives. The real significance of the dictum of Clausewitz that war is only a form of political intercourse is seldom understood or, if understood, is largely forgotten. It frequently requires major retraining to make the soldier understand that not only is his ultimate objective a political one, but that it is his duty to contribute to the achievement of that objective by all the means at his disposal.

The politician is the least difficult to convince of the importance of *the* mission of government, of the importance of creating an effective government the people will support. However, the politician must, periodically, secure the support of enough people to keep him—or place him—in office. It is difficult, therefore, for him to lose himself in a cause. Viewed cynically, the politician's objective must always be capture of the next hill—the winning of the next election. If he is to help the cause of good government, he must use all means at his disposal to become part of that government. So he must forever be caught between the ideal the people seek and the practical means he must resort to. At best, it is more difficult for the politician than for the soldier to engage in a sustained effort clearly intended to further the mission of government.

The personnel of government must understand not only the mission of government, they must understand also the necessity for making their every action further that mission. Finally, they must convince the governed that they are effectively seeking to advance that mission. This has perhaps never been better demonstrated than in the Philippines during the years 1946–52. Those were the years when the vicious guerrilla rebellion, the Hukbalahap movement, sought to overthrow the democratically constituted government in the name of the "New Democracy"; years when the government fumbled and nearly failed in its attempts to quell the rebellion; years when the government finally solved the problem.

To the Philippines, and to the Filipino, the ultimate objective of government was clearly stated in 1900 by William Howard Taft. Summarized, it is the establishment of a stable, popular government, ruling in accordance with the needs and desires of the majority while protecting the rights of the minority. That objective has never changed appreciably. Schools, free press, free speech, and all mass communications had made the purpose of government widely known for more than forty years, to such an extent that the overwhelming majority of Filipinos believed in a democracy as the only acceptable purpose of any government.

It was Japan's ruthless contempt for this concept that set tens of thousands of Filipinos marching as guerrillas even before the Japanese completed their occupation of the islands, in 1942. The chorus of the favorite marching song of one large unit was, "Come and fight for democracy." Tens of thousands died between 1942 and 1945 for the (to them) inextricably intertwined ideals of patriotism and democracy, for government "of the people, by the people, and for the people." It cannot be doubted that this was the original motivation of many of the followers of the Hukbalahap *Supremo,* Luis Taruc.

If the purpose of government was as stated and was so widely understood, how then were the Hukbalahap able to launch a thriving rebellion in the name of "New Democracy"? How could they so long disguise their Communist ties? It cannot be explained by the fact that the Communist Party of the Philippines and the Communist International had a long-range plan ready to put into effect calling for the overthrow of the established government and the installation of a Communist state. That is true. They did have such a plan. But the desire to achieve these objectives—which Communists in every country desire—is not in itself a sufficient base from which to launch an effective guerrilla movement. Perhaps the real reason their guerrilla movement achieved viability—and was well on the way to success—was that nearly all that the Huk publicly said and did was compatible with their claim of trying to attain the kind of government all Filipinos wanted.

Why were the Huk slogans—"Land for the Landless," "Equal Justice," "Honesty and Efficiency in Government"—so appealing, so immediately effective with the people? For one thing, these were slogans deeply rooted in political history, dating back to the days of Spanish occupation. That Hukbalahap leaders believed these were ideals that could best be achieved through the establishment of a Communist form of government was not generally understood by their sympathizers. Filipinos supporting the rebellion were not fighting over details of administration, over the right to put—or not to put—the significant label "People's" before the title "Republic of the Philippines." Relatively few of the Hukbalahap would have been willing to fight for Communist dialectics or Mother Russia.

Was it failure of—or betrayal by—the legally constituted government that gave strength to the Huk guerrilla movement? It was not, despite widespread Huk charges. Basically, the long record of the government's failure to eliminate the Huk was due to the failure of men at all levels of government to understand their mission, their failure to concentrate on the main objective of government and to make their actions clearly compatible with service to the people. There were sins, but they were sins more of omission than of commission, a situation that threatened at one time to give the Huk victory by default.

There was a breakdown in communications between people and officials. The officials' words were not always consonant with their deeds—and where there was a conflict, the people believed the deeds rather than the words. Huk propagandists seized on every misdeed within government, proclaiming the occasional dishonest or inefficient official typical of the men in government. The many worthwhile achievements of the government were not effectively and convincingly brought to the attention of the people. The press and radio were largely filled with charges and defenses, with promises and denunciations.

More deep-seated and far-reaching than the failure in communications, however, was the failure to clarify the mission and the urgency of that mission, a failure that very nearly caused the collapse of the government. The mission— to protect, represent, and defend the interests of the people—was taken for granted. Stress was placed instead on the myriad secondary objectives, each treated as a crisis, with any success hailed as the end of crisis. None of these "crises" had the broad appeal that would have opened the way for a crusade— the appeal necessary to engage the people and to persuade them to subordinate their individual aims.

Those individual aims differed widely, as human objectives must, since they are directly related to the interests and beliefs of the individuals themselves. Essentially, the concern of the individual in government was to ensure the well-being of himself and his family. To the soldier, this meant compliance with orders. To the politician, it meant securing his appointment or re-election to an office. To the lesser government employee, it seemed that his very presence on the job should be regarded as contributing in some measure to the general welfare.

The Filipino soldier and politician may or may not have realized how important liquidation of the Huk movement could be, but no one was reminding him of this from 1946 to 1950. No one was impressing on him the importance of his individual contribution or delineating the areas of that contribution. Inevitably, the power and capability of the government were progressively weakened as the years passed.

The individual citizen not actively concerned in the Huk movement found himself in a morass. In a culture that placed great emphasis on democratic government, he often had the reaction that there was little difference between the existing government and the government the Huk professed to offer. Weren't their claims almost the same? To put the welfare of the people above all else? Possibly one was better, possibly the other, but by and large, the ordinary Filipino cared little for either one. He was not convinced of the sincerity of either, so his natural inclination was to pursue his own interests and hope that both sides would leave him alone. In this he was not unlike the average man in any country, at any time, whose emotions and instincts for self-preservation have not yet been aroused by either protagonist in a national struggle. To be stable and popular, above all to be successful in eliminating a guerrilla movement that threatens its very existence, government, and the people who compose it, must do three things:

1. Understand the primary mission—the provision of effective government that represents the wishes of the governed and respects their rights.
2. Ensure that all actions of the government, and its personnel, clearly further the primary mission.
3. Convince the governed that the government is earnestly and effectively seeking to accomplish the functions stated.

The blunt fact is that because it failed to do these three things, the government of the Philippines from 1946 to 1950 failed to suppress the Huk movement.

Success in these three things was the greatest contribution of Ramón Magsaysay to the Philippines and to the operations against the Huk. To him, the mission was clear and unmistakable: The establishment of government of, by, and for the people was the single major objective to which everything else must contribute. He never let anyone forget this or permit secondary objectives to appear more important than the primary one. He realized, of course, that many things must be done to achieve this objective, and that one of the most immediate tasks was elimination of the threat to the stability of government and to the welfare of the governed that the Huk movement presented.

More, he sought by every means possible to make it clear to everyone from President to uncommitted citizen, from Senator to General to private soldier and individual voter, that the real ultimate objective of government was the one to which his and their energies must be devoted. Once the people of the country were convinced that the government earnestly and effectively pursued *the* mission, was indeed seeking honestly and intelligently to promote the welfare of the people, the Huk movement became scarcely more than a petty nuisance.

Nevertheless, it still demanded the accomplishment of many difficult tasks. These tasks involved, for the most part, changing the ways in which things were done; securing the adoption of tactics consonant with the mission and with the necessity for securing public support. Many military practices had to be changed radically to secure popular acceptance of the concept that the military were the protectors of the civil population.

Obviously, such practices as area clearance by slaughtering every moving thing could never be employed against the Huk, for this was only the most stringent of various techniques that would have inflicted undue hardship on people not proved to be guerrillas or guerrilla supporters. The suspension of civil liberties traditional to the culture was similarly excluded, unless the people could be persuaded that such measures were needed for their own protection.

Typical of practices that had created widespread ill will for the forces of government in the Philippines was the establishment of checkpoints, where all traffic might be stopped along main arteries of travel and commerce. Theoretically, these were a safeguard to civilians—a method of making the highways more hazardous for guerrillas and their supporters.

In reality, checkpoints became collection points; too often the soldier found that by collecting a "toll," he could increase his scanty pay and allowances. The commanding General of the Armed Forces, traveling in civilian clothes, was asked for "coffee money" by a soldier who did not recognize him. Before it was finally abandoned, the permanent checkpoint not only had proved utterly inadequate as a limitation on Huk movement, but had created widespread corruption among troops and commercial truckers. What was almost as serious was the fact that the military—representing the government—had worsened relations between the people and the government.

Even military measures directed solely against the enemy—the guerrilla and his supporters—must be weighed for their effect on the attitude of the people toward their government as well as for their military value. For example, from 1946 to 1949, some of the most effective military action against the Hukbalahap was taken by the Nenita unit and its successor organizations under the same commander. The Nenita unit was organized as a small semi-independent hunter-killer detachment to seek out and destroy top leaders of the Huk. Openly based in the heart of the strongest Huk area, it sought by disciplined, ruthless action to strike terror into the guerrillas and their supporters. It was popularly (but erroneously) thought to take no prisoners, to grant no quarter. By dint of hard intelligence work and clever ruses, the unit did succeed in capturing or killing many Huk, in substantially dampening the fighting spirit of many more, and in reducing the effectiveness of local support organizations. The Nenita unit certainly contributed in no small measure to the Huk decision to accept—or pretend to accept-an amnesty proffered by the Philippine Government in 1948.

But the over-all effect of the Nenita operation, and of the reputation it established throughout the country was, on the whole, to increase support for the Huk. How could a government claiming concern for the welfare of the people and protection of their interests support a gang of ruthless killers, many of whose victims were not proved traitors? The political repercussions were serious, as might be expected in a democratic country. Even more damaging to the government was the condemnatory attitude of the press, cunningly intensified by Huk propagandists. In the end, many Filipinos were convinced that the government, by the use of such a force showed itself to be at least as bad as the Huk, and perhaps less deserving of support than the "agrarian reformers."

There were other practices of the military, such as the *zona,* or village-screening operation, which created great ill will toward the armed forces, yet were undeniably effective means of hitting active guerrillas. It was essential to make the armed forces more effective in hitting them, and this could scarcely be done if techniques of proven utility were summarily abandoned.

The answer lay in changing the attitudes of the soldiers toward the civilians, toward the guerrillas—in fact, toward the war. The lack of success in suppressing the Huk movement had adversely affected the morale of members of the armed forces as much as it had that of other government servants and the governed themselves. The armed forces were thoroughly committed to conventional doctrine and to conventional methods of waging war. To the military theoretician, the purpose of the armed forces was to repel, or to prepare to repel, external aggression. The Huk campaign appeared no more than a lengthy and tiresome diversion from that objective. To many of those in the field against the Huk, in a campaign that the government seemed unwilling to support sufficiently to make possible its successful conclusion, a state of desultory combat had become a way of life. Worst of all, soldiers in the field had come to look upon the civilian population in the area of operations as composed largely of enemies or enemy supporters, people whose protection was no part of their mission.

These attitudes had to be changed. They were—in many ways. Essentially, the changes meant instilling in the soldier, at all echelons, an understanding of *the* mission of government, and the true mission of the armed forces. This was not a simple process, for it involved convincing the soldier that the government was dedicated to, and aggressively pursuing, its mission, which necessarily included effective support for the soldier. It involved, too, demanding that the soldier effectively accomplish his mission in all its aspects, from protecting civilians to aggressively pursuing and imposing his will on the guerrilla.

One of the moves that convinced the soldier was the emphasis the government placed on neutralizing support for the enemy by actions other than military. The soldier realized, at least intuitively, that the wide acceptance won by Huk slogans (he was at least tempted to believe some of them himself) meant that the government itself was generally disliked and distrusted. There were many reasons for this, but at the time Magsaysay became Secretary of National Defense, the greatest single cause was widespread indignation over the last Presidential election.

The 1949 election was marked by many fraudulent actions. To what extent these occurred at the direction of, or with the knowledge of, the highest officials of the country cannot be determined and is not really important. Political analysts have found it probable that whatever frauds were committed, they did not significantly affect the outcome of the election. However, knowledge of fraud was sufficiently widespread, the protests of losers were so loud and so persistent, and the propaganda by the Huk so effective, that the people of the Philippines were to some degree persuaded that the chief executive had stolen his office. And the chief executive himself believed that nothing he could say or do, nothing except his re-election, would convince the people of his right to hold office.

Throughout the government, officials had reached a state of mind compounded in roughly equal parts of frustration, justifiable indignation, defeatism, and self-justification. So many of the charges made against them by the press (and the Huk, whose purposes were very often served by the press) appeared palpably untrue to those in a position to know, and so many imputations of evil intentions were known by the accused to be false, that responsible officials had concluded that efforts to disprove the charges against them would be construed as a tacit admission of their truth.

A wholesale change in attitudes was clearly necessary. This might have been effected much more efficiently, with much better utilization of government resources, had the leader of the counterguerrilla movement been the chief executive or if there had been a master plan. Only in an antiguerrilla effort directed or, at least, wholeheartedly supported by the chief executive is it possible to use all existing government agencies. In the very propaganda slogans the guerrillas find successful, one may often find the clue to which department of government should take countering action.

For instance, when the guerrillas make profitable use of the slogan "Land for the Landless," then the ministry responsible for allocating and/or developing land should proclaim the government's intention of making land available within the limits of its resources for those who honestly desire it and will work for it.

If an effective slogan of the guerrillas is a demand for "Equal Justice for All," then the ministry of justice must find some dramatic way of demonstrating that justice is in fact dispensed equally to all.

In the Philippines, no Cabinet minister denied the desirability of such actions when Ramón Magsaysay took office as Secretary of National Defense. But none of the high officials in government understood the urgency for action in his own department. Their situation was not easy. The Secretary of Agriculture, for instance, was concerned with restoring normal agricultural production in a country largely devoted to agriculture, a country whose agricultural productivity had been greatly reduced, even to the extent of rendering many fields unusable, during the period of Japanese occupation. The enormity of these tasks blinded the Secretary of Agriculture to the urgency, if his government was to survive, of responding to the desires, to the demands so skillfully elaborated and exacerbated by the Huk, for land for the landless. The Secretary's answer was truthful and totally inadequate: A resettlement program was in progress, but it was not important in comparison with other agricultural emergencies.

The same sort of reaction came from the Department of Justice. That department was staggering under an overwhelming work load. Officials were for the most part sincere, even efficient, but they were much too busy to expend time and attention on petty cases, much less on publicizing their actions on such cases. And the occasional instances of dishonesty or inefficiency in the administration of justice did not warrant the broadside attacks being made on the whole department. The Secretary was not inclined to dignify such attacks by any dramatic action.

Into this atmosphere of dissatisfaction and recriminations, the new Secretary of National Defense swept with no planned action beyond his sincere and dedicated conviction that the people must be assured of the intention of the government to promote their welfare and of the effectiveness of the government in doing so.

What were the resources—political and military—on which Ramón Magsaysay could draw in 1950, when he was appointed Secretary of National Defense and charged with eliminating the Huk guerrilla movement?

The Philippines had a government and a people universally committed to the objective of a government elected by the people, dedicated to their welfare and protection, based on widespread democratic institutions. There was a fairly well-developed system of communications, a relatively high standard of literacy, and a tradition of political discussion and of popular participation in government. There was a notably free-spoken press of large circulation, which, whatever its faults, could not seriously be suspected of being under government control or even of being susceptible to control. The Philippines had a small but relatively well-trained and well-disciplined armed force. Not least, the individual Filipino was accustomed to taking personal action, to fight, if need be, for the establishment and the maintenance of liberty.

The situation in the Philippines will not have an exact parallel in any other country. However, a surprising number of similarities will probably be found to exist in greater or lesser degree in any country faced with a serious guerrilla problem. Perhaps the greatest difference, likely to be found in some of the newly emerged nations, will be a general lack of understanding of the institutions essential to representative government (i.e., a free press, schools, means to guarantee civil liberties, civilian-military balance, etc.). Any such lack of understanding or appreciation of the necessity for these institutions will offer a real challenge, but one that can be turned to the advantage of the (presumably) better-equipped counterguerrillas, if they can understand these requirements.

The basic plan for counterguerrilla action must provide for immediate and effective action to: ensure national security and effective administration; keep actions of government compatible with the objectives of government; inform and convince the people (including the guerrillas) that the Administration has a cause and that they should help that cause (an effective and desirable government).

At various times and under certain circumstances, one of these three elements may take precedence over the others, but none can be forgotten. The task becomes one of organizing and employing all available resources for translating these elements into positive action, positive achievement.

Magsaysay was the only high official in the Philippine Government who realized the necessity for—or could implement—these three approaches. Others in the Administration unanimously agreed on the validity and the desirability of the mission, but they failed to relate it to their own activities.

To obtain the balanced effort necessary to win for the government the necessary popular support, especially from the apathetic or uncommitted majority, Magsaysay was forced to use the armed forces, the press, public-spirited citizens. Everyone and everything possible was made to serve this purpose.

It was not coincidence that most of the private citizens who joined his effort were men who had themselves fought as guerrillas (against the Japanese) and for the same objectives. Further, as a former guerrilla, Magsaysay realized not only the necessity for obtaining maximum commitment to the struggle, he realized also the basic imperative of successful counterguerrilla war: the need to seize the initiative from the guerrilla on all fronts, psychological as well as military.

Understanding also that only active reform in the government could win the people to its support, Magsaysay himself became the most convincing argument that reform was in process. His youth, his exuberance, his decisiveness, his confidence in himself and in his country, the humorous temperament that kept him from self-aggrandizement—all these helped to convince the people that a new era, their era, had dawned. No one, seeing him in action, could doubt his determination to make good the claim that the soldiers were the protectors of the people, the members of government the servants of the public. He inspired, as well as required, those under his leadership to prove their dedication and sense of mission.

This rededication to the ultimate mission of government obviously imposed limitations on the actions that could be taken. Protectors of the people could scarcely operate checkpoints to extort coffee money. More, it imposed stiffer requirements for effective action—action to demonstrate effective protection—against those whom he denounced as enemies of the people. Otherwise, his claims were but empty words, he himself another demagogue, and the Huk virtually assured of easy victory.

To dramatize the intention to afford the maximum assistance and protection to those who wished to be good citizens, and its corollary of relentless action against those who wished harm to good citizens, Magsaysay announced the policy of "All-Out Friendship or All-Out Force." The Hukbalahap who would work for, rather than against the people, i.e., who would surrender, would receive a friendly welcome and the help he might need to rehabilitate himself. The Hukbalahap who continued to fight against the people and their government would be repaid in his own currency—force.

The color and magnetism of a Magsaysay are not an essential prerequisite to success as a counterguerrilla leader, although they are very helpful. It is essential that he understand, and pursue, *the* mission of government, as well as the immediate political and military actions necessary to defeat the guerrilla. It is imperative that military actions contribute to the over-all mission of convincing people of the good faith of their government.

In counterguerrilla warfare, as distinguished from conventional operations, the military is thrown into close contact with the civilians in the area of operations—since the guerrillas use the civilians as a shield and as a source of supplies. Whether his mission is to attack the guerrillas, or to protect the people from guerrilla attacks, the soldier must act in such close proximity to the people that the most significant part of the environment of antiguerrilla warfare is neither the terrain nor the weather; it is the ever present "sea" of civilians.

In moving in this sea, military personnel must, of course, be effective if they encounter guerrillas. More, they must so act as to carry conviction to the civilians that they are not sharks seeking to snap up guerrillas and any other "fish" that come their way; but that, instead, they are seeking to drive away the guerrilla sharks, and to help in other ways as well.

Militarily, this makes sense when it is put to the test of practice. The critical military need in antiguerrilla operations is to obtain information about the guerrillas, and to deny them information about friendly forces. This is most effectively and economically accomplished by securing civilian cooperation. With such cooperation, military forces need not greatly exceed the numbers of the guerrillas. Without cooperation, an overwhelming numerical superiority (historically, sometimes as high as 200 soldiers to 1 guerrilla) must be achieved.

A form of military organization must be provided capable of effective acceptance of responsibility in a given region for operations against the guerrillas, and for the inhabitants. Whatever form of organization is chosen, it must be one that will prove to the local citizens that the primary mission of the troops is the welfare of the nation and the protection of its citizenry. Effective action against the guerrillas is essential, but effective action against the guerrillas that simultaneously alienates the people is self-defeating. However, effective action that gains the support of the people for the armed forces will almost certainly lead to effective action against the guerrillas.

Planning and organizing effective action to gain the support of the people for the armed forces parallels the steps needed to gain the support of the people for the government. Both may often be achieved by dramatic attack on conditions that have given rise to effective slogans of the guerrillas.

A popular grievance that was once prevalent in the Philippines, and is usually to be found in countries subjected to prolonged guerrilla and antiguerrilla effort, is the behavior of the troops. Troop misbehavior under these conditions results not alone from lack of discipline; more often, it is traceable simply to inadequate appreciation by the command of the requirements of antiguerrilla operations. This last has many aspects, all of them militating against troop success.

Food for soldiers, especially for troops on patrol or actively engaged in operations, is often a problem that generates unnecessary civilian hostility.

Frequently, soldiers are forced for want of supplies to forage, to levy on the inhabitants of the area, for their food. Usually, this food is neither graciously sought nor willingly given; rather, it is taken and yielded in ways creating ill will on each side. Foraging and stealing by counterguerrillas must be stopped if popular support for them is to be achieved. It can easily be stopped, if the command will take the trouble to supply them with rations or money.

Magsaysay said that every member of the Armed Forces had two missions: He must be an ambassador seeking to build good will for his outfit and his government; he must also be a fighter seeking to kill or capture at least one enemy.

Effective action to gain popular support usually necessitates many activities not in the normal role of the armed forces. Some of these should be undertaken by other more appropriate agencies of government, were it not advantageous to highlight the accomplishments and dramatize the role of the armed forces. These actions (although often prompted by grievances exploited by the guerrillas) must not appear to be taken because of guerrilla demands, but must rather seem to prove the futility or malice of the guerrillas.

Thus, for example, "Land for the Landless" was an effective battle cry for the Huk. The reaction to this was so highly emotional that the slogan could not be countered; it had to be captured by dramatic government action. The need for land-settlement programs, at least as a political measure, had long been acknowledged by the government and a program of land settlement was actually under way. But the program lacked emphasis, drama, and popular appeal. The officials in charge of the program could see no need for exploiting their tasks as part of the antiguerrilla effort. Ideally, they should have expanded this program with a coordinated publicity program to drive home the realization that anyone who claimed to be fighting to get land of his own needed only to surrender, and demonstrate his sincerity, in order to be helped to his own farm. This the officials could not, or would not, do, so an agency of the Armed Forces did it. It is not a recommended solution, but it was one that was necessary then and it succeeded. It may be that other governments will find the same solution the most feasible.

Another plea, "Equal Justice for All," had found widespread support. Traditionally, there were complaints that the agencies of government, and especially the courts, listened only to the rich and influential. Peasants believed that they could not hope for a fair hearing, much less justice, in court unless they could hire an expensive lawyer. Obviously, an effective, aggressive, public defender program, such as had been initiated many years before, was in order. Obviously, too, if this program was really to pay off in terms of winning support for the government, it must be effectively publicized. Such a program could not be initiated by the Secretary of National Defense, and he could not get other agencies of government to implement it.

Magsaysay's solution was this: He made it known that the services of the Judge Advocate General's Corps, the legal branch of the Armed Forces, were available to peasants who had substantive grievances and could not afford adequate representation in court.

It was widely believed that government officials in general were not responsive to the needs of the poor and those without influence, that more often than not, the poor man was abused by military and civilian officials alike. Magsaysay announced that any man who believed he had a legitimate grievance against an official of government, civilian or military, need only go to the nearest telegraph office and send a telegram to him, the Secretary of National Defense, in order to receive fair play. Since this cost was often regarded as prohibitive, Magsaysay arranged that these telegrams could be sent to him for the equivalent of five cents. Further, he promised, and made good on it, that each telegram would be answered within twenty-four hours and that an investigation of the complaint would be initiated within the same period. This was so successful that when Magsaysay became President, he established a special agency within the Office of the President to continue the practice.

The Philippines is a country where people have a passion for education. Many of the schoolhouses had been destroyed during the Japanese occupation. Many of those that were left, especially in Huklandia, were either destroyed during the campaigns against the Huk or were used by the military as troop headquarters. Realizing the importance placed on education, Magsaysay ordered the troops out of the schoolhouses—except for those soldiers who could act as teachers. More than that, he encouraged troop units to build schoolhouses in their spare time, and when the national situation permitted, he organized a special unit of Army Engineers that prepared 4,000 prefabricated schoolhouses to be erected by troops or civilians.

Who gave the Secretary of National Defense these many missions? As he saw it, the limited mission given him of eliminating the guerrilla rebellion was inextricably linked with the national mission. Accordingly, he felt free to do anything that, in his judgment, would advance the national mission.

In his letter of resignation from the post of Secretary of National Defense, written to the President February 28, 1953, after it had become apparent that he could no longer act freely in improvising solutions to existing needs, he said:

Under your concept of my duties as Secretary of National Defense, my job is just to go on killing Huk. But you must realize that we cannot solve the problem of dissidence simply by military measures. It would be futile to go on killing Huk, while the Administration continues to breed dissidence by neglecting the problems of our masses.

The need of a vigorous assault on these problems I have repeatedly urged upon you, but my pleas have fallen on deaf ears. To cite an instance, some eight months ago I informed you that the military situation was under control, and I offered to leave the Department of National Defense in order to speed up the land-settlement program of the government. My purpose was to shift our attack on Communism to one of its basic causes in our country, land hunger.

This letter was obviously written with a shrewd eye to its use later when he announced his candidacy for the Presidency, but nevertheless it hit too close to home. For two and a half years, Magsaysay had been free-wheeling, taking actions far outside the scope of his normal duties, with the result that in less than two years, the rebellion had been brought under control. If the value of these actions had by that time been still so little realized that such a letter could be written and used with telling effect, it may be safely assumed that no one else would have undertaken them.

The leader of antiguerrilla operations in a nation should be the chief executive. Only he can assure that the necessary actions are taken by the appropriate agency of government, that existing organizations, plans, and assets are used to the best effect. If undertaken in this way, the actions necessary to counter the guerrilla threat can better be fitted into the long-range programs of government, and presumably assigned to the men best fitted for the tasks. There will be less waste motion and duplication of effort; and there will be far better assurance of a continuation of long-range programs, such as land settlement.

The accomplishments of the Secretary of National Defense of the Philippines and the wide range of action he undertook have been stressed to emphasize the truth of the old adage that there are more ways than one to skin a cat, an adage which could well be emblazoned on the escutcheons of the effective guerrilla and of the effective counterguerrilla warrior alike. If one agency of government cannot accomplish a function necessary to successful prosecution of the counterguerrilla effort, another agency, or even a civilian organization, must do it. If no organization for a purpose exists, one may be improvised, or the task accomplished without organization. If a needed law does not exist, and cannot be secured, there may be ways to accomplish the task with no other law than the consent of the people.

There has been much discussion of the proper relationships between military and civilian authorities at provincial and lower levels, in "counterinsurgency" situations. The British have evolved a system, apparently their standard, of formal committees, chaired by the civilian executive, including military, police, and intelligence chiefs of the area, augmented by civilians. This is undoubtedly effective under the conditions of respect for law and mutual trust found in their territories. In many parts of the world, such a set-up would be almost a guarantee of delay and ineffectiveness.

Counterguerrilla operations in the Philippines were carried out without any formal arrangements governing military and civilian relationships on the working level. Local executives, military or civilian, possessed police powers. The judiciary was, often fiercely, independent. To the extent judged practical by local leaders, civilian functions of government were carried on in normal fashion. Since the local executives were either elected by the people under their jurisdiction or appointed by the next higher elected official, the civilians had political influence that they did not hesitate to use. The military officials might or might not have political influence, depending on their inclinations and on their family connections.

Until the end of 1950, the soldier without powerful political connections was almost sure to lose in any disagreement with the politicians. The Huk leader, Taruc, probably escaped capture on at least one occasion when an operation was summarily called off at the request of a provincial Governor. After Magsaysay became Secretary of National Defense, the officer who was trying to do a job was assured of political backing if he was right in what he was doing. That backing was not always enough to ensure that the officer won, however.

One incident demonstrates the difficulties inherent in such an informal situation when politics rears its ugly head. A town Mayor was proved to be supporting the Huk. He was arrested, formally charged with offenses ranging from illegal association to murder, and placed in jail without bail pending trial. In spite of this, he was believed to be such an effective vote-getter that the provincial Governor, together with the National Chairman of the party in power, decided that he should be released and become an endorsed candidate for re-election. Learning of the plan, the military commander responsible for the province visited the Governor, warned him that the man could not be legally released, and secured a verbal agreement that no attempt to do so would be made.

A day or so later, the officer learned that the man had been released and was, in fact, about to appear at a political rally. With a few trusted officers, he went to the scene, found the Mayor on the speakers' platform together with the Governor and the Chairman of the party. Forthwith, he rearrested the Mayor. To the barely concealed chagrin of the military at the scene, the politicians confined their reactions to threats.

Almost immediately, the commander, then a lieutenant colonel highly esteemed by Secretary Magsaysay, was ordered by him to return to Manila, in tones that boded no good. Once assured of the facts in the matter, the Secretary visited the President and worked out a compromise. The officer was relieved of his command and "exiled" to the United States for a time, in lieu of the drastic action on which the politicians were insisting. The Mayor stayed in jail, was convicted on some of the lesser charges, and was only recently pardoned—coincidentally, shortly before an election.

This incident is typical of the problems that exist when there is no formal division of authority between civilian and military commanders. It emphasizes even more the problems that may arise in a democratic society when the military commander (who has no interest in votes, especially those of guerrilla sympathizers) is placed under the authority of one who must seek votes wherever they exist.

There is another side to the coin. Had the Governor been under the command of the Colonel, the incident might well have caused a rupture that would have placed the majority of the residents of the province in active political opposition to the local army chief, perhaps on the side of the guerrillas. All in all, the *ad hoc* solution reached in the Philippines, where military commanders and provincial Governors had approximately equal political influence with the chief executive (after the Constabulary was attached to the armed forces) was perhaps the best possible for their situation. It may well be the best solution in other areas faced with an insurgency problem that is complicated by popular respect for formal, elective government. The important thing is the accomplishment of the mission by means not inconsistent with national purpose, with *the* mission of government.

Who does what, and how the activities are organized (in counterguerrilla or guerrilla warfare), is far less important than understanding the mission and being determined to accomplish it by means not inconsistent with the mission. So long as a sufficient number understand the mission and what it implies, seek to accomplish it with a dedication and an intelligence not substantially inferior to that of the enemy, and receive adequate political support, the counterguerrilla effort should not usually be difficult. The counterguerrilla, whether working on the national or the local level, must assess the resources available and employ them as may be necessary to accomplish the mission.

The mission: to establish a political base, to protect it from the physical and psychological assaults of the guerrilla, and absorb within it the political base of the guerrilla.

NOTE

1. Joint Chiefs of Staff, *Dictionary of United States Military Terms for Joint Usage* (Washington, D.C.: JCS Pub. 1, February, 1962), p. 144.

Chapter 8

TARGET—THE GUERRILLA

THE AVERAGE guerrilla met personally is so unimpressive that mounting a conventional military operation against him seems as unfair, as inappropriate, as sending a platoon of soldiers to shoot an overgrown tomcat wandering in 10,000 acres of forest. And one operation is about as likely to succeed as the other. Like the tomcat, the guerrilla may be more a nuisance than a threat, a nuisance constantly renewed if the conditions that permit him to develop and go wild are not changed, if his habitat is not rendered hostile to him.

Action with the guerrilla as the immediate, direct target will seldom if ever eliminate a viable guerrilla movement. However, some success in hunting the guerrilla must be achieved for the government he opposes to be able to make plausible its claim to be an effective guardian of the popular welfare. Effective action against the guerrilla target is essential.

Initially, actions against the guerrilla are likely to be full-dress hunting trips, conventional military (or police) operations. After a few such hunting trips, in which the guerrilla (or tomcat) has probably not been seen, although he may have been felt, the target begins to take on the attributes of a superman (or super-beast) in the minds of the hunters. Political authorities, and the press, begin to regard the government forces as incompetent sub humans, too lazy and too stupid to find anything except, perhaps, their rations.

Until a record of continuing success in killing or capturing guerrillas is established, public and government opinion will probably oscillate between viewing the guerrilla as a pitiful victim and as a superman. The image projected will vary with the interest of the projector, but denigration of guerrilla capabilities will be useless until the hunters can point to victories.

The truth is, of course, that the guerrilla is a man, capable of acting boldly in concert with other men (i.e., as a member of a military organization) or of acting singly or in small packs like a wild animal, capable of killing but interested most keenly in self-preservation. The competent guerrilla when hunted will usually adopt the animal role, striking back viciously if given a chance.

The hunter must understand and accept these facts of life. He must expect contumely until he has established a record of success. He must understand also that the guerrilla, if allowed the initiative, may attack him or his charges in overwhelming strength. On the other hand, if the guerrilla is not allowed to concentrate his forces, he will be as elusive as the cat in the forest. Understanding this, the guerrilla hunter will be prepared to meet an attack made by a (usually) poorly organized, poorly equipped force numerically superior to his own, even while he is dispatching parties of qualified hunters.

Action directly against the enemy is usually thought of as being designed to kill or capture him, or to make him surrender. In antiguerrilla operations (as well as in the last stage of conventional warfare), one other form of action must be added: action intended to make the enemy quit and go home—permanently.

To kill an enemy, it is necessary to use a weapon on him. To capture him usually requires demonstrating the imminent effective use of a weapon. To cause his surrender—or resignation from the war—it is necessary only to overcome his will to continue to fight. This may be the easiest and cheapest solution, like luring the cat out of the forest with a trail of valerian or scaring him out with dogs. So with the guerrilla. He may be persuaded that he can better serve his purpose by giving up the fight, or he may be convinced by words and deeds (reducing his rations and arms supply, lessening his choice of targets or his mobility, increasing the skill and numbers of hunters) that continued guerrilla activity will be increasingly unpleasant, unprofitable, and, ultimately, fatal.

Actions taken by the Armed Forces of the Philippines (AFP) against the Hukbalahap between 1946 and 1950 cannot properly be considered failures. Accurate figures are not available, but during those five years, the AFP undoubtedly killed, captured, or caused the permanent submergence into the civilian population of at least half the guerrillas originally in the field against them. The AFP's own losses during that period were negligible. For an armed force with relatively little logistic support, operating against a guerrilla enemy at least half its own strength, that is not a record of failure.

Conversely, its actions cannot be called successful. The AFP, during this period, eliminated only two top leaders of the Huk. They permitted the Huk guerrillas to inflict heavy casualties and heavy losses on the people. Worst of all, the guerrillas gained in strength; during that period their number increased by probably 3,000–4,000.

The forces initially arrayed against the Huk were Philippine Constabulary[1] companies, with a nominal strength of ninety-eight officers and men, armed at first only with billy clubs, side arms, and carbines. These companies could not, militarily speaking, engage an armed, organized, hostile group. Politically as well as militarily, the Constabulary was restrained from initiating action against the Huk. After the Constabulary secured more adequate weapons (rifles, some machine guns, and mortars) and was encouraged to seek and destroy Huk units, it was still fettered by political considerations. Most damaging of these were calls to protect villages, towns, and large estates by garrisoning them. As a result, most of the personnel of each company were more or less permanently tied down by guard duty, in detachments of five to fifty men.

From one to fifteen Constabulary companies were assigned to each province, under the command of a Provincial Provost Marshal, later called the Provincial Commander, who was the chief military authority of the province and had a small staff. Not directly under the control of the provincial Governor, he was, nevertheless, under a practical compulsion to cooperate with him and win his good will. If the Governor belonged to the political party of the Administration, or if the Governor's support for that party was desired by the Administration, military considerations often had to defer to political realities (nowhere more real than in the Philippines).

Under these circumstances, the offensive capabilities of the armed forces were substantially diluted; in fact, they often seemed nonexistent. Worse, the troops pinned down to guard duty were, for the most part, unable to secure tactical information about the guerrillas since the civilian population—the best source of such intelligence—had been antagonized by the troops' behavior, which reflected the lax supervision and discipline inevitable when small detachments are long in one place. Although the troops encountered intelligence problems, the guerrillas had no difficulty obtaining information about the troops. Patrols usually neither saw nor heard of guerrillas, unless the guerrillas decided to ambush them.

Such conditions are not conducive to aggressive patrolling or to aggressive action of any kind against the nominal enemy. The psychological hazard of the defensive, so often cited by past military writers, is seldom greater than in counterguerrilla warfare. If the enemy is aggressive, troops on the defensive begin to picture him as ten feet tall, with a magic cloak of invisibility. If the enemy is not aggressive, why pick a fight? Building morale, *esprit de corps,* an aggressive attitude, is the problem that every commander at every echelon must face and solve many times in any continuing counterguerrilla war. This was one of the difficult tasks in the early period in the Philippines.

The situation was discouraging. Patrols were seldom successful. Demands for troops to act as guards were too heavy. There seemed to be neither a reason nor a capability for antiguerrilla action. The civil branch of government appeared to have no real determination to defeat the Huk, at least no determination expressed in terms of moral support and matériel for the men arrayed against them. More and more, the troops took a defensive attitude. They went through the motions; they maintained garrisons. At times, they furnished heavy escorts for rice harvests being moved from the field to town. They investigated reports of Huk concentrations if the source seemed reasonably reliable and if there was a chance of making contact. Aside from these sporadic efforts, the Constabulary and the army units attached to them were sitting out the war.

This was not true of all units at all times, of course. Some units took up an aggressive posture immediately. Sometimes this was successful. Sometimes when they seemed on the verge of success, they were called off by civilian authorities. Sometimes the aggressive commander caused so much trouble for the politicians or committed so many abuses against civilians in his efforts to get information that he was relieved of his command.

This pattern had begun to be quite recognizable by the end of 1946. Then, near the end of that year, the assistant intelligence chief of the Philippine Constabulary obtained permission to form a hunter-killer team and take it into the field to "find and finish" the Supreme Commander, Luis Taruc. This team was the Nenita unit.

The commander did not manage to catch Taruc, but in the next two years, his group operated aggressively—a group at times augmented by two or three companies of Constabulary, at other times made up of only forty to fifty men. They pursued the hunt relentlessly, seeking information about Huk units, contacting them by one ruse or another and then destroying as many as they could. Militarily, this effort was an unqualified success, in comparison with what was accomplished by other forces in this period. Politically, it was less than successful.

Most armed-forces action against the Huk was still confined to garrison duty, some patrol activity (not infrequently carried out in company strength), and more or less routine police activities. Checkpoints were set up along the main highways; occasional screening, or *zona,* operations were carried out. These actions seldom met with success, but they did at least keep some pressure on the guerrillas. There were several large-scale operations during this period—the encirclement of Mount Arayat, already described, which involved around 3,000 troops. Usually, these resulted from pressures generated by the chiding of a high government official or from scathing newspaper comments. As might be imagined, they did not meet with much success, nor did the participants really expect to do more than make a show of force in order to ameliorate what they felt to be unjust criticism.

The first effective large operation against the Huk developed in reaction to an ambush. The rich central plain of Luzon is bordered on the east by a range of extremely rugged mountains, the Sierra Madres, which extend for twenty to fifty miles to the east coast of the islands. On April 28, 1949, Doña Aurora Quezon, widow of President Manuel Quezon, was motoring with a large party on the northernmost road traversing the mountains from west to east. About midway through the mountains, the ambushers struck, killing Doña Aurora, her daughter and son-in-law, and several others of the party.

For the first time, widespread popular wrath flared against the Huk. The armed forces were told in no uncertain terms that they must eliminate the ambushers, and the officer placed in charge was virtually told not to come back unless he accomplished his mission. Fortunately, he was given a free hand and overriding authority throughout the whole area of operations.

To this operation were assigned nearly 4,000 men, organized as two provisional battalions of Constabulary and one army battalion. The ambushers were reported to have withdrawn northward into the mountains, an area never before penetrated by troops. There was, of course, no assurance that the Huk would continue to move north; in fact, there was every likelihood that they would try to evade the troops and get back down to the lowlands, where food and shelter would be available from local sympathizers.

Accordingly, the command was divided into three task forces, with sectors roughly corresponding to the areas delineated by the principal east-west highway across the mountains and the principal north-south highway, which skirts the west side of the mountains from Manila almost all the way to the northern end of the island. One task force was assigned the inhabited, cultivated area west of the north–south highway, in which it was to block the escape of the Huk, prevent supplies getting to them in the mountains, and forestall possible diversionary attacks by other Huk elements seeking to relieve the pressure on the ambushers. This mission was assigned to the Second Battalion, First Infantry, Philippine Army, with attached reconnaissance-car company and field-artillery battery.

The mountainous area south of the principal east–west highway was assigned to a hastily organized provisional Philippine Constabulary battalion with a composite reconnaissance-car company.

There remained the northeastern sector, into which the ambushers had withdrawn, a solid mass of mountains shown on most maps as a blank (unexplored) space. The pursuit mission in this difficult area was given to the First Provisional Battalion, Philippine Constabulary. To it was attached many of the nearly 2,000 civilian-guard auxiliaries from the province of Nueva Ecija who had also been mobilized for the vengeance operation. Since the emphasis was on covering this portion of the Sierra Madres with experienced, hard-fighting foot troops, they were given a commander known for determined, aggressive leadership, Major Mariano Escalona.

Initial emphasis was on patrolling, especially in the western and southeastern sectors. Intelligence activities were also pushed in an unprecedented manner. Great emphasis was placed on personal inspection of the task forces at all hours of the day and night to determine if patrols had performed their assigned tasks and had actually reached designated objectives, and if all available personnel were assigned to patrolling as continuously as humanly possible. Each group was required to keep a detailed account showing how many patrols were out, how many men on each and how long the patrol took. There were, in effect, daily time sheets for every officer and enlisted man.

For two weeks, the task groups concentrated on patrol activities and on gathering intelligence about Huk activities in the area. It was learned that a little north of the ambush site there was a base supported by a regular supply route from the lowlands. It was further determined that many members of the ambush party had been fed by three Chinese storekeepers in a town on the mountain fringe the day before the ambush. These Chinese confirmed the presence of a major Huk base in the mountains and identified a key Huk liaison officer in the lowlands, Pedro Mananta.

When he was picked up, three weeks after the ambush, Mananta was persuaded to disclose the location of the Huk commander, Viernes, who had commanded the ambush, as well as the position of the mountain base, Mount Guiniat. He also revealed that the commander of Reco 1 (Regional Command 1, the major Huk command, which included this area), Commander Dimasalang, was with Viernes at the mountain base. Perhaps the most important of his disclosures was that Huk units in the neighboring lowlands had been ordered to attack isolated towns to relieve the pressure the task forces were placing on the Huk who had taken part in the ambush or who were supporting the ambushers.

Despite the lack of terrain information, the approximate position of Mount Guiniat was determined and an operation against it initiated. The plan was for five company-size columns to try to converge on the mountain from different directions, launching a synchronized attack when all were in position—if possible. By extraordinary good fortune, all five companies reached substantially the proper positions and by the agreed time. The attack was launched at dawn on June 1. The Huk knew the troops were in the area, but one of the disadvantages to guerrillas of bases in such extremely rugged and uninhabited terrain was manifest: The Huk were unable to keep track of all the columns or even to identify their objectives until too late.

The attack was surprisingly successful, although most of those in the objective area managed to escape. Eleven Huk were killed, five captured, at a cost of only two casualties. It was discovered that the objective of this operation had been only an outpost; the main base lay two miles away.

An attack on that base, covered by mortar fire, was launched on June 2. The Huk resisted initially, to allow time for their leaders and the bulk of their party to escape. The vegetation was extremely dense, the terrain all stood on end; these conditions and their effect on radio communications made control difficult. The attack was carried on into the night by small parties, squads and half-squads, moving through the dark, seeking to push forward on a compass bearing that was intended to bring it to the objective.

The determination with which this attack was carried on produced results. By early morning, the task group succeeded in entering a settlement of twenty-three shacks hidden under tall trees. This settlement actually was the buildings and campus of a Huk "university." The area was immediately saturated with patrols. Within a week, 37 dead Huk were tallied and several taken prisoner. From the prisoners, it was learned that Commander Viernes, with an estimated

250 guerrillas and perhaps 200 unarmed followers, was located in another site about 14 kilometers farther to the northeast.

Another infiltration attack by small patrols, each proceeding on an azimuth, was launched. A mortar barrage was laid down to cover these patrols when they came in sight of their objective. Other units followed up, seeking to throw a cordon around the site. This rather unorthodox operation netted twenty-one Huk dead and the capture of seventeen wounded as well as three women and a child. Counterguerrilla casualties were one man killed by falling off a cliff and four wounded, of whom two died while being evacuated.

Commander Viernes and Commander Dimasalang were not among those killed or captured. Interrogation of prisoners revealed that there was supposed to be another base some forty-odd miles farther to the north, still in the mountains, in the vicinity of a remote valley known as Kangkong. It was determined that the pursuit should continue, even though this appeared a tremendous task, one which might well take a day for each of the forty or more miles to be covered.

Another provisional force, composed entirely of armored cars and vehicles, was formed to patrol the north–south highway continuously and probe as far as possible into the rudimentary trails running east into the mountains. The Second and Third Task Groups, reinforced by the bulk of the civilian guards, were deployed in the lowlands flanking the mountains to keep up maximum pressure on the Huk there and on Huk suppliers and sympathizers. This pressure was exerted largely through intensive patrolling. The operational pattern became one of patrolling by half-squads of soldiers. Such patrols in areas where Huk might be encountered were followed by a platoon of auxiliaries close enough to reinforce them if a serious fight should break out.

While preparations were under way for resuming the hunt, several incidents occurred indicating that the denial operations were indeed effective. Survivors from the mountain bases who reached the lowlands often found their contacts already arrested or neutralized by government forces. They also found that anyone who might have participated in the ambush of a widely beloved old lady was unwelcome to civilians in general. Suspected members of the ambush party had two alternatives—surrender or death.

Those who surrendered furnished information, sometimes no more than two days old, on happenings among the armed elements of Reco 1 still in the mountains. The guerrillas, they said, had broken up into small units, which, in accordance with their standing orders, were working north toward Kangkong Valley.

A small but experienced undercover intelligence team, equipped with radios, was sent to Kangkong. The team members claimed to be lumber cruisers or mining prospectors. By the middle of June, they began to report that residents of small settlements in the area were becoming nervous as a result of the appearance of many strangers from the south who posed as hunters or wood-gatherers. A store in the principal settlement of Kangkong was identified as the liaison and rendezvous point of these strangers and placed under surveillance.

Supplies and porters for the pursuit through the mountains were finally assembled. On June 28, four columns, each of company size, struck north on parallel routes through the mountains. There were no trails and few guides. The guides who could be found were tribal inhabitants of the area who seldom knew what lay more than one or two mountain ridges beyond their homes. The pattern of advance along the axis assigned each company was unorthodox. Every morning, each company sent out from four to ten small patrols, each instructed to head generally north. The patrol that found what seemed to be the best route for the advance of the company sent back guides to bring up the rest of the column. This made for slow going, but had the advantage, at least, of so blanketing the area as to discourage any guerrilla exfiltration to the south. Not a day passed without one or two encounters with Huk who were probably lost themselves, and each day one or two more Huk were eliminated.

It took more than two months to move forty miles in airline distance through the mountains. Finally, the base near Kangkong was located and successfully attacked on September 11. Commander Viemes, Commander Dimasalang, and twenty-five of their men were killed, seven were captured, and one surrendered. This marked the end of the pursuit, the end of the ambush squadron, and the end of the headquarters command of Huk Regional Command 1. The list of those killed, captured, and surrendered showed clearly that virtually every man who had been in the ambush party was accounted for, and not one was again found in action.

After this, anti-Huk operations slacked off somewhat until the 1949 elections were over. No politician cared to risk antagonizing any possible voter, whether Huk or Huk-hunter.

For both government and guerrillas, 1950 proved to be the year of decision. The guerrillas proved to be completely wrong about what the outcome of their decision would be. The government saw itself well on the way to victory before the end of the year, but the victory was achieved in a way it had not anticipated.

As the year began, the Armed Forces of the Philippines decided that company-size units were no longer sufficient to cope with the Huk; larger units capable of slugging it out with powerful enemy forces seemed necessary.

The Central Committee of the Communist Party of the Philippines had similar ideas. Now, they decided, the time was ripe to follow the precepts of Mao Tse-tung: to establish a conventional army and take the offensive against government forces. They publicly announced their leadership of the Huk; more, they renamed them grandiosely and in the best Communist tradition, "People's Liberation Army" (Hukbong Mapagpalaya ng Bayan, or HMB). They established also a timetable for expansion and for the seizure of national power.

The effects of these decisions of government and guerrillas were not decisive, but they were significant. The decisions of the guerrilla leadership were manifested in raids that seriously alarmed citizens and government and guaranteed that attention would be focused on the guerrilla problem. The decision of government resulted in the building of the basic military machine for hitting the guerrilla effectively, not through major combat actions but through many coordinated small actions.

The Armed Forces of the Philippines decided that the answer to their organizational problem was the formation of battalion combat teams (BCTs). This was accomplished with the advice and assistance of JUSMAG (Joint U.S. Military Advisory Group). As quickly as possible, existing units were grouped into BCTs, retrained, and placed in the field with area responsibilities. Until virtually the end of the campaign, the BCT with area responsibility remained the basic operational unit, although in the later stages, two or more BCTs were often placed under so-called sector commands, comparable to brigades. As they were required, BCTs or elements of them were assembled for special operations in task forces.

A BCT was normally composed of a Headquarters and Service Company; 3 rifle companies, each of 110 men; a weapons company armed with mortars and heavy machine guns; and a reconnaissance company at least partially equipped with armored cars. A field-artillery battery was often attached to the BCT. Other groups often attached, usually to the Headquarters and Service Company, included MIS (military-intelligence) teams, Scout-Ranger teams, and, if needed and available, scout-dog teams. Personnel of the weapons company and of the field-artillery battery were often employed as riflemen.

This basic organization proved to have great flexibility and utility. It seems well adapted to counterguerrilla operations almost anywhere, especially when responsibility for protection and clearance of an area is to be imposed on a commander.

As will often happen under such circumstances, several of the first BCTs were organized in the field from companies (in this case Constabulary) already assigned counterguerrilla missions. The 7th BCT met problems that will often be encountered in counterguerrilla operations. Because the solutions they developed have wide applicability and enjoyed enviable success, their experiences merit consideration.

The 7th Battalion Combat Team, composed of three rifle companies, a Headquarters and Service Company and a reconnaissance company, was given responsibility for counterguerrilla operations in the province of Bulacan and certain adjacent areas—altogether about 1,200 square miles. Their area was delineated largely by political boundaries imperceptible on the ground. In some places, the boundaries followed the natural terrain divisions made by river or forest that offered natural paths and refuge for the guerrilla. There was a passable network of all-weather roads, linked occasionally by secondary roads useful only in the dry season. The province embraced swamp and mountain, both grasscovered and forested, with lonely settlements—isolated hummocks thrust up in the swamps, small households clinging to hillsides. In the lowlands, there were wide expanses of rich rice lands under paddy-field cultivation (which meant that the fields lay outside the villages of the cultivators and that they were flooded part of the year).

The conditions found by the commander who took over the 7th BCT in Bulacan Province in July, 1950, will be encountered by many commanders assigned to similar commands. Many of the actions he took will be applicable to the problems of area control by a battalion-size unit in many counterguerrilla situations.

The BCT was scattered throughout the province. Each company had its headquarters in a different municipality. Each company furnished a number of garrisons, ranging from half-squads to platoons in size, scattered throughout the area of company responsibility. Communications were poor. Civil guards existed but were under virtually no supervision by the Armed Forces. Municipal police, in the larger towns, were similarly without direct contact with the army. About 1,500 active Hukbalahap made this area their home, their training ground, their supply center, in short, theirs. They were supported by thousands of active civilian sympathizers. Not a few towns were under almost complete Huk domination. Pandi, which lay in the crossroads of many access routes to Manila, was a principal Huk rest area, under the command of its municipal Mayor.

The 7th BCT had relatively few encounters with the Huk before the new commander took over, and only one of these was significant. Some four months before, when the BCT was first formed, a patrol ran into a large Huk band which engaged them in a fire fight. The patrol fled, leaving behind one man wounded and two dead.

Under the circumstances, with the dispersion of the command and the strength and freedom of initiative of the Huk, there was only one reason why there were not daily encounters with the Huk. The Huk did not want encounters. The Huk were busy recruiting, developing their strength, setting up support systems, extending their control of the area. The little half-squad and squad detachments of the BCT, which they could have snapped up easily, they left unmolested. How better could they show their contempt, their superiority over the Armed Forces of the Philippines? In fact, this military force with an authorized strength of 1,100 officers and enlisted men (actual strength was about 950) continued to exist only because the Huk did not wish to eliminate it.

This situation was not entirely the fault of either officers or men of the 7th BCT, nor will such conditions often be found to be solely the fault of any officer or group of officers, although correction must be their responsibility. Such conditions arise only from the apathetic, defensive attitude that pervades an entire command, if not the entire administration, in a nation faced with an unchallenged guerrilla movement. When that threat goes unchecked, it will be found elsewhere, as it was in the Philippines, that few are imbued with a sense of mission, a sense of urgency. The supply system is usually bad. The liaison with civilian communities and civilian authorities is almost inevitably poor or nonexistent. Weapons and equipment are in poor condition, buildings are shabby, everything is marked by failure, disintegration.

The new commander set out to reverse the process. First, he checked on the information available about the enemy in the area. He found that a good deal was known about them. Many of the units and commanders were identified, and it was known that frequent visits were made by Luis Taruc, the sometime *Supremo.* The most significant thing he learned was that the Huk were not on the offensive against his command, and seemed unlikely to be, so long as his troops offered them little threat. It was clear that his command was in no imminent danger of being wiped out.

The commander surveyed the general condition of his troops; he visited every detachment (many of which had never before been inspected by their battalion commander). He looked into their tactical situation, their living conditions, and their knowledge of the enemy in the immediate vicinity. He checked on their liaison with civilians (and found it almost nonexistent). His headquarters had little or no knowledge of the activities of municipal police forces or of the civil guards in the area.

The commander immediately assigned an officer of his staff to establish liaison with civilian authorities for gathering data on all agencies that might be of assistance—specifically on the civil guard and the municipal police. The commander wanted to know everything about them—identity, organization, strength, armament, equipment, particularly communications equipment. And he wanted this information yesterday.

At the same time, he ordered the withdrawal of all the small detachments that could be swallowed up by the Huk. He clamored for transportation, for vehicles to move the troops along the good roads available. He got transportation by every conceivable means, some of them scarcely within the purview of army regulations.

As fast as his civilian liaison officer came up with information about the civil-guard units, these units were brought into the tactical plan. The provincial Governor was persuaded to give the commander authority over them. Capable soldiers were detached as liaisons (actually as instructors and commanders) for major civil-guard units. They were given radio communications. Whenever a civil-guard unit became capable of putting up substantial resistance to attacks against its town or village, of holding off an attack until it could communicate with the army and receive needed reinforcements, troops were withdrawn from the area.

As troop units were drawn together, they went into intensive programs of training and patrolling. Comprehensive patrol plans were instituted and their execution carefully supervised. Intensive intelligence operations of all types were begun. No longer did the army exist by the toleration of the Huk.

Within three months, there was no garrison in the field smaller than a company. Within another month, there were only three companies on field-garrison duty. The rest were assembled at headquarters, undergoing training and constituting a mobile reserve ready to be moved to any part of the area on report of Huk incidents.

By October, it was possible to send three companies into combat operations against the Huk, dislodging them from their lairs and guiding them into an ambush. In December, the whole Battalion Combat Team was employed in an operation so shrewdly planned, with three separate forces, each apparently moving independently, that the command echelons of the Huk were deceived, drawn into a trap, and largely destroyed. Throughout the province, the only defensive forces in place during this fight were civil-guard units and the municipal police forces. These were able to maintain adequate security because reinforcements for them could be detached, motorized, and dispatched to any part of the area within hours.

No other combat-team commander faced an identical situation. Probably no commander anywhere will face an identical situation. But any commander ordered to fight guerrillas while protecting the citizenry in a large, partially inhabited area will find many of the same problems and can apply many of the same remedies.

This pattern—the assignment of an area responsibility, and the accomplishment of the mission through extensive patrolling while mobile parties are kept ready to reinforce local defense forces—seems the best basic approach to the guerrilla target.

Many reasons dictate maximum utilization of civil- (or home-) guard units for defense of civilian communities. First, they represent economy of force. One good noncommissioned officer serving as liaison, trainer, and inspector, with half the equipment of a platoon, can make an effective combat unit of a platoon of civilians fighting for their families, their homes, perhaps their very lives. Thirty soldiers are thereby released for offensive action against the guerrilla. The cost in training, equipment, and supervision is negligible, but all, especially the supervision, must be adequate.

Second, an effective civil-guard unit represents the commitment to the side of the government of many people—people who otherwise might be at best apathetic; at worst hostile to it. The value of this commitment manifests itself in many ways, from assistance to troops in nonmilitary aspects, such as provision of porters, to the furnishing of intelligence and guides.

There are, of course, disadvantages to the use of civil guards, but these can usually be overcome by careful selection of personnel and adequate supervision. In the first years of the campaign against the Huk, the disadvantages were very apparent. Although identical precedent conditions may not exist elsewhere, similar conditions may, and the results can be virtually the same as in the Philippines.

To understand the Philippine situation, it is necessary to know that during the Japanese occupation of the rich rice lands of Huklandia, there were actually four fighting forces operating. There were the Japanese troops. There were the Japanese-sponsored (or Japanese-tolerated) Filipino units, both those of the Bureau of the Constabulary and privately financed outfits formed to protect the estates of landowners cooperating with the Japanese. These two groups were proper targets of the legitimate guerrillas and of the Hukbalahap.

The legitimate guerrillas (called USAFFE because they claimed allegiance to the United States Armed Forces in the Far East) were fighting the Japanese and their puppets. Frequently, they also of necessity fought the Huk, since the Hukbalahap, under cover of their pious claims to be fighting the Japanese were actually fighting to establish Communist domination of the area. This was interpreted to the Huk in the ranks as fighting "all those who own land," or fighting "to establish a legitimate government." To justify their attacks on the legitimate USAFFE guerrillas, the Huk called them "Tulisafle" (thieves) and "puppets of the landowners."

Although the legitimate guerrillas disbanded after the liberation of the Philippines, many small groups in Huklandia held together under arms. Some were supported by landlords, some by municipal governments, some had no money or visible support. In many instances this continued quasi-military posture was not so much for the protection of the landowners or the municipal officials as it was a matter of self-protection for the ex-guerrillas. The Huk, of course, did not disband. Not infrequently the preliberation war was continued.

In at least one instance, soon after liberation, ex-guerrillas of a civil-guard unit rounded up a number of Huk and shot them out of hand. Perhaps this was justified; whether it was or not, it vastly increased bitterness and tension in Huklandia. As time wore on, some civil-defense units involved themselves more and more in politics and in activities to promote their sponsor's welfare, by legal means or otherwise. Some units, short of pay and equipment, turned to levying informal taxes on those they protected. Guard-operated checkpoints came to be toll stations for all who passed. The result was to make the home guards highly controversial, both locally and nationally.

When Magsaysay took office as Secretary of National Defense, he first sought to disband all civil-guard units. This proved to be impractical: There were not enough troops to replace all of them, and some units had long rendered necessary services, so the order was quietly rescinded. Soldiers were detached from army units and assigned to train and control civilian units. The results were excellent. Some units became models. They not only protected their own villages but went out looking for the Huk. They performed both combat and intelligence operations that greatly relieved the pressure on the troops.

Under Magsaysay's encouragement, some units went even further, taking on civic-action projects—repairing roads and building schoolhouses—as part of the duty of village civil guards. This often brought whole villages actively to the government side.

Civil guards form part of the spiral of success (or failure) in counterguerrilla operations. More civilian support plus better enemy information plus better civil guards plus effective troops equal still more civilian cooperation plus still better information, and even more effective civil defense equals more and more effective patrolling, etc., until the final phase in the spiral: no more guerrillas.

The importance of small-unit actions in conventional warfare is greatly enhanced by the weapons of mass destruction. These small actions reach their greatest importance when the weapon is the ultimate—man, acting largely on his own responsibility, acting as a guerrilla.

The guerrilla is necessarily one of the principal targets of the armed forces engaged in counterguerrilla operations. He is an elusive target, really dangerous only when he is allowed the initiative. To deny him the initiative, it is necessary to get him, and keep him, off balance; to confront him as often as possible with an enforced choice between running and accepting proffered combat. This was accomplished in the Philippines by incessant patrolling. Patrols always had three missions: obtaining civilian cooperation, gaining information, looking for the Huk. Patrols proved to be by far the most effective weapon for applying force to the Huk. Obviously, saturating an area with active patrols reduced the requirements for defensive garrisons. Reducing the number of soldiers needed for garrison purposes made more soldiers available for offensive action against the Huk.

Patrols were of all types, but they usually had one thing in common: They were small—half-squad, squad, perhaps platoon size. The most effective patrols were the smaller ones. There were regular patrols which passed through specified areas almost on a schedule, following roads or trails. There were unscheduled, unexpected patrols, sometimes following an expected one by fifteen minutes. There were patrols following eccentric routes, eccentric schedules, moving cross-country at right angles to normal travel patterns, which often unexpectedly intercepted scheduled patrols.

In areas where the Huk could maintain or could easily concentrate strength greater than that of the patrol, two factors prevented wholesale slaughter. One was the routine use of reinforcing patrols, that is, patrols moving in coordination, separated by limited space and/or time, juxtaposed so that if one patrol ran into the enemy, the others could come to its assistance. The known use of random patrols moving according to no discernible pattern increased Huk uncertainty as to the number of enemy who might respond to an attack. The other factor was the superior training and discipline of the patrolling troops, who could be counted on to inflict heavy casualties if attacked.

By saturating an area with patrols, guerrilla intelligence nets could be partially eluded, partially overloaded with patrol reports. This made it difficult for the guerrilla commander to make any decision other than to run. Any alternative was likely to be too risky. Competent guerrillas are seldom willing to attack an observed enemy who will resist, no matter how weak he may be, unless they can be certain their victim has no chance of reinforcement.

There are many ways by which this guerrilla characteristic can be turned to advantage. If an enemy is known to be so posted that he will receive warnings of any approaching force, a small patrol can be used to draw him into pursuit and into an ambush. Or patrols may be sent out in such number as to make the guerrilla withdraw—with an ambush waiting along his anticipated route.

The classic patrol method, the use of mounted cavalry, was attempted briefly in the Philippines and found effective. Unfortunately, it was not used until late in the campaign and met with many difficulties, from scarcity of mounts and lack of forage to stubborn opposition from the orthodox military. As a result, the efficacy of horse cavalry in campaigns of this nature was not adequately demonstrated.

Light armor was extensively used for patrolling roads. Terrain and crop considerations seldom permitted it to patrol off them. Heavy armor was not used at all.

Operations against the guerrilla were by no means confined to small-unit actions, although these were the most profitable. A number of large-scale operations were launched after Magsaysay became Secretary of National Defense. Their principal value was in harassing the guerrilla. True, each operation resulted in the capture and destruction of a headquarters, of supplies, of matériel, perhaps of garden areas where the guerrilla grew some of his food. These small results could have been accomplished equally well by much smaller units. Large operations did, however, have the advantage of causing a major "flap" among the Huk in the area, of increasing the psychological pressure on them. The sight of so many well-armed, well-fed soldiers made the Huk's own chances of success seem small. Not infrequently, the large operations also resulted in the subsequent capture of Huk whose enjoyment of life had been sadly disrupted and who were apprehended either accidentally, or by small stay-behind units, left in the area after all troops had supposedly departed. This, incidentally, was the way the American Communist William Pomeroy and his wife, Celia, were captured.

In seeking ways to hit the guerrilla, or to assist in hitting the guerrilla, a military commander will naturally look toward the air for assistance. In some situations, as in the Philippines, air-force personnel may be eager to cooperate. All they ask is for a target area to be designated so they can "clobber" it. Unfortunately, "clobbering" a target area seldom does much good as far as hitting guerrillas is concerned. Often, some presumably innocent civilians, or their crops, or their property, are "clobbered" instead, which naturally results in public "clobbering" of the military and the air support.

The value of air in counterguerrilla operations probably is primarily in its use as transport, especially for supplies. In the Philippines, the L-5, an artillery observation plane of World War II, was extremely effective in this role. Two L-5s completely supported two battalions of the Philippine Army in a month-long march through mountain areas where it was believed Huk might be based. The effects on the enemy could not be tested, because he had never gotten that far back in the hills, but the operation was successful because it dramatically proved the great value of aerial resupply by light aircraft and the great reliance that could be placed on this method.

Another highly significant use of light aircraft is for liaison and communications: telling troops on the ground where they are; picking up messages—radio, visual, or physical—from troops and civilian informers.

The abundant vegetation characteristic of many areas of guerrilla operations substantially reduces the value of direct aerial observation. This drawback can be offset to a considerable extent by using pilots with long, and almost daily, experience in an area. It has been found that such pilots will detect signs of activity absolutely imperceptible to a trained observer who is new to the area. This is one of the reasons that it is desirable for pilots to be assigned permanently to the unit (ordinarily at BCT level) they support. Another, and more important reason is that only by such assignment will pilot, fighting man, and commander develop the feeling of mutual support, concern, and interdependence that permits the most effective action. Few experienced patrol leaders care to rely for their food, their communications, their ammunition, in fact, perhaps their lives, on either a commander or a pilot they do not know. The pilot, too, is much more likely to make that little extra effort if he knows that it is Sergeant Paladin, of his own outfit, who needs that radio battery.

Too often aircraft, by their flight patterns, reveal to enemy observers the positions or probable intention of the ground troops they are supporting. This can be avoided only by careful planning and pilot indoctrination. Preferably, an area of operations should be saturated with aircraft, if they are to be employed at all. In an area such as that of the 7th BCT, it is desirable that at least one light aircraft be in the air throughout the hours of visibility. Each flight should follow generally a predetermined route on which expected contact points are indicated, as well as the areas where the aircraft may indulge in deceptive maneuvers. If a supply drop is planned under circumstances that make it probable that it will be observed, the flight pattern must be such that the aircraft can make each drop behind local concealment without noticeably changing its course, or else it must make dummy drops and engage in deceptive maneuvers that will saturate guerrilla intelligence nets with misleading information.

Only two light reconnaissance helicopters got into action during the major campaign. These, acting in the casualty evacuation role, had a tremendous morale effect. Troops who know that casualties can and will be evacuated from the most remote area act with vastly greater aggressiveness.

Troop-carrying helicopters were obtained too late to play any significant part, and it is doubtful if they could have been of very substantial assistance. They are too noisy to use against any guerrilla except one foolish enough to try to hold his ground, unless available in such numbers as to permit their almost continuous airborne operation on deception missions. Their role as transport for reinforcements of beleaguered troops is probably less than might be supposed, again because of their noise and because their characteristics make them such an easy target for ground fire. Their utility in direct support of ground forces seems limited in the present state of the helicopter art.

The value of artillery in counterguerrilla operations has been hotly debated. From 1946 to 1950, artillery was not infrequently used to shell suspected Huk concentrations. There were few instances when Huk concentrations were actually in the impact area. Too often, artillery bombardment, like aerial bombardment, inflicts casualties and damages only upon presumably innocent civilians. This not only brings hostility from civilians, but also develops contempt in the guerrilla for the armed forces.

One BCT commander decided to take advantage of artillery, using it as a deceptive measure, by which he sought to channelize the withdrawal of Huk alerted by cannonades into routes passing prearranged ambush points. He met with some success. However, one of his most daring opponents, Huk commander Linda Bie, soon grasped this use of artillery and made it SOP in his unit that when an artillery barrage was heard, the unit should move toward that barrage. This action was based on the theory that when the fire ceased, they could withdraw through that area safely and avoid ambush parties, which were almost certain to be placed elsewhere. The BCT commander learned of this and discouraged the practice by lifting a bombardment and then putting it down again on the same area. Linda Bie countered by moving his troops near the bombardment area, sending out scouts to make sure there were no troops between the target and the batteries, and then moving in almost under the muzzles of the guns.

When this was detected, the commander of the BCT worked out a new plan. He would start a desultory bombardment, sufficient to alert Linda Bie. Then, when he thought the guerrillas had drawn into their position between the impact area and the battery, he started a "rolling" mortar barrage, moving the impact area out from immediately in front of the mortar tubes, while drawing the artillery barrage in even closer. The idea was to form a vise that could squeeze Linda Bie's men into one barrage or the other. The scheme was only partially successful, but the whole process exemplifies the constant battle of wits that goes on between guerrilla and counterguerrilla.

In addition to actions designed to kill or capture the Huk—or failing that, to make him move, to get him and keep him on the run—there were, of course, operations designed to cut off his supplies, and operations designed to weaken or to destroy his will to resist.

In the early stages of the campaign, actions intended to cut off Huk supplies were directed primarily against the civilian supply sources. Such operations amounted to harassment of civilians and, generally, boomeranged. Actions to protect the rice harvest, or to ambush Huk coming in to take part of the harvest, were continuous and, on the whole, beneficial, although their direct effect on the Huk was probably limited. These two observations seem to be characteristic of food-denial operations. If effective, they alienate the civilian population. If they do not seriously annoy the civilians, they do not seriously afflict the bellies of the guerrilla (but they may be worthwhile for their effect on civilian morale).

As early as 1948, the Huk had begun to establish so-called production bases to grow their own food. Initially, they were primarily to supply training camps or "schools." These farms and the camps they were intended to supply were located in areas not ordinarily cultivated, usually populated, if at all, only by tribal people. As the anti-Huk campaign gained momentum, every effort was made to identify production bases through the use of aircraft, intelligence reports, and patrols. Once they were identified, attacks were made that sought both to eliminate those tending them and to destroy the crops. In timing such an operation, some commanders were so unsporting as to deny any knowledge of a production base until a crop was ready to harvest.

A large-scale arms-purchasing program was launched about 1951 to cut off Huk supplies. Civilians had long been prohibited ownership of firearms other than shotguns or rifles and pistols of not larger than .22 caliber. In the postwar years, however, enforcement and respect for this law had broken down to such a degree that almost anyone could get a temporary permit for possession of military-type weapons from some government authority. These permits were withdrawn when the purchase program was instituted. Anyone whose license to possess firearms was withdrawn usually claimed he had lost the weapon, transferred it, or turned it in. Such assertions were almost impossible to disprove. However, if the individual was offered a fair price for a weapon with no questions asked, a weapon was likely to appear. Many thousands of arms were recovered, but there is no conclusive evidence that the Huk were seriously handicapped by this campaign. Even when arms were plentiful, some of the Huk preferred to carry home-made weapons; others already possessed weapons in abundance. Always, it seemed, there were those who could steal ammunition which would get into Huk supply channels.

It is reported that one quite unorthodox, and unsanctioned, measure was practiced that substantially diminished the flow of arms and ammunition through illicit commercial channels. This was a device dating back to the operations against the Moros (Moslem Filipinos) in the early part of the century. During that period, a certain platoon leader was observed to have a careless habit of dropping cartridges—the old 45-70 shells roughly the size of a man's thumb. The Moros also noticed his outfit's carelessness with cartridges—cartridges that were eagerly collected, of course. However, when the Moros tried to use these cartridges, they found that cartridge, gun, and man issued their final report simultaneously. The cartridges had been loaded with dynamite.

No such activity was authorized during the campaign against the Huk. It appears that in some instances, however, officers who knew of this old device did insert into Huk supply channels cartridges that destroyed the weapon that fired them. The psychological and physical effects of such cartridges were reported as substantial. First of all, a weapon was destroyed, and usually, the man firing it was seriously injured or at least rendered permanently gun-shy.

There were many secondary benefits. It was not readily clear why the weapon was destroyed, whether it was the fault of the cartridge or of the gun. Accordingly, everyone who knew of the incident—particularly those in the same outfit—immediately became suspicious of his own weapon and his own cartridges. Guns were taken apart and painstakingly cleaned two or three times a day. Inevitably, somebody would lose a critical part of his weapon, and another firearm would be out of action. Cartridges, too, were taken apart and examined—that is, if they were not simply thrown away. Taking a cartridge apart, checking its contents, and then putting it together again can seriously reduce the reliability of the ammunition. It is almost guaranteed to cause stoppages of automatic weapons.

Finally, there is the question of where the cartridges came from. The purveyor of the ammunition comes under suspicion. In one instance, it was reported that four middlemen were eliminated because certain ammunition had passed through their hands, and a market for stolen cartridges was put out of business.

It must be reiterated that such operations were at no time authorized or approved. If they did take place, it was without the sanction of the government, which could scarcely justify the use of such indiscriminate measures. However, there is no doubt that this tactic was effective. It may be argued that the impact was chiefly psychological. This is probably true. It is true of most activities targeted against guerrillas if they are successful. Their greatest value lies in influencing the thinking of other guerrillas, potential guerrillas, and guerrilla supporters as much as in terms of guerrillas killed or captured.

Ordinarily, guerrilla thinking may best be influenced by actions ostensibly directed against the civilians who support the guerrillas. There is, however, a role to be played by direct appeals, so-called tactical psychological warfare aimed at the guerrillas in general, or at specific members of the guerrilla movement. Such efforts were used with considerable success in the Philippines after 1950. Leaflets of both "canned" and "spot" varieties were extensively air-dropped and hand-delivered. Themes ranged from appeals from mother or wife, through safe-conduct passes, to warning or threatening messages. Portable reproducing equipment in the field enabled battalion commanders to have spot leaflets prepared for immediate distribution.

Loudspeakers—hand-carried, jeep-mounted, and airborne—were used to advantage. Always, success in these, as in other tactical operations, depended largely on the accuracy of the information on which the operation was based, the intelligence with which it was prepared, and the effectiveness of its delivery.

Radio, press, and movies were sometimes used in tactical psychological war, perhaps most often for "leaking" or "planting" stories about projected operations or troop movements. Such stories caught the attention of the Huk, whose leaders had found news reports their most reliable source of strategic intelligence, and not infrequently diverted their attention from operations actually being conducted.

These mass media (press, radio, etc.) were also used to gain credibility for tactical psychological warfare themes, and for appeals distributed by other means, such as surrender leaflets. Timing was important. When surrender leaflets were used, their impact was substantially augmented by the appearance in the commercial media, long hostile to the armed forces, of recognizable pictures of Huk who had surrendered and were obviously receiving good treatment.

Psychological-warfare monies were useful in ways far beyond those ordinarily thought of, for they constituted one of the principal sources of the most critically needed auxiliary weapon of counterguerrilla warfare—MONEY. Money to be spent at the discretion of unit commanders, and money for specific purposes, such as purchase of rations or information, hire of guides and porters, emergency repairs to radios or vehicles, is very nearly as necessary as small-arms ammunition for fighting guerrillas effectively, and almost a prerequisite for winning civilian support.

The company or battalion commander who does not have both discretionary and specific-purpose funds legitimately at his disposal is almost irresistibly tempted to acquire them illegitimately, most often as "contributions" or "requisitions" in cash or in kind from the civilians in his area. Sometimes the needed funds are obtained by levying on the soldiers' pay, or even by hiring out the soldiers as guards or laborers. Bad as these practices are, if applied in moderation they are probably better than trying to fight guerrillas without money to buy critically needed items not available through normal supply channels, or without money to make on-the-spot recompense to injured civilians or emergency advances to soldiers and their dependents.

Ironically, a junior officer is routinely entrusted with 30 to 150 men, whose time in the field he may waste for days, or whom he may expose to unnecessary casualties, with probably no worse punishment than a reprimand. Yet if he is lucky enough to be entrusted with an equal number of dollars, he will probably face court-martial if he cannot account rigorously for the expenditure of each dollar. This condition must be changed if maximum effectiveness at minimum cost is to be achieved.

A simple rule of thumb for the allocation of discretionary funds is to withhold (i.e., not assign) 5 of each 100 men authorized to a unit. Give the company commander the cost (i.e., pay, allowances, etc.) of 4 of these men, and give the battalion commander the cost of the fifth. Require only the simplest accounting, subject to simple (and flexible) ground rules, such as that without special authorization, no more than one-third of each monthly allotment may be spent for a single purpose. Make readily available, also, specific funds for the purchase of information, pay of guides and porters, etc. The value of these discretionary and specific-purpose funds—used with the same discretion as is used in the deployment of individual soldiers *and on the same level*—is likely to be greater to the commander fighting guerrillas than the value of an additional platoon in his company.

This standard of fund availability was not achieved in the Philippines, although its desirability was well demonstrated. Enough funds were made available, at Magsaysay's insistence, to meet the most urgent requirements without levying on civilians. The only serious problems encountered in their use were those created by overly meticulous finance officers, or an occasional overenthusiastic commitment to win civilian good will, such as an officer's overrash bid for the crown of a local fiesta queen, which had the result of putting his fellow officers on short rations for some time thereafter.

There is one essential ingredient of success in hitting the guerrilla—or counterguerrilla—target which was overlooked by AFP and CPP planners alike in the plans and decisions made at the beginning of 1950. It has scarcely been touched on here. It is to the credit of President Elpidio Quirino that he supplied the missing ingredient on September 1, 1950.

That ingredient? Dedicated, aggressive leadership!

To the troops, and to the nation, Magsaysay soon became the personification of leadership. He had outstanding ability to inspire effective action by small units, to rally to his support leaders at all echelons; and he had an equally uncanny gift for identifying inadequate action and causing regrets among those who were responsible for it. Most important, he had the knack of inspiring emulation of the example he set. This is not to imply that there were no capable leaders in the Armed Forces before Magsaysay. There were many. His predecessor as Secretary of National Defense had been a capable leader of guerrillas against the Japanese, as well as a fine officer of the old school. Magsaysay was new, dramatic, infinitely energetic, determined to overcome, by any means necessary, the obstacles to effective action against the Huk.

In addition to setting an inspiring example of leadership, Magsaysay made two outstanding contributions to the military effort against the guerrilla target. One was to put adequate military forces into the field, ensure them the best possible support, and imbue them with a sense of urgency in effective action against the guerrillas. Ultimately there were twenty-six BCTs activated in the Philippine Army. Not all of these were given area responsibilities; in fact, not all of them were needed.

Nevertheless, each received the best support he could give it, and each was made to understand the requirement for continuing aggressive action. Better results might have been obtained with fewer men, and at less expense, had more emphasis been placed on specialized counterguerrilla units, and on better logistical support tailored for counterguerrilla operations. Of the value of aggressive BCTs as the basic quasi-independent formation for fighting guerrillas there seems little doubt.

Military effectiveness against the guerrillas was enhanced more by improving the morale, motivation, and combat techniques of the soldiers than it was by the increase in their number. Efforts to improve supply and training had their most significant value in raising morale and aggressiveness. Magsaysay spared no effort to impress on the soldier the importance and urgency of his missions, and to demonstrate to him the support the government desired to give him.

One of Magsaysay's most effective actions in this field was to require that the designated beneficiary of a soldier receive, within twenty-four hours after confirmation of his death, a cash payment of 1,000 pesos, less funeral costs. This money was deducted from the benefits (insurance, arrears in pay, etc.) to which the beneficiary was entitled and so represented little additional cost to the government. It meant a great deal to the widow, however, to be able to get the money when she needed it, rather than having to wait for the long, slow bureaucratic paper mill to grind out the finished papers, perhaps after a dozen visits from her and a lapse of six months. Later, specific provisions were made for immediate cash assistance to the dependents of seriously wounded soldiers. The influence these actions had on the combat aggressiveness of the troops was surprising.

Magsaysay's second major contribution toward hitting the guerilla target was to convince the troops that the guerrilla was not the only target; that, in fact, the guerrilla was not a target of overriding importance. Magsaysay emphasized, and demonstrated through the "Attraction Program" he implemented, that actions designed to win the cooperation of civilians actually increased the effectiveness of actions against the guerrilla. This idea was not new, but impressing it on the troops, and making them act in accordance with it, was new and effective. From the time Magsaysay became Secretary of National Defense, to win his approval, every military operation had to have three objectives: to get civilian cooperation, to get information, and to get guerrillas.

NOTE

1. Called Military Police Command (MPC) from 1945 to 1949.

Chapter 9

FOOL 'EM

"Fool 'Em, Find 'Em, Fight 'Em, Finish 'Em!"

The old motto used in training for conventional war contained only the last three elements. The addition of "Fool 'Em," an outgrowth of experience in guerrilla fighting in the Philippines, supplies a significant new note, one supremely important in counterguerrilla warfare. First in importance, and first in difficulty, is fooling the guerrilla enemy, misleading, eluding, or blinding his information and observation screens.

His information service is often the one palpable military advantage the guerrilla possesses. He may be inferior in training, in number, and in armament, but if he has intelligence superiority, he will be able to bring superior force to bear on his selected targets, and he will be able to evade superior enemy forces. The assumed—and, all too often, actual—greater determination of the guerrilla to endure and to win will not save him from military defeat if his information about enemy presence, capabilities, and intentions is repeatedly insufficient or incorrect.

Fooling the guerrilla requires the coordination of many actions often placed in distinctly different categories. First and foremost there must be effective counterintelligence action—denial to the guerrilla of accurate information about the strength, locations, capabilities, intentions, and actions of the counterguerrilla. Requisite counterintelligence actions range from detecting guerrilla spies who seek to penetrate high government offices to approaching villages against the prevailing wind so that the dogs will not be alerted.

It is often useful to fool the guerrilla by letting him fool himself; it is *never* useful to fool him by lying to him in the name of the government. The distinction between legitimate ruses of war and treachery must always be maintained.

If a counterguerrilla doubts the legitimacy of a deceptive action, he will usually be wisest to abandon it. The statements of government must be credible, and the actions of its representatives must maintain this credibility. It is legitimate and often useful to disguise soldiers as guerrillas and to have such disguised soldiers penetrate guerrilla elements and attack them. It is not useful, not legitimate, for identifiable soldiers to secure surrenders under promise of good treatment and then kill the surrenderers.

Finally, fooling the guerrilla involves defeat of guerrilla counterintelligence measures—that is, penetrating or deceiving his organizations in order to collect information about him. Actions in this category run the gamut from placing spies in guerrilla headquarters to establishing simple systems for the collection of reports from informants without disclosing their role to the guerrillas.

Very often, success in fooling, finding, and fighting guerrillas follow one another as closely as the words follow each other. How rapidly and how successfully this can be accomplished has seldom been better exemplified than in the operations of the unit known as Force X. Here is the story, and an analysis of the lessons learned, as told by the commander of that operation:

> When we organized Force X in 1948, the Huk were running freely all over Central Luzon. Their command structure was not well organized or well understood by the Huk themselves. Just prior to this time, the Huk in Southern Luzon had thought themselves to be independent. When their commander, a Colonel Villegas, died, some of their units tried to establish contact with the more highly developed and organized forces in Central Luzon under Taruc, who was also eager to contact them. This was obviously a very favorable opportunity for a deception operation.
>
> I assigned the 16th Philippine Constabulary Company the duty of forming Force X. The commander, Lieutenant Maraña, after receiving his instructions, quietly screened his entire company, selected forty-four enlisted men and three officers, and at night moved to a predesignated training base in the rain forest. Force X was in existence and was completely isolated from the moment they moved into that base, which only three officers from my staff were authorized to enter.
>
> The training given there was designed to enable the men to conduct what we called "Large-Unit Infiltration." The basic idea was to make this specially trained force into a realistic pseudo-Huk unit that could, in enemy guise, infiltrate deep into enemy territory. The men in training were divested of all items that could identify them as soldiers. They were dressed in civilian clothes and armed only with captured weapons that had been accumulated by my S-2 [intelligence officer]. They were given indoctrination booklets, propaganda publications, and other reading material of the sort carried by Huks. They were given the things generally found on Huk dead, such as soiled handkerchiefs and love mementoes from girl friends. During the four-week training period, all conver-

sation was conducted in terms of the preassigned enemy identities—the enemy ranks, aliases, and pet names commonly used in guerrilla units of Southern Luzon. The men were addressed as comrades, brothers, members of the proletariat. They were taught Huk songs. They learned how to deliver speeches in Huk style.

They became familiar with the descriptions of the leaders of Southern Luzon guerrillas. Some, who resembled known guerrilla leaders, posed as those individuals. All men were required to take on the appearance of hunted guerrillas during those days. They became, and stayed, dirty, unshaven, badly in need of haircuts. Like the enemy, these soldiers were unhappily forced to renounce bathrooms, shaving cream, and razor blades.

Sometime during the second week, my S-2 smuggled in three ex-Huks who had been captured in Southern Luzon and subsequently incarcerated in our national prison. They had been tested, screened, and reindoctrinated to our side and were brought to the training base to serve as instructors. They became round-the-clock critics of mannerisms, speeches, customs. We knew that Huk were taught certain methods of addressing a superior, certain ways to eat, certain general practices for their daily ablutions in the river. The same training was now given to the men of Force X.

While this training was going on, my troops were making a reconnaissance of the area through which Force X would supposedly pass while en route from Southern to Central Luzon. A disguised patrol, led by a sergeant, actually covered the route. It noted the trails, observed the attitude of the inhabitants, and identified the obstacles encountered. All this was incorporated into the cover story of Force X to ensure that that force would be accepted when it entered the proposed operational area, the Candaba Swamp.

When everything was set, my S-2 went to Manila to recruit several walking wounded men from our army hospital. He finally found two rugged enlisted men who wanted to join Force X in spite of their wounds. With the addition of these men, the operation was ready to roll and it was launched at 1700 hours, 14 April 1948.

The force almost precipitated a pitched battle when passing near a Philippine Constabulary company in another province while en route to the line of departure for their operational area. The operational departure was from a small town about four miles east of the highway, where they fought a carefully staged sham battle with two of my uniformed PC companies. From this they withdrew in good order, carrying with them their two wounded. Four hours later, they contacted the first Huk outpost, which was of course informed of their approach and very curious as to the identity of this unit which had been fighting the PC.

They were carefully interrogated as to who they were, where they came from, where they were going, etc. Their cover stories stood up well, and their wounded lent an invaluable semblance of authenticity to their accounts. They were given guides who took them on into the Candaba Swamp until they linked up with Huk Squadrons 5 and 17, under Commanders Tomy and Vergara. There they were again interrogated and asked about their route from Southern Luzon. Much interest was taken in them and they were promised that top leaders, possibly the *Supremo,* Luis Taruc, would see them. Force X and the two squadrons (with an estimated strength of about 120 men) fraternized for more than a day and a half, exchanging experiences, boasting of their respective commands. Naturally, Force X was talking about the prowess of the South Luzon Huk. Squadrons 2 and 17 were talking of the prowess of the Huk *Supremo.*

During these conversations, Force X accumulated a lot of information. Individuals selected in advance deliberately engaged visitors in lively discussions about local conditions, propaganda, supply systems, etc. They found that most of the town Mayors and Chiefs of Police were in collusion with the enemy. They discovered that there were enlisted men in the PC company on the other side of the swamps who were giving information to the Huks. They learned that supplies were left by women in selected spots along the road to be picked up at sundown by the Huks.

The fourth day after they crossed the line of departure, two more Huk squadrons joined the combined group. These new squadrons—4 and 21—were special killer groups. One in particular, under Commander Bundalian, was unique in its organization and its assigned mission. It was called the enforcing squadron, assigned by the Huk *Supremo* to enforce Huk justice. Actually, it was a band of well-trained executioners; their specialty was kidnapping civilians suspected of disloyalty to the movement.

By the end of the fifth day, Force X was outnumbered 1 to 3. During those 5 days, the Huk squadrons showed no indication of suspecting that Force X was other than what it seemed to be. No one detected the 4 60-mm. mortars, 2 light machine guns, 200 hand grenades, and complete voice radio that Force X concealed. How was all this hidden? Some enterprising enlisted man found that mortar tubes fitted inside bamboo water tubes, as did light machine guns. Others took delight in hiding grenades and mortar shells inside watermelons, papayas, etc. The radio was inside a sack of rice.

About breakfast time on the sixth day, according to the story of the force commander, Lieutenant Maraña, they noticed that the Huk, the real Huk, seemed to have become cool and distant in their attitude, so much so that breakfast was eaten in complete silence. Lieutenant Maraña decided that the time had come to strike. On a prearranged signal, the members of Force X unobtrusively separated from the Huk groups, and Lieutenant Maraña gave the order to strike.

It was a slaughter. Two Huk squadrons were practically deactivated as of that moment. The mortars came into play within the first two minutes after the strike. The men were instructed to throw hand grenades before using their weapons. And within five minutes, the radio was in operation and was in contact with me and with three Philippine Constabulary companies that were alerted around the operational area, ready to move in.

Such an operation is not easy, as several commanders who sought to copy it learned too late. There are many problems to be solved, many prerequisites to be met. Assuming that personnel are available, they must be screened for suitability and carefully trained until they know enemy procedures and personalities as well as the members of the enemy unit they are to impersonate. This means that before their training is finished, a favorable situation for their employment must exist and must be known in detail.

What is a favorable situation for the use of such a unit? It is one in which communications between enemy units are not yet well developed, or have been thoroughly disrupted for a long period. It is a situation where the enemy knows less about the unit to be impersonated by your men than you do. Such situations most often arise when the enemy is expanding his organization vigorously, when there is as yet little contact between the different centers of expansion.

Above all, the entire operation must be planned and conducted, from the start to the moment of the final strike, in absolute secrecy. Information must be given only on the strictest "need to know" basis.

Once the tactical opportunity has been determined to exist, an appropriate cover plan must be developed. Most often, we found, the cover story for the infiltration unit will be that of being a known unit from a distant area with which communications are poor, a unit which has come on a liaison and reconnaissance mission. Needless to say, every man in the unit must know the cover story in great detail, must know more about his supposed unit than any enemy whom he may contact.

To some extent, the cover story will depend on the target—or targets—selected for the operation. Targets can be only tentatively designated and assigned priorities in advance. Much should depend upon opportunities encountered. The killing of leading enemy personalities may be far more important than the destruction of a certain enemy unit. An appropriate order of priority might be: (1) killing enemy leaders or outstanding fanatics; (2) destroying enemy elite organizations; and (3) penetrating and destroying especially devoted and/or effective enemy support elements.

All these targets may be found in the area of a single operation deep in enemy territory. Time involved in preparation of counterguerrilla infiltration units is variable. Don't be tempted into throwing in half-trained units. In our experience, four to six weeks of intensive training was usually necessary. Careful screening and selection of operational personnel is of paramount importance. Personnel selected on the basis of combat experience and physical condition are segregated in a secret training base. Training should stress physical condition and adoption of enemy "personalities" (of enemy units being represented) in dress, speech, manners, customs, etc. Divested of any article of clothing identifying their own force, personnel are reissued captured weapons, equipment, personal articles, and other matériel. This is important. Where possible, captured enemy insignia, uniforms, documents, ID cards, propaganda publications, songbooks, indoctrination booklets, etc., are freely distributed to operating personnel.

There should be no uniformity of wearing apparel, with the possible exception of the two or three ranking members of the disguised force. Armament and equipment must show signs of wear and tear, or poor upkeep, which is characteristic of guerrilla weapons. Well-kept weapons and an abundance of ammunition with the disguised force are a dead giveaway. However, the newer and gaudier weapons, such as pistols with pearl handles, should be given to leaders. This is common with guerrilla units.

The maximum number of ex-enemy personnel are recruited. Through careful screening and tests to establish loyalties, the services of these individuals can be invaluable during training and operational phases. During the training of the troops, they are useful and instructive critics. With individual cover stories, they are assigned to command, security, or advance elements during actual operations. After training, the disguised force should be made to undergo rigid tests with unwitting friendly troop units. These tests will require special precautions to prevent mistaken encounters.

We considered this activity one partial solution to a major problem of counterguerrilla warfare, that of finding and finishing enemy units in large force. Usually, guerrilla enemy-intelligence and warning systems are too efficient to permit major encounters.

The major objectives of this activity are to effect surprise contact with the enemy in force and to take advantage of this contact to destroy him by close combat. There are many other obvious objectives. First in importance is to gather intelligence, especially verification of the enemy order of battle. Second is the penetration and study of existing enemy systems of security. Third is the study of enemy signal communications and the extent and nature of civilian support and liaison methods. Fourth is the appreciation and study of enemy supply methods and extent of local area support to enemy units. A special added bonus is the final identification of local government officials secretly in collusion with the enemy.

Fooling the guerrilla, like charity, begins at home, a home not infrequently shared with the guerrilla, or at least his supporters. Since guerrilla and counterguerrilla often have so much in common in cultural and physical heritage, it follows that, much more than in any other type of war, counterguerrilla warfare requires the strictest security consciousness at all times. It must be taken for granted that any civilian may be an agent of the guerrilla, witting or unwitting, and that his information can reach the guerrilla very quickly. The fact that the most significant element of the combat environment is the human element—the people, people who can give information, people whom the counterguerrilla, like the guerrilla, must seek to exploit—infinitely complicates the security problem. The difficulties are great, but good security discipline of troops must be maintained, or all other efforts of the campaign may fail.

The security of camps, both permanent installations and temporary bivouacs, is a major consideration. There is a widespread tendency to locate troops in existing facilities or at least in close proximity to them. In the early stages of the anti-Huk campaign, the tendency invariably was to post troops in schoolhouses or municipal buildings because there they had shelter, often electricity, and water. Communications facilities were usually good. Of course, they were right in the heart of the enemy espionage nets.

Ordinary military-security precautions are ineffective as long as the troops are quartered among the civilians, or even near civilian installations. Ideally, every military installation in a counterguerrilla campaign would be located behind a wide buffer zone, where it would be invisible and where no civilians might enter. Such an encampment, on the other hand, would almost certainly deny the troops a most important source of information, the people.

Where camps cannot be located in a position that eliminates chance contacts with civilians and that is secure from the observation of guerrilla sympathizers, elaborate security and deception procedures must be employed. This usually calls for virtually continuous troop movements, fooling the guerrilla into thinking that the entire unit, or at least substantial portions of it, are shifting.

One BCT in a Huk area had a standard operating procedure (SOP) that required its units to move their operational bases on a regular schedule. Detached companies had to move at least once every five to seven days; platoons every two or three days; squads or half-squads at least twice a day. This was arduous, but it may be the only way the enemy can be fooled so that the tactical initiative can be wrested from him.

Denying the enemy information is one way of fooling him. Another is to saturate his intelligence nets. The frequent shifting of troops serves both functions. If troops are security conscious, and if the commander does not tell them of moves until the last possible minute, the soldiers cannot disclose information to their sweet-hearts, wives, tailors, barbers, or favorite bartenders. Thus, the enemy intelligence system does not learn of the proposed move until an hour or less before it begins. The guerrilla information net may not even learn where the unit is bound until it actually arrives at its destination. Finally, if several units are on the move simultaneously, the number of reports reaching the guerrilla intelligence-collecting stations, with their imprecise data (reports from untrained informants are imprecise about time and numbers), may confuse rather than clarify the situation for the guerrilla. If uncertain what troops are where, knowing only that troops are on the move, the guerrilla must choose between accepting the risk of surprise attack and taking unnecessary precautions. He makes possibly unnecessary moves, which may bring him into a surprise encounter with the enemy he has lost.

Of course, fooling the guerrilla involves far more than denying him information about his enemy. It also means eluding his elaborate warning systems. To understand the problems of evading his warning systems, one may look at the fairly elementary but effective techniques commonly used by the Huk in the Philippines.

The Huk warning system combined detection and transmission elements in one operation, that is, everybody observed, and everybody passed on the word. There were usually certain individuals specifically charged with keeping watch or listening for signs of enemy approach. If the Huk were in a village, such watchers might be posted in isolated houses or in fields two or three miles away, apparently pursuing normal activities—plowing, cutting wood, washing clothes, etc.

In daylight hours, the signals would often be visual, compatible with the natural occupation of the signaler. A woman washing clothes might suddenly decide that nature was calling, step off to one side and turn around two or three times before proceeding. A farmer plowing might observe the approach of an army patrol, whereupon he would find it necessary to unhitch his plow to mend one of the ropes or the plow itself. Of course, houses facilitated signaling. All that was needed was to go out and open or close the gate; or to open or close the windows—any small activity might provide the clue that would make the next watcher in line hasten to give the alert to the guerrillas.

At night, these signals could be supplemented by the natural use of lights. What is more natural than for a farmer to come out with a lantern to find out if his *carabao* has enough feed, or needs untying, or should be moved to a new feeding area. The Huk also encouraged the villagers to keep dogs, the maximum number possible. Naturally, when strangers approach, dogs bark—and the sound carries. It was some time before troops learned to "read the wind" before approaching villages or houses at night. Couriers, church bells, truck and bicycle horns, beacon fires, smoke signals, and anything else that could transmit information or sound an alarm was used at one time or another.

Ordinarily, at least two warning "shells" were constructed by the Huk around villages they were occupying so that signals not only would be rapidly picked up and repeated, but would be augmented by reports from the inner ring of watchers if the enemy (the army) approached closer to their resting place.

To some extent, slightly more sophisticated devices were adapted from military practice. Trip wires with tin cans attached to them were strung around or across possible avenues of approach, ready to rattle at a touch. The Huk made relatively little use of booby traps or mines. It has never been determined why. Probably, it was partly technical difficulties and partly the risk of injuring civilians, with consequent loss of their support, that caused them to neglect such antipersonnel tactics.

The Huk did use radio to some extent immediately after the close of World War II, but this equipment was soon replaced by the famous "bamboo telegraph," which proved more reliable, less expensive, and more flexible, as well as advantageous in implicating more civilians in direct support of the guerrilla.

Such warning systems could transmit information with some accuracy and with considerable speed over many miles. To elude them was a major challenge. Some of the methods have already been described, such as the emplacement of "stay-behind" parties by troop sweeps. Surreptitious night movements conducted with all the care one would use in stalking big game often, but not too often, circumvented these warning nets. The bamboo telegraph at night has its disadvantages. Alert soldiers, expecting their presence to be signaled, can detect light signals and surmise the identity of Huk sympathizers and the direction in which they are transmitting their information, hence the location of the Huk elements.

Since they could seldom be effectively eliminated or disregarded, guerrilla warning systems had to be nullified whenever possible. This could be accomplished by saturating them, avoiding them, or deceiving them. Saturation was most often accomplished by troop movements or patrols. So many patrols would operate at such irregular times that the guerrilla intelligence nets would be filled constantly with reports of patrol presence. Not infrequently, a guerrilla would be so confused by the multiplicity of reports, so tired, or so overconfident, that a patrol of which he had learned long before would find him still at rest, or making a frantic last moment effort at escape. At other times, the effort to avoid a patrol would take the guerrilla into an encounter with still another patrol.

Evading the guerrilla information net, as contrasted to deceiving it, is largely a matter of proper scouting and patrolling techniques, principally effective under cover of darkness or where enemy observers are few (or sleepy). In relatively uninhabited areas, the habitual use of mutually supporting small patrols may permit one or more to avoid detection. Patrol formations that employ existing cover or concealment to prevent elements of the patrol from being seen from probable observation points will often be able to outflank guerrilla units and engage them by surprise.

Minuscule patrols of especially selected and trained personnel, moving surreptitiously, are extremely valuable in counterguerrilla as in other forms of war. Operating in areas inhabited only by enemy personnel, especially if these enemy are in a quasi-military status, they frequently meet amazing success in evading observation. The value of two men on such a patrol— whether employed for collecting information, destroying enemy and their supplies, or simply increasing psychological pressure—is often greater than that of a platoon or more of conventional troops.

Most often, penetration of the guerrilla counterintelligence and warning screens can best be effected by deceptive measures. For this purpose, patrols disguised as civilians are particularly effective. One BCT in the Philippines secured several panel trucks belonging to Manila businesses (complete with business signs on the trucks), with which they actually carried on appropriate business activities. Usually, the drivers and the "women" riding with them all were soldiers. Sometimes more soldiers, and certainly weapons and radios, were hidden inside the truck. This, however, was disclosed only to operatives among the civilians. Sometimes these trucks were stopped by Huk foraging patrols. The results discouraged future Huk foragers from stopping trucks.

Ordinary carts drawn by oxen or water buffalo were frequently used. Such a cart, carrying four to eight people off to attend a fiesta or to visit relatives or to shop in town, was a common sight in the countryside. Usually, the bed of the cart was filled with hay to feed the animal that drew it. The hay was an ideal place for troops to hide weapons and radios, just as it was an ideal place for Huk supply personnel when they were making a delivery to the guerrillas.

These disguised patrols were only too willing, as a rule, to encounter guerrilla sympathizers. They were always eager to stop and talk with anyone. These casual conversations yielded much information about the enemy. Chance encounters often produced a real surprise. Not the least of those surprised was an officer of the Joint U.S. Military Advisory Group who found it difficult to believe that the pretty girls he saw leaving a BCT headquarters were actually soldiers, until one of them reached inside "her" blouse and produced one of the hand grenades serving him as "falsies."

Although these patrols in disguise sought encounter with the enemy and tried to get information through observation or talk, their principal value, perhaps, was in transmitting instructions to informants and receiving their reports. These informants might be local people who had volunteered their services or who had been induced to volunteer during a village screening, or they might be agents who had been sent in for the purpose. Not infrequently, they were small storekeepers, whose cooperation had been enlisted after several visits and possibly with such inducements as price reductions on supplies furnished them by the patrols.

Actually there was a third purpose for such disguised patrols. Each time their presence was revealed, tension was increased among the Huk. In time, the Huk grew suspicious of everything moving in the countryside, every truck, every oxcart, every strange vehicle. If the party looked too strong, or if for some reason the Huk were unwilling to attack, or even to stop a party because they feared it might be composed of soldiers who were better armed, or who had access to reinforcements, the Huk had to leave the area lest their presence be detected. Always, it added to their uncertainties. And if they did stop a cart or truck, they risked losing friends and supporters in the countryside if the party was innocent. Any way he approached this problem, the Huk lost.

Operations having possible repercussions in the form of guerrilla actions against civilians must always be carefully considered and conducted. No deceptive measure should be undertaken that will, of itself, harm the civilians directly. Indirect harm, through guerrilla reprisals, cannot always be prevented, and may be allowed if it is not too clearly provoked by government forces, and is not merely a way for government forces to evade open warfare with the guerrilla.

Efforts to deceive the guerrilla are so much a part of successful counterguerrilla warfare that there are few effective operations that do not include a good deception plan. Some operations in the Philippines included a broadly based deception operation, which ranged from making use of the everyday commercial press and radio for planting stories to running convoys of trucks, supposedly carrying troops on carefully timed decoy runs. Other operations depended on no more than a sweet smile, an indiscreet word, and a careful avoidance of impertinent hands.

Flares were particularly helpful in hasty deception operations. If it was desirable for tactical purposes to block off possible withdrawal routes of a Huk group, three or four men, sent in under cover of darkness with flare pistols and a good supply of flares, could make that area seem so heavily infested with troops as to be extremely unhealthy for a Huk unit trying to avoid combat.

At other times, flares were used when Huk were supposed to be in the vicinity but had not been located, and when insufficient troops were at hand to make a proper search. A few men with flare pistols could break up the night's sleep for a much larger number of Huk and possibly cause their withdrawal.

The use of artillery fire and of light aircraft in deception operations has already been discussed. Combat aircraft can be similarly employed, but the risk of injury to the nonguerrilla must always be carefully considered. The counterguerrilla, like the guerrilla, must never stop trying to find new ways of misleading his enemy.

Also, like the guerrilla, he must always consider the intangible value of fooling the enemy, of creating and strengthening distaste or fear of continued activity in his role. Tactical psychological warfare—directly influencing the behavior and attitudes of the enemy—is not infrequently effected by measures directly or indirectly intended to fool him.

The patrols that saturated guerrilla warning systems hoped to find an enemy, but they were nearly as effective if they did not. The reports of their presence effectively increased the psychological pressures on the guerrilla. A band might be able to stay in an area of ten square miles for a week or two weeks without being found by an army patrol. However, if a patrol entered that area every night and every day, it meant an alarm every night and every day. It meant that the Huk could never relax, must always be on the alert, always on the move or ready to move. Always there was the risk of clash with the patrol. The patrol might be the vanguard of a platoon or a company, might be going to rendezvous with a patrol guerrilla informants had not spotted, or might simply be trying to push the guerrilla into the arms of a waiting ambush.

Appeals to superstition probably should be classified as attempts to fool the enemy. They can be surprisingly useful, if soundly based and carefully implemented. The field is broad, and the possibilities range from tangible actions aided by complicated equipment to simple gimmicks.

One useful gimmick used in the Philippines consisted merely of a picture of a staring eye enclosed in a triangle, printed on a four-by-five sheet of paper. This was secretly posted in places Huk were known to pass or take shelter. The picture bore connotations of ethical and/or religious groups not well known to the average Huk, but respected by them and by most people. The appearance of the posters was unexpected, and their purpose quite mysterious. They seemed certainly to have more meaning than was apparent. Could it be some strange new scientific device, possibly one that was taking a picture, or making a report or a recording? Did it have some magical significance? Who was doing this and why?

This little device certainly killed no Huk. It is not known to have caused, directly, any Huk to surrender (although it did cause some Huk supporters to surrender). It is known that it caused Huk to give up the use of favorite shelters, to make detours around places where this eye could be seen. It did contribute to the feeling of harassment that lessens the offensive spirit; to the feeling of frustration and futility that can ultimately lead to the dissolution of a guerrilla unit and the surrender or submergence of its members.

It must be emphasized that the only real limitation on fooling the guerrilla is one that must be scrupulously observed. Measures taken in deception operations must be in clear conformance with the over-all mission of the armed forces and the government they support. The deceptions must not be of a kind that may harm the essential establishment of faith and confidence in the armed forces and the government as the protectors and friends of the governed, as honest men dedicated to the public welfare.

Chapter 10

FIND 'EM

"FINDING 'EM"—learning soon enough, and in enough detail, the position and actions of the guerrilla—is perhaps more essential to success in counterguerrilla operations than in any other type of war. "Finding 'Em" requires intelligence. Intelligence in both senses of the term is necessary, but here it refers to information about the enemy, properly assembled, evaluated, interpreted, and disseminated.

"Fool 'Em, Find 'Em, Fight 'Em, and Finish 'Em." To the novice, "Finding 'Em" may seem the most difficult of the tetralogy, especially in trying to take the initiative from the guerrilla. Actually, "Fooling 'Em"—deceiving or escaping their surveillance and getting into a position to use weapons against the guerrilla—is really the most difficult.

As in other types of warfare, the primary source of combat intelligence is the combat soldier; but in counterguerrilla operations, the soldier draws his best information not from the enemy himself but from the civilian population, which is also the best source of information for the guerrilla. Many civilians are reluctant or absolutely unwilling to give information, especially in the early stages of counterguerrilla warfare. Their reluctance may be due to sympathy with the guerrilla, to distrust of the troops, or as is most often the case when the guerrillas have been active in an area for some time, to fear of reprisals from the guerrillas. This is so characteristic that it is often regarded as a virtually insurmountable barrier to the antiguerrilla forces.

There are many ways to overcome this reluctance. The best is to convince the civilian that the armed forces can and will protect him from the guerrillas. This is far easier said than done; until the enemy is found, the civilian cannot be protected from him.

The most useful and reliable way to collect basic combat intelligence is active, extensive patrolling. Every patrol is exposed to much potentially valuable information. Whether this information is perceived and is reported by them so that it can form intelligence depends almost entirely upon the emphasis placed on intelligence by their commander. Enthusiasm and ability in gleaning useful information will develop rapidly under guidance. A comprehensive standard operating procedure for the guidance of patrols, specifying the action they must take to note down information, the information they must seek, and the manner in which they must report it, is essential. Equally essential is a standard operating procedure that calls for proper briefing of patrols before their departure and proper debriefing upon their return. (An example of an appropriate SOP appears as Appendix I of this book.)

Patrols should do far more than go from Point A to Point B and return. Obviously, all patrols should report their route, any indications of enemy activity, any unusual incidents among civilians, and similar matters. Routine overt patrols should visit villages and isolated farmhouses along their routes, talking to the people in each place, reporting not only what is said, but also how it is said, and the apparent attitude of the people contacted. Unscheduled overt patrols may do the same. Patrols in disguise usually follow this procedure; covert patrols must not risk detection and compromise.

In the Philippines, a special patrol force known as the Scout-Rangers was organized, made up of small teams, each consisting of three to ten men. These teams were used principally for surreptitious penetration missions, entering forests or swamps to locate reported guerrilla concentrations or installations in so-called safe areas (areas from which no reports of guerrilla activity emanated). Occasionally, these Scout-Ranger teams were engaged in combat, most often when they were spotted and identified by the enemy. So far as possible, however, their operations were entirely covert, designed to secure information on which larger forces could operate. Similar missions were carried out by elements of the regular forces but generally with less success than those of the specially trained Scout-Rangers. Even the use of such units can be futile unless the commander places continuing emphasis on the collection of all available information and unless enthusiasm for collecting information is generated.

There are many ways to secure information from civilians unwilling or afraid to give it. The most obvious way is to disguise the soldier as a civilian or a guerrilla. There are many others, appealing to the patriotism or the cupidity of the individual or acting in a way that makes him fear the soldier more than he fears the guerrilla. This latter approach—fear—adopted systematically, inevitably redounds to the benefit of the guerrilla. Selectively employed, it can be of value, but the risks of a negative effect are so great that fear-producing tactics are better outlawed.

During the 1946–50 campaign against the Huk, the standard technique for obtaining information from a presumably hostile village, and discovering

Huk or their supporters who might be hiding there, was to "screen" the population, the practice generally called *"zona."* The term originated during the
Spanish occupation of the country, and the technique was erroneously believed
to have been invented by them. Actually, it is as old and as widespread a practice as war. The *zona* was violently abhorred, primarily because of the high
pitch of cruelty to which it was brought by the Japanese during their antiguerrilla operations. Here is a victim's description:

> During Japanese-conducted *zonas,* the people witnessed all kinds of barbarity
> and butchery; those thought to be guerrillas were summarily beheaded in the
> presence of their family and friends; suspected youths were used for bayonet
> practice; women were abused while their husbands were forced to watch, etc.

After the Japanese occupation, *zona* connoted unlicensed brutality, which
Huk propaganda exploited. The uncontrolled use of the *zona* system during
the early years of the anti-Huk campaign did not really help the pacification
effort, even though Philippine Constabulary units did not resort to Japanese
brutalities and were, in fact, much more restrained than the Huk themselves in
collecting intelligence from those who did not wish to give it.

The following report well illustrates the value that can be derived from a
well-planned *zona* operation, and simultaneously illustrates why a villager
will scarcely react sympathetically to government forces after such an action.
This report was written by a participant who later became convinced that it
was imperative for such village-screening practices to be greatly modified or
completely prohibited.

> In the early morning hours of 11 May 1947, Lieutenant Rizalino del Prado's
> patrol flashed a radio message reeporting that the inhabitants of the *barrio*
> [small village] of Pulong Plasan, of the municipality of Baliuag, in Bulacan
> Province, were observed suddenly to have broken normal village routine.
>
> Del Prado and a five-man patrol equipped with voice radio had for ten days
> been posted secretly near the *barrio* with a surveillance mission. This action
> was based on reports that Pulong Plasan was a heavy contributor to the Huk,
> with almost all the able-bodied men serving actively in the ranks of Huk Squad-
> rons 21, 26, and 104. Squadron 104 had recently been activated by Huk Lieuten-
> ant Colonel "Mallari," a native of the *barrio.* ["Mallari" was his *nom de guerre;*
> he, like most Huk leaders, usually used a *nom de guerre*]. Previous observation
> reports submitted by Del Prado indicated that the *barrio* people followed the
> typical village life: rising long before dawn, attending to the work animals,
> working in the fields, stopping heavy labor when the sun is high in the sky,
> retrieving the animals just before dark, lights out by 8 o'clock in the evenings.
> Except for the occasional barking of dogs, or babies crying, or sometimes whis-
> pered conversations inside dwellings, no sign of life was to be noted in the
> evenings.
>
> But it appeared that some "visitors" had sneaked into the barrio the previous
> night (May 10), probably coming from an unguarded side, without alerting Del

Prado's group. A radio conversation with Del Prado gave further details of his impressions of the abrupt change of routine in the village. Del Prado suspected either that the village was deeply involved in collecting and packing food supplies, or that a Huk VIP had arrived to visit relatives and/or to conduct the customary Huk indoctrination rallies.

Del Prado was ordered to stand by with his group until they could be reinforced. A strong patrol (about thirty men), under Lieutenant Constante Cruz, was rushed to Del Prado's OP site, with orders that both patrols be combined under Lieutenant Cruz and then enclose and screen the village, keeping headquarters posted by radio.

The combined unit conducted village screening according to the standard operating plan, which called for the screening force to be divided into two main elements during the first phase. During this phase, the enclosure group, which was the larger, sealed off the village, covering all known entrances and exits, throwing out a cordon that moved in gradually until it reached the edges of the village itself. (All previous patrols covering the area had been instructed to include in their reports simple, detailed sketches of villages visited, which facilitated screening plans and operations.)

Meanwhile, during this first phase, the second element hurried to the center of the village (again according to standard operating procedure) to gather all the inhabitants, regardless of age or sex. They were assembled in the open space in front of the school building and were divided into small groups so dispersed that conversation between villagers, or even between families, was made difficult.

The screening of Pulong Plasan commenced in the middle of the afternoon of May 11. An ex-Huk commander, "Totoy Bondoc," who had served as a government agent for a year and a half, accompanied Lieutenant Cruz and immediately recognized some of his former comrades when the second element began gathering the villagers in concentration. Lieutenant Cruz ordered the immediate segregation of the three identified men: Guillermo Sagum, alias "Mallari," a lieutenant colonel of Huk Regional Command 3 and a reputed Huk combat organizer; Jovito Maravilla, alias "Marvel," assistant squadron commander of Squadron 104 (Maravilla enlisted in the Armed Forces two years later and, proving to be a courageous Scout-Ranger, was decorated in 1951); and Pascual Palma, a Bataan and Death March veteran who had joined the Huk guerrillas originally to fight the Japanese.

As soon as the villagers had been rounded up, the operation moved into its second phase. The enclosure element was swiftly and silently divided into three new elements—a sentry group, a search party, and a support group. Two-man sentry units with automatic weapons were posted around the periphery of the village, each unit within visual range of the sentries on either side. This sentry line was thoroughly inspected to ensure that attempted sneakouts would be impossible or, at least, extremely hazardous.

The search party, under its leaders, reported to the force commander. He then dispatched parties, accompanied by one or two village elders (usually the *barrio* Lieutenant and the most influential citizen), to make a methodical search of all the houses, sheds, barns, public buildings, yards, and any other places inside the enclosure that might hide subversive materials, weapons, food caches, or even people. The presence of these village representatives with the search parties was mandatory. Past experience had shown that enemy propaganda frequently alleged that screening forces of the government committed robberies, etc., during this search phase. After the search, these village representatives were required to draw up certificates, in their own handwriting, attesting to the manner of the search, conduct of troops, items seized (if any), and other pertinent details.

The security group from the first element also reported to the force commander and was posted under arms at a suitable location, ready to rush to support of the sentry line or to offer protection to the civilians congregated in the enclosure. As soon as the situation was stabilized, some of the security group was designated to service the civilians (fetch drinking water, furnish escorts, etc.), but most of them reinforced the activities of interrogators in order to hasten the screening.

As the three visiting Huk VIP's were marched away to the security group for detention, the villagers of Pulong Plasan watched expressionlessly, evidencing the silent resistant attitude normally encountered by government troops during this period (1946–50). The people were obviously determined to remain silent, were obviously afraid or unwilling to give any truthful information that might help the government.

This attitude was expected. The force under Lieutenant Cruz had brought in several informants, ex-Huk and others, all wearing hoods so they could not be identified. In accordance with procedures based on experience, several interrogation points were set up, widely enough separated so that proceedings at one interrogation point could not be seen from another or by those awaiting their turn. As quickly as possible after the village search, information obtained thereby was passed on to the interrogating personnel (who had been making preliminary inquiries in the meantime), and the formal interrogation commenced.

One by one, the adult members of the village passed under the scrutiny of the hooded "Magic Eye" informants and were brought to an interrogation point, sometimes accompanied by one of the hooded informants. A firm stare, a quiet, determined voice, and evidence of knowledge about his activities persuaded almost everyone to tell what he knew. The interrogation usually began with questions about the activities of the individual and his family, questions susceptible to confirmation or denial on the basis of observations made during the search or by questions to others in his family. The development of contradictions to his statements and the obvious determination of the interrogator to get at the truth were usually sufficient to break down opposition. With some villagers, it was necessary to resort to a dramatic action to shock them, to convince them that the interrogator would not hesitate to use any methods necessary to extract the truth.

Lieutenant Cruz ordered one of his interrogators to resort to a tested ruse in order to push a particularly stubborn villager to speak frankly. The interrogating Sergeant first arranged for two individuals to be marched off in sight of the stubborn subject, to the interrogation point; then the villager heard loud, threatening voices coming from the interrogation point, then a few pistol shots, then silence.

Soon the Sergeant came back into sight, reloading his pistol, after which he took the villager from those congregated and marched him off for interrogation. There, the recalcitrant one saw two bodies, bloody, covered with banana leaves.

Quietly, the Sergeant explained that he didn't believe in "horsing around" with stubborn civilians—he had no time for it—and that the Lieutenant would in turn shoot him if he could not come up with the information required, etc. Therefore, he could allow the subject only a few minutes, including time for prayers, to determine for himself whether to cooperate with the Sergeant by furnishing correct information.

What had really happened was that the Sergeant had the preceding individuals, immobilized and silent, liberally drenched with chicken blood and covered with leaves, during the entire period of the "drama." This ruse worked successfully during the early period of the anti-Huk campaign, but it was too dangerous a stunt to pull after Magsaysay became Secretary of National Defense. By no stretch of imagination could it be considered part of his "Attraction Program."

Several villagers of Pulong Plasan were bluffed into telling the truth about the visit of Huk Colonel Mallari and his companions by the above-described trick. Declarations tallied with what was already known: that Mallari had made this visit in order to organize the support system of Squadron 104 from Pulong Plasan and to recruit for the new force pending the arrival of weapons expected from some unknown source.

Five days later, the village was visited again by the same screening personnel, this time accompanied by the Huk prisoners, Mallari, Marvel, and Palma, who were by now in a cooperative mood. When the villagers saw their repentant leaders working on the side of the government, they in turn offered information voluntarily, which led to further apprehensions and investigations missed in the original screening. Pulong Plasan eventually changed to a strong base of anti-Huk resistance. An NCO, with a team of three men (later relieved from this duty) plus Marvel, was left behind to organize local resistance. This team successfully organized an armed volunteer group that proved to be helpful government auxiliaries.

An interview with the detainees after two days of arrest revealed that Mallari had been caught so unawares that he did not offer any resistance in spite of his vows never to be taken alive by government troops because he believed that his high rank in the Hukbalahap would ensure his execution. Further, he was stunned to find an intimate comrade, Totoy Bondoc, was really a trusted government intelligence agent, who unhesitatingly identified him. Bondoc later persuaded Mallari to emulate him in cooperating with the government, and Mallari contributed importantly by identifying Mayors, town councilors, and police forces who were in secret collusion with the Hukbalahap, contributing heavily in food, supplies, and government information.

Of special interest among Mallari's contributions to our side was the help he gave in the solution of the Plough ambuscade-murder a year later.[1] He guided troops to secret hideouts (which on two separate occasions nearly resulted in the capture of top Huk commanders, including the *Supremo,* Taruc). This information, his descriptions of Huk tactical organizations, tactics, techniques, signal and warning systems, recruiting procedures, and disposition and care of their wounded became the basis of many operations by our organization for almost two years.

Marvel, the youngest of the three detainees (he was eighteen when arrested), turned out to be the normal village youth impressed into Huk service with no special antigovernment feelings. Young, bright, and a natural leader, Marvel was being groomed by Mallari for the eventual command of Squadron 104, a newly activated unit at the time of their arrest. In 1949, Marvel enlisted in the Armed Forces and served meritoriously.

Pascual Palma, a Visayan and actually a stranger in Luzon who had originally joined the Huk in order to fight the Japanese, showed no special desire to return to his home province in the Visayas, to the south. When he was released, in late 1950, with admonitions to become a better citizen, he returned to the sweetheart he had found in Arayat, in Central Luzon, married her, and settled down there as a tenant farmer. In 1950, when he was asked to join the town defense corps, he left the farm and led the townspeople in the defense of Arayat. On several occasions, Palma was officially reported by the army as having led attacks with civilian armed volunteers against Huk foraging parties. In 1953, Palma accepted a position as a regular patrolman with the municipal police force of the town, in recognition of services rendered, and he discharged his duties faithfully.

Screening operations were not always so carefully planned as the one in Pulong Plasan, or so successfully concluded. One spur-of-the-moment operation was conducted when Huk ambushed a Philippine Constabulary jeep on a lonely road in Pampanga Province early in 1947. The company commander of the 26th PC and two enlisted men were riding in the jeep. Fortunately, due to the failing light and to faulty execution of the ambush (by a party of ten or twelve Huk), no PC personnel were hit or injured. A senior officer moving with thirty men in a motor convoy heard the firing and, suspecting an ambush, rushed to the scene. The ambush party withdrew precipitately upon hearing the convoy's approach, and a chase began.

After a running fire fight of some two miles, through cultivated rice fields, irrigation ditches, patches of tall cogon grass, and bamboo thickets, the Huk suddenly vanished just after pursuing elements passed the village of San Patricio, northwest of the provincial road. The officer suspected that the Huk had melted into the village, and he ordered an enclosure of the entire village.

All those interrogated denied the presence of any guerrillas when the screening began. By chance—as it was not a standard item carried by Armed Forces—the officer had a paraffin-test kit, borrowed from friends in the Manila Police Department. All able-bodied males were put through the paraffin test, a standard police technique for determining if suspects have recently fired a gun. Three people out of about seventy-five tested as "positive." As the three were being marched off to the vehicles that would carry them to camp, they suddenly bolted. A guard fired and killed one. A second escaped. Another guard, startled by the maneuver, fired at the third escapee, who was running through the assembled villagers. The shot killed one woman bystander and wounded another seriously.

However, the open demonstration of the paraffin test on suspects, who were told that it would pinpoint the guilty, apparently discouraged guerrillas from seeking refuge where they might be picked up in a screening operation. Despite the limitations and known inaccuracies of paraffin testing, it can be used to advantage by the armed forces, especially if the people can be persuaded that it is infallible.

But such operations, however effective, were scarcely feasible for an army that stressed respect for the rights of citizens and professed to be their friends and protectors. After Magsaysay became Secretary of National Defense, he severely limited the use, scope, and methods of the *zona,* which had been one of the greatest sources of bitterness and complaints against the Armed Forces.

Nevertheless, until both intelligence and communications services are highly developed, it will scarcely be possible to conduct active counterguerrilla operations in inhabited areas without occasional village screenings. These are especially necessary in areas where the guerrillas hold some initiative and are capable of entering villages at night to obtain supplies and to liquidate "traitors." Often, a screening operation can be combined with a major military action as an integral, and therefore relatively justifiable, part of it. The system adopted in the anti-Huk campaign after 1950 is described in the following account by the officer who wrote the report above on the 1947 screening of *barrio* Pulong Plasan:

On the morning of 9 May 1951, as part of a special intelligence operation conducted by the 7th BCT S-7 section under Major Medardo T. Justiniano, troops under Lieutenant Lauro del Rosario surrounded the small *barrio* of Balatong, in the municipality of Plaridel, Bulacan Province. The screening force carried its normal complement of interrogation and investigation personnel from the S-2 section and was accompanied by the 7th BCT Civil Affairs Officer, Major Roberto Belen, and a small group of technicians from the Civil Affairs section. In addition, Major Belen brought a representative of the Provincial Governor, the Mayor of Plaridel, two reporters from the Manila press, and other local civil-government dignitaries. The presence of these representatives of civil government followed the current 7th BCT standard operating procedure.

As soon as the cordoning force was in place, the command group entered the village, and went to the house of the *barrio* Lieutenant, the village leader. He was informed of the purpose of our visit and asked to call all the villagers together. After they were assembled, the commanding officer of the cordoning troops informed them that he had heard there were Huk hiding in the village and asked if the report was true. When he was assured by several people that they knew of no Huk or Huk-sympathizers in the village, he asked if there would be any objection to a search of the village in the presence of witnesses. The searching parties were, accordingly, dispatched, each accompanied by a civilian representative.

Meanwhile, Major Belen, the Civil Affairs Officer, arranged for the villagers to be seated in the shade, in such a way that they were not readily able to talk with one another. He then gave a brief explanation of the mission of the troops; their duties as the protectors of the people from the Huk. The commanding officer directed the establishment of interrogation points and then said to the people:

"We know that most of you are loyal to the government. We know also that some of you have been giving assistance to the Huk. We know that some of you would like a chance to reform. We are going to give each of you a chance to show where your true loyalties lie. Each of you will go to one of those interrogation points, where you can speak freely. If you have supported our enemy but now sincerely repent, or if you are a loyal citizen, no harm will come to you. If you remain loyal to the Huk, you must go to the stockade and await trial for your crimes against the people."

The Civil Affairs Officer then asked the representative of the Governor to speak and called on the other speakers in turn until the screening was completed.

As soon as the searching party returned, having found evidence of visitors in three houses, they joined the interrogation teams. During the interrogation, five active Huk were discovered, three of them by their own spontaneous confession. In addition, the local Huk finance-corps representative confessed, asked for protection, and named three other active supporters—all supply officers. One of these, Juan Bantay, confessed also and was taken into custody at his own request. The other two did not confess, so they were released.

Altogether, we took into custody the five active Huk, the two confessed supply officers, one other civilian who desired protection—our principal informant. We released the two supply officers who did not confess and a man who had been visited by two Huk but claimed he knew nothing about them, as well as the other villagers. Four men volunteered to give information in the future and arrangements were made to contact them.

When we were through, the Civil Affairs Officer again spoke to the people, thanking them for their cooperation, especially for that given by the two Huk supply officers, who, he said, had repented and were being released; he assured them that the others who had been arrested would be treated fairly and asked if there were any complaints. There being none, he informed the villagers that since there would be an active operation in the vicinity, it would be wise for them not to go to the fields that day and that he was leaving a squad of soldiers and the Civil Affairs representative for their protection.

There are benefits to be derived in the technique by which screening ceases to be *zona,* advantages that may recommend its use even in areas where the armed forces have already built up substantial good will. Thus, requiring all the inhabitants to pass, singly and privately, through an interrogation station enables those who wish to volunteer information to do so without being detected, and allows arrangements for secure transmissions of future information to be made. Because of the announcement that persons known to be collaborating with the Huk would be released if they gave information to the government troops, any Huk collaborators immediately released—in Balatong, the two unregenerate supply officers—became suspect to the Huk. Those who were detained were not subject to Huk suspicion, and since those who betrayed their Huk friends were held until after action was taken, the informants could continue to function for the army.

Screening operations were also conducted through checkpoints posted along well-traveled roads and highways. In the initial stages of the anti-Huk campaign (1946–50), military-operated checkpoints were generally static. Out of inertia and lack of imagination, checkpoints were often established and operated at a fixed place, usually in or near a town. Naturally, the Huk soon identified and found ways to bypass them. Furthermore, examination of travelers was often so cursory that Huk documents captured in the field spoke of these checkpoints as being operated by the military personnel primarily to line their pockets rather than to detect and apprehend subversives.

Mobile checkpoints were found to be effective in disrupting guerrilla courier activities and in intercepting shipments of weapons and subversive propaganda. Mobile checkpoints were particularly valuable when operated on lonely rural routes, which, during the later stages of the campaign, were often used by guerrilla couriers, VIP's, or escapees. If these checkpoints were placed so that the traveler suddenly stumbled into them, he had no alternative but to go through the careful screening, which brought about the arrest of several important guerrillas. A courier intercepted in 1951 carried documents that contributed substantial military intelligence and aided in the conviction of the Huk Politburo members.

One packet of intercepted documents showed plans of alternative lines of communications, secret routes to be used in the event government pressure made them necessary. On another occasion, vehicle inspectors found, tucked into a piece of luggage, a map of Bulacan Province with several markings in cipher and code. One was a map that showed four points in the Sierra Madre mountains marked in red. This map was forwarded to battalion headquarters, where the S-2 section discovered that the plottings coincided with known or reported Huk "production bases." This ultimately resulted in a large operation that ended in the destruction and deactivation of Huk Regional Command Number 3, considered the best-equipped and the best-led Huk field force at the time.

Usually, a mobile checkpoint was situated so that it startled travelers. It might be near a hairpin turn, a curve, or hidden under the shadow of mango groves, bamboo thickets, etc. No signs were posted in either direction to indicate the imminence of the checkpoint. A security element would be posted far enough away to intercept any who might try to turn back when they learned of the checkpoint. Vehicles were directed to drive off the road, out of sight from the highway, and park under the trees or in a neat arrangement on open ground. Passengers, including drivers and their assistants, would then be marched off from the parking area to the area where the interrogation team took over the screening.

In the meantime, the search element would methodically examine the vehicles, while cargo, including luggage, was unloaded. The luggage and other cargo were opened in the presence of the owner. The army usually recruited volunteers—local hospital nurses, schoolteachers, and social workers—to search women travelers. Their services proved invaluable in raising the prestige of the Armed Forces. The 7th BCT procedures called for certificates testifying to the proper behavior of the searchers in order to offset possible malicious Huk allegations and to ensure the good behavior of the troops.

There are, of course, many other ways to get information from uncooperative civilians. One technique that frequently gave good results is described in an operation report by Sergeant Onofre Oblenida:

Sir, as directed, my patrol, consisting of seven men and myself, visited a *sitio* of the *barrio* of Mantang Tubeg, in Candaba Municipality, Pampanga Province, 7 April 1947. In compliance with the unit procedure, we entered the *sitio,* after studying it for some time, just before the men returned from the fields. We visited each of the seven houses, in each case going up the house only after we got permission from the housewife. All seemed scared. Each was asked how many in the family were expected home for supper, and in each house, it was noted that more rice was being cooked than was accounted for by the number supposed to be fed. In each house, we were assured that there were no Huk known to be in the area, and that all in the *sitio* were peaceful, loyal farmers. We pretended to accept this and marched off toward the highway without giving any indication of our suspicions.

Before reaching the highway, we had to pass through a field of high grass, where we believed no one could see us. So we hid there until half an hour after dark, then moved quietly back, downwind, taking up ambush position about a quarter of a mile outside the *sitio,* on a heavily traveled trail that led through the fields to what appeared to be a clump of trees at a stream. This, of course, we had noticed while studying this *sitio* and visiting it.

At about 2300 hours, three men were seen coming down the trail toward the houses. I decided to keep our patrol hidden and risk waiting until they came back, for I was sure that they would have to deliver the surplus rice I had seen being cooked. When they came back, about half an hour later, they were laughing and talking, carrying what we later found to be rice for about ten men. Since they were so noisy, we decided that we could capture them without revealing our position to the people in the houses. We hit each one over the head with a rifle butt. This made no more noise than they themselves had made, and after making sure we left behind no signs of the scuffle, we reset our ambush.

As we hoped, four more men, all armed, came in about half an hour to look for the missing three. We could hear them talking before we saw them, arguing about whether the three had decided to have a party or had run into trouble. When they reached our position, they were proceeding very cautiously. We challenged them and opened fire when they attempted to escape. Since it seemed unlikely that we could cut off the escape of the others, we immediately returned to the command post, and I am reporting to you, sir, as soon as I arrived.

Next morning, as soon after daylight as possible, while the prisoners were still being interrogated, the assistant intelligence officer visited the sitio, accompanied only by two interrogators and his driver-radioman. He found the people very frightened; the men were not expecting to go to the fields, but were discussing with their wives whether to make for the hills and hide out or to evacuate to the town. Lieutenant Justiniano, the young intelligence officer, called them together and said:

"You people have been very foolish and have placed yourselves in grave danger. Our soldiers came here to see if you needed any help. You lied to them. You said there were no Huk here. They knew you lied, and so they waited for the Huk to come. They killed some, and captured some, but others got away.

"You know what those Huk are thinking now—the ones who got away. They are thinking that somebody here betrayed them. They are planning now to come back here and take revenge on the traitors. Probably all of you will be killed, or at least have your houses burned, because you helped your enemies instead of the soldiers who came here to protect you. If you had told the truth, the soldiers would have found a way to get the Huk so they would never suspect you.

"We, too, should punish you for helping the enemies of the people instead of the friends of the people. I think the best punishment will be to make you stay here and keep the soldiers away until your 'friends' have showed you what they think."

This, of course, did not appeal to the people at all. The soldiers agreed to talk with them individually; each story was compared with those of the others and with the reports by the prisoners. It was decided that there was a substantial possibility of a Huk vengeance raid, so that night two squads of soldiers were smuggled into the town. They remained, hiding in the houses during the day, for two weeks, while an alert force was maintained ready to reinforce them if they radioed the approach of the enemy. At the end of two weeks, it was decided that chances of a raid were small, and the soldiers withdrew, over the inhabitants' protests. A warning system was set up, by which the people could notify the troops secretly if Huk were observed in the vicinity. Some information was later received and patrols visiting the village afterward reported that the people showed a marked desire to cooperate with them.

Patrols against guerrillas, like guerrilla patrols, need many skills besides those of the diplomat, the spy, the cross-examiner, and the mess sergeant.

They need the skills of the soldier, especially in the estimation of terrain, of its potentialities for concealment or disclosure, of its suitability for travel, of the likely spots for observation posts or bivouacs.

They need also the skills of the hunter, and of the hunted. Trackers may be invaluable, so may outdoorsmen, often tribal hillsmen or professional hunters, who can spot a leaf turned the wrong way or interpret animal cries. Soldiers long in the field can acquire these skills to an amazing degree. One, Felix Jabillo, ex-Sergeant of Philippine Scouts, after two years of fighting as a guerrilla against the Japanese twice demonstrated the ability to smell a single enemy soldier more than fifty feet away.

Patient observation is often the key to finding guerrillas. Frequently, getting the observation group into position without detection poses serious problems. One of the easiest solutions to this is the use of troop activity to cover the observers, who form staybehind parties.

A typical operation was conducted in Pampanga Province in early January, 1948. Three companies of troops mounted on trucks drove into San Luis, Pampanga, early one morning. They stopped, dismounted, crossed to the east side of the Pampanga River, and spread out along a line of skirmish, moving off into the swamp (fairly passable at that season). They were carefully observed by the citizens, many of them dedicated to the Huk cause.

The line of skirmishers kept moving until they were sure they were well out of sight. There they halted, with outposts in position. Three groups of four men each changed to civilian clothes (carried in the troop's packs along with rations). The three groups were supplied with clothes and a month's rations. The now-empty packs were stuffed with swamp grass to make them appear untouched. The troops assembled, marched back carrying the packs, got into their trucks and departed. Needless to say, they had seen no Huk. The townspeople could hardly hide their amusement at the valiant soldiers who had marched out into the swamp and then marched back again. No one bothered to count the men getting into the trucks.

For nearly a month, the three parties stayed in the swamp, each in radio contact with headquarters. They were able to report the movements of couriers and supply parties; in fact, as a result of their reports, the entire system of courier-supply routes was disclosed. There were no military operations in the area during this period, but the patrols operating to the west of the river seemed to have uncanny success in picking up couriers. The operation as a whole was considered markedly successful.

One of the interesting minor items of information they picked up from first-hand observation was the system used by Huk tax collectors in the little villages that dot the hummocks near the Pampanga River. They watched Huk tax collectors slip into the village late at night, placing under the household ladders (of the highbuilt Filipino houses, or nipa huts) one, two, sometimes as many as six, stones. It took a little patience to reveal the purpose. When householders were found putting a one-peso bill under each stone, it became obvious that each stone represented a one-peso tax assessment.

Obviously, "Finding 'Em" involves more than screening villagers, sending out numerous patrols, or setting up observation posts. It requires infiltration of agents into the ranks of the guerrillas, into the midst of guerrilla sympathizers, and getting the reports of these agents back in time to be of use. To some extent, these too can be done by combat units, but usually require greater resources and greater autonomy than are granted to a combat unit.

The development of adequate intelligence about a guerrilla movement is far too big a task for any combat unit. Adequate intelligence about the guerrilla means determining what orders he takes, and the way in which he receives them. It means tracing the possible links of the guerrilla governing body with outside nations. It means determining whether aid is coming from outside sources, and if so, how much, and by what channels.

Even more, adequate intelligence about a guerrilla movement means collecting rapidly every bit of information that may be relevant, from the identification of members in the smallest unit of the most remote guerrilla command to the pattern of the propaganda. This can be done effectively only by a nationwide organization, given full access to every scrap of information collected; more than that, a national organization with its own means for collecting and verifying information. Finally, it means that this national organization must process this information into useful intelligence and get it as quickly as possible to those who can use it. And that means, in many cases, getting it down to the squad leader.

The intelligence picture in the Philippines from 1946 to 1950 would have frightened any organization-minded intelligence officer. The Philippine Constabulary was charged with police action against the Huk and maintained its own intelligence organization. The Philippine Army, as the principal instrument of national defense, had its Military Intelligence Service (MIS), with branches for collecting intelligence about the enemy and for counterintelligence. The National Bureau of Investigation (counterpart of the United States FBI) felt that since the FBI was charged with investigation of U.S. Communists, the NBI should also have this same function in the Philippines, so it maintained its investigating branch. Since the center of Communist activities was in the capital, Manila, the Manila Police Department believed it had a primary interest in collecting intelligence about the Communists. Nearly a dozen other agencies, ranging from the special agents of the Office of the President to the Customs Secret Service, thought they had a proper role in the collection of intelligence about Communists, or the Huk, or both, and they too engaged in it.

The overlapping was, of course, phenomenal; jealousy was rampant. Despite this, by informal coordination, a very respectable job of intelligence collection was accomplished. The basic intelligence data on the principal figures in the Communist Party and their subordinate organizations (including the Hukbalahap) were at all times available to the President of the Philippines. Unfortunately, dissemination downward was poor. All agencies were eager to pass information up; they were reluctant to pass information down, especially if it meant going through an organization other than their own.

When it was determined that the Armed Forces should take the principal role in operations against the Huk, MIS was substantially strengthened and reorganized. It was given primary responsibility for collecting information on the Hukbalahap and the Communist Party, preparing it and disseminating it as intelligence.

To do this effectively, MIS was organized to include a conventional headquarters, a metropolitan detachment for the city of Manila, and two major types of field units. The plan was that in each area, usually a province, there would be an MIS team permanently stationed. This team was responsible for setting up intelligence and information nets throughout the province.

In addition, tactical MIS teams for attachment to BCT were organized. These teams were attached to the BCT in the area of operations and directed by the BCT intelligence officer. Each team included intelligence analysts, interrogators, and agents capable of undertaking limited covert operations or of organizing such operations through informants. They were also charged with maintaining close liaison between the BCT intelligence officer and the area MIS detachment. All information, in general, went both to the BCT intelligence officer and to MIS headquarters in Manila. If the BCT were transferred and another BCT replaced it, the MIS-BCT team was usually detached from the old battalion and attached to the new, although this practice was not invariable.

There were, of course, also operations conducted directly from MIS headquarters in Manila—largely of the long-range, or deep penetration type. There was considerable flexibility in this organization, and command lines were not always too closely drawn—nor can they always profitably be closely delineated in intelligence matters. The important thing was that primary responsibility for intelligence was placed where it should be: with the Armed Forces, who were responsible for defending the country against any threat, foreign or domestic. This pattern might well serve as a model for any nation that either has a domestic insurgency or is subject to enemy invasion. It is the only one by which the men who do the fighting (if it comes to that) can be assured of having the intelligence they need.

The other intelligence agencies were not taken out of the picture altogether, and quite properly not. They were given clearly to understand that their information effort was considered secondary and that primary responsibility and authority went to MIS, but their reports were welcome and were indeed often most useful. The competition that remained was far from being harmful. True, it caused some duplication, some overlapping, some "blowing" of other operations, but it served effectively to keep all on their toes.

Since the MIS as a really active field service came into the picture rather late, some combat units that had long been in the field had developed excellent intelligence services of their own. Wisely, the MIS did not attempt to disrupt their procedures; rather, they joined them. Operations undertaken after 1950, in some units, blended MIS and unit intelligence officers to the point where no distinction was made. This worked very well. One of the more significant operations of such a joint effort was the penetration of the Communist National Finance Committee, the tax-collection and supply arm of the Party and of the Huk, by an agent from a combat unit. The following is an account by one of the participants:

"Relatives Project" was aimed at the Huk organization in the Mount Arayat section. We found it necessary to contact the relatives of several Huk commanders in order to find a suitable person for infiltration. We did this, without identifying ourselves, until we finally located a cooperative man who was the cousin of a Huk commander. (This Huk commander, incidentally, had joined the Huk not for ideological reasons, but for personal reasons.) The infiltrator had about two months' intensive training. While this was in progress, arrangements were made for cover and protection. It took the burning of his house, the imprisonment of his brother, and eventually the evacuation of his mother and family, to ensure his cover and protect the infiltrator. We had to fool the Huk, and the government naturally had to pay for this.

His mother did not know her son was an infiltrator. The brother did not know he was being put in jail because we were working a scheme. But the news of these activities made them very effective. Slowly, on the basis of his obvious grievances against the government, our agent was able to reach the Huk.

He was made a collector of the National Finance Committee, the organization that supplied Huk in the field with money, medicine, ammunition, weapons, and other equipment. For two months, our supplies—medicine, ammunition, and weapons—were flowing into the Huk lines through this infiltrator. The purpose, of course, was to enable him to implant himself firmly into the organization. Soon he was promoted, and our effort and our supplies paid off because he was able to reach Taruc himself.

Our man was finally appointed a bodyguard to Taruc, the Huk leader of field forces, but for security purposes, he had this duty only on and off. Nevertheless, this fellow was able to take secret pictures of the entire membership of the organization in the Candaba Swamp. In all, only Secretary Magsaysay and five Filipino and American officers knew of this project.

The supply operations I mentioned went on for two months—and we got our reports back. Then, in the third month, it was decided the time had come to strike. It was very easy to simply pick out of the files the material this fellow had submitted. From his information, we were able then and there to apprehend 1,175 members of the National Finance Committee. That destroyed the Huk supply line.

This agent, like many other agents and informants, found that his most difficult task was communication with his true superiors. The tactic adopted to aid in getting instructions to him is rather ingenious, as described by the same participant:

In order to let our man know that he must pick up instructions, we used ordinary kites. At certain prearranged points in the area where he operated, we would fly kites simultaneously at three different places, at certain times of day exactly on the hour. The kites were not flown continuously or at random times in order to relieve him from having to keep constant watch for them; if he were always seen scanning the horizon, suspicions might have been aroused. So we did things on the hour. We would fly the kite at seven o'clock in the morning, eight, nine, and ten to make sure this signal had been received. The moment he saw the kite he would know a contact was to be made within the swamp.

The troops, of course, couldn't be told anything about the operation. As a matter of fact, I lost two men when the area commander in this area attacked my men, and I nearly lost my life, too, but I couldn't tell him.

Very often, there wouldn't be anyone to meet our infiltrator, but he would find his messages concealed, perhaps in a carelessly abandoned mess, or first aid, kit.

Using this system, how could we make an emergency contact at night? What we did was fly the kite with a battery-operated light. That is one way he got the message. The other was by the use of flares. In other words, if we believed that he had not been able to see this small light from the kite, we supplemented it with flares fired on the hour at the same designated spots. The moment our man saw this signal, he knew it meant that he had to be very careful because the troops were going in fast. We told him now to find a way to save himself. It was my biggest concern, to be sure this fellow was safe.

It is similarly difficult for the agent to have his information delivered. One of the most effective ways of obtaining reports from informants in guerrilla-infested areas is through the use of aircraft. It was found that the L-5 aircraft was especially useful for picking up reports from ground observers. Operating on a flight plan prepared jointly by the S-2 and S-3 sections, the pilots were directed to observe certain specific points—houses occupied or used by informants who gave their information by prearranged signals. These signals were improvised to suit the local environment: an open gate, an animal tied in the southeast corner of the yard, two windows of a house open. This particular combination of signals gave three items of information: the enemy's direction was noted by the relative position of the animal to the house; the open gate indicated that the enemy planned to stay in the area;

and the two open windows indicated there were about two hundred Huk in the area.

When reports of this nature were received from two or three informants, accurate plotting of the enemy position was possible and an attack could be mounted.

Aircraft observation of ground activities must usually be confirmed on the ground before action is taken on them. This is especially true of observations of new plantings and similar activities in supposedly uninhabited areas. These must be verified by ground patrols before action is taken against what may well be the farm patches of honest citizens. Indiscriminate aerial attacks may turn otherwise potentially valuable guides and informants into guerrilla sympathizers with just cause to hate the government.

Any lover of mystery stories will remember the classic conversation between Sherlock Holmes and Inspector Gregory:

> "Is there any point to which you would wish to draw my attention?"
> "To the curious incident of the dog in the night-time."
> "The dog did nothing in the night-time."

Then the memorable comment:

> "That was the curious incident."

This point, so well made by A. Conan Doyle in "Silver Blaze," has remarkable pertinence to counterguerrilla intelligence operations. It was the dog that did not bark, the "quiet" zone, that brought about "Operation Cover-up," which was conducted in Pandi, Bulacan Province.

The municipality of Pandi covers many of the back doors to Manila; it is sparsely populated and is not as well developed as the surrounding areas. For some time—since 1950—the S-2 section had consistently found Pandi a "quiet" sector, while neighboring municipal areas drew high operational priorities because of frequent Huk troop concentrations and other guerrilla activities. Personal interviews with municipal authorities drew blank stares and invariably a denial of any information about Huk or guerrilla activities in the town of Pandi or the municipal area itself.

On the other hand, G-2 reports indicated that Huk couriers and Huk VIPs habitually traveled through Pandi on commercial buses without being molested or challenged. Huk wounded were sheltering and convalescing in Pandi. This was obvious, because at this time the home guards and police forces in other municipalities around Pandi were on the offensive against Huk foraging parties. To cite one instance, an encounter took place between a civilian guard unit led by an MIS operative of the 7th BCT and a fifteen man Huk band at Sapang Palay, a village about eight miles east of Pandi. During this encounter, two Huk were killed. The Huk band fled westward with the home guards in pursuit. The withdrawing Huk completely disappeared, leaving no trace. As a result, "Operation Cover-up" was launched. An elaborate report was ultimately submitted on its activities:

> Four teams, consisting of six to eight members of MIS and Charley Company (a specially trained unit like Force X), with radio sets were organized, with the ranking NCO in charge of each team. Later, six more teams of the same composition were added. Assigned missions were varied, but essentially the teams were dispatched to penetrate the suspect area secretly and report by radio all observations on the people there. Contact frequency was every other hour on the hour. S-2 rented a house in the town of Pandi and hired a family to occupy the house as a cover for MIS operatives. The MIS group was assigned to effect surveillance on the Mayor and the town Chief of Police, already suspected by S-2.
>
> It was possible for the 7th BCT to detain suspects indefinitely, if there were good grounds, because of the temporary suspension of the writ of habeas corpus in Huklandia since 1950. On the theory that the people were being subjected to a deep-covered "terrorism," it was recommended that several people be "snatched" and brought to the 7th BCT headquarters for interrogation, in the hope that these people could be convinced of the protective intent of the government and would tell the truth about Pandi.
>
> The teams were able to kidnap no less than seventy people from different parts of the area without being detected by the inhabitants. Suspicions about the hidden power of the Huks in Pandi grew, since in not a single case did either the Mayor or the Chief of Police report the disappearances to the Philippine Constabulary or to the 7th BCT.
>
> With good treatment, frequent appeals to the detainees (in these, the Secretary of National Defense, Magsaysay, participated), and promises of rewards, the knowledgeable eventually came up with startling information. However, all detainees agreed on their fear of Huk reprisals. Allegations from detainees were radioed back for verification or confirmation to field teams covering Pandi. The statements were carefully classified and analyzed and compared with intelligence files as far back as 1948. Out of these painstaking efforts, S-2 was able to establish the following intelligence:
>
> 1. Pandi was important to the Huk organizations in Luzon due to its proximity to Manila, the center of underground activity of the Communist Party of the Philippines.
>
> 2. Therefore, it was important that Pandi should not draw the attention of the Armed Forces or the Constabulary. To keep from being garrisoned by either, the area must be kept a "quiet" sector, free from raids, ambuscades, or any Huk activity that would draw troops.
>
> 3. It was commonly known in the area that Huk troop concentrations were prohibited. The area was even supposed to be avoided by traveling units. Foraging was done only through supply agents, specifically appointed by

the Mayor. Direct approach to houses or inhabitants was punishable by death.

4. Huk wounded or fugitives desirous of seeking shelter in Pandi first had to get proper permission from their superiors, who would in turn make proper arrangements with Pandi authorities.

5. Huk couriers traveling to or from Manila received briefings from Pandi Huk intelligence officers on the current situation at their destinations, were given passwords, and were taught new countersigns.

6. Pandi inhabitants adjudged "reactionary" or recalcitrant were not disciplined within the municipal area, but in accordance with long-standing practice, secretly kidnapped and killed outside of Pandi. Several instances were cited where the Mayor and the Police Chief conspired in Communist-style kidnap-murders of those the Huk high command ordered punished.

7. During the past years, Philippine Constabulary garrisons had occasionally been set up in Pandi. Although, because of their small size and poor security they could have been wiped out by local Huks, these garrisons were left unmolested to mislead government intelligence appraisals.

8. Names of individuals were submitted as active Huk agents in Pandi, starting off with the Mayor, policemen, rich and prosperous businessmen, etc.

With several sworn statements, each corroborating others, criminal actions were instituted against all individuals cited or involved.

The liquidation of the Pandi sanctuary broke the Huk secret refuge near Manila, which, in a larger way, hamstrung their clandestine activities in the city and their liaison and control lines with active field units in Central Luzon. Travel for Huk couriers and VIP's to and from Manila became, at the very least, more difficult.

Finding the guerrilla is a dangerous and difficult task, but it must be done. It can be done only through the continuing action of many devoted men, plus the most intense command emphasis and unstinted command backing.

"Finding 'Em" in the Philippines was well performed. Most of the accomplishments still cannot be told, nor can some of those who contributed significantly, and at great risk of their lives, their reputations, and their families, be identified. However, any discussion of the efforts and the accomplishments in finding the guerrilla—and more particularly, his leaders—cannot be complete without mentioning the names of three devoted men. The senior, in point of service in this campaign, is Lorenzo "Pop" Alvarado, onetime Sergeant of Philippine Scouts, whose attention was first directed to Communist activities in the Philippines in 1922.

Most significant were the services of two gallant senior officers: Colonel Agustín Gabriel and Colonel Ismael Lapus. Both were active throughout the entire campaign against the Huk. Colonel Gabriel was active against them from the days of their predecessor organization, the prewar Sakdal. Without the efforts of these two gentlemen—which too often seemed unappreciated by their superiors—the final success against the Huk might have been long, perhaps even too long, delayed.

NOTE

1. This was a Huk ambush of an isolated vehicle, in which the wife and child of an American officer were killed.

Chapter 11

FIGHT 'EM

FIGHTING THE guerrilla—the use of force against individuals or units—is very much less difficult than the two elements that have just been discussed; it is much easier than "Fooling 'Em" or "Finding 'Em." When the counterguerrillas have the initiative, the guerrillas they meet can only die, run, surrender, or try to hide. They may try to postpone acceptance of one of these choices, but if the counterguerrillas who encounter them are reasonably well led and supported, the guerrillas must do one of these four things.

Ordinarily well-trained and well-disciplined troops with competent aggressive leadership have a tremendous advantage over guerrillas in actual combat. A platoon of such soldiers, armed with commercial .22-caliber sporting rifles, should be able to drive before them a company of guerrillas, in normally overgrown terrain.

The competent guerrilla leader knows that ordinarily he cannot hold terrain, should not try to keep his position in the face of aggressive troops. If surprised, he may fight long enough to determine if the troops are aggressive or to cover the withdrawal of his main force and his auxiliaries or his VIP's. Even if not surprised, he *may* offer resistance, hoping to inflict sufficient casualties on the enemy to dampen their aggressive spirit.

"He who fights and runs away can fight again another day" is a cardinal guerrilla axiom. Successful offensive combat tactics against the guerrilla are those that seek to prevent him from running away, either by cutting his route of withdrawal or overwhelming him by sudden assault. Successful defensive tactics are those that lure him out to be killed (only rarely possible) or those that cause him to run away—again, immediate assault, or a threat to his route of withdrawal.

These words are easy to say; the principles are easy to prove. Their implementation is another matter, as the history of every guerrilla war shows. Time after time, guerrillas have successfully held their ground against larger bodies of troops, or have successfully attacked military installations. Occasionally, as in the Boer War, this has been a matter of superior marksmanship and clear fields of fire. Most often it has been due to the mental attitudes (or incompetence) of the counterguerrilla forces.

The principal considerations limiting effective combat against guerrillas are the attitudes of the participants. Of these, an unwillingness to accept reasonable combat casualties in counter-guerrilla operations is the most serious drain on the combat effectiveness of counterguerrilla forces. This tacit attitude usually may be found to prevail at all echelons, from the troops actually engaged up through their entire military structure to its political chiefs, the national administration, and back down to the people that administration represents. It is indeed rare to find counter-guerrillas willing to accept, in engagements of their own seeking, casualties proportionate to those they can inflict on the guerrillas.

Only the British in Malaya seem to have been wholly successful in overcoming this attitude in modern times. Their doctrine was immediate all-out assault, whenever, and as soon as, they were sighted by the guerrillas. Militarily, this is probably the best tactical doctrine, but it is one not likely to be effectively employed in most circumstances. Perhaps even the British found this tactic feasible only because their forces usually greatly outnumbered the guerrillas they encountered.

Sometimes it almost seems that nobody who "counts" is really mad at the guerrilla. A large army training camp in Huklandia was, in 1948, the target of nuisance attacks by roaming Huk. The Provincial Provost Marshal responsible for operations against the Huk in that area, an aggressive Lieutenant Colonel, received many complaints about these attacks from the General commanding the camp. The Colonel suggested that the camp might contribute to its own defense; that patrols around its boundaries would be extremely good training. The General made it very clear that he was not mad at the Huk, and that he hoped they would not get mad at him. One could scarcely have blamed the Colonel for being madder at the "brass" than at the poor hard-working guerrillas.

That General's attitude was perhaps less common in the Philippines than in many other countries with a serious guerrilla problem. When those whose mission is to fight know that members of the public, of the government, of the armed forces have such an attitude, a certain reluctance to accept casualties is inevitable and understandable. Under such conditions, the counterguerrilla feels that he is a policeman with a lot rather worse than that characterized by W. S. Gilbert as "not a happy one."

Basically, the counterguerrilla's reluctance to accept combat casualties arises from a tacit realization of the worth of the guerrilla attitude, of the desirability of living to fight another day. It is a seemingly realistic appraisal of the situation; of the consensus that the guerrilla does not pose the threat to national existence that would be presented by a conventional army. No matter how brave he may be, no matter how aggressive his leadership, it is an unusual counterguerrilla who will behave as he would in a "regular" war—unless the people for whom he fights show an enthusiasm and devotion comparable to that shown during a "regular" war. Often, getting the people who "count" to realize and show by their actions that the guerrillas do represent a deadly menace to the nation is the most difficult task of the counterguerrilla.

Even the most aggressive units engaged in counterguerrilla operations find their combat tactics almost unconsciously restricted by this unwillingness to accept casualties. Consider the 7th BCT, Armed Forces of the Philippines, one of the most aggressive and effective units in the campaign against the Huk, one that has furnished many examples of how guerrillas should be fought. Any soldier, any officer who knew that unit would be justly proud of service in it.

During the five-year period 1950–55, the men of the 7th BCT were almost continuously in the field. They met the Huk at the height of his strength; they broke his strength in every area to which they were assigned. Exact figures are not available, but they killed more than 500 Huk, they captured nearly as many, they received the surrender of many more. They were a fighting outfit. One commander was twice wounded, another commander (just after the period covered) was killed. Their total casualties during these five years: 53 men killed; 1 man missing in action, believed killed; 29 men wounded. At least half of those killed were not on combat missions when they died; they were conducting intelligence or reconnaissance operations in which they tried to avoid contact with the enemy but were surprised and overwhelmed. Four were chopped to pieces, and the pieces were strewn down the road as a warning to their comrades.

Counterguerrilla reluctance to engage in actions that will probably result in the loss of men is just as real and significant a fact of life as the reluctance of guerrillas to engage in combat unless they have an obvious advantage over their opponents. Both must be accepted as the rule rather than the exception. Combat tactics in counterguerrilla operations must seek to avoid friendly casualties while concentrating on forcing the enemy to fight until he is killed or surrenders.

The temptation always, the practice too often, is to avoid decisive aggressive action by proceeding as though the guerrilla were an orthodox enemy determined to fight. It is all too easy to follow the tactics and troop-leading procedures for conventional warfare. The first action upon encounter with an enemy is usually to establish a base of fire, that is, a line of men parallel to what is believed to be the enemy front, shooting in the direction where the enemy is believed to be. Until the situation is clarified, most or all automatic weapons and mortars are used to augment this fire. The base of fire established, the commander makes a reconnaissance, makes an estimate of the situation, and formulates his plan of maneuver. This he communicates to his subordinates, who must make their own reconnaissance, etc., etc., and eventually an attack may be launched.

In due course, the positions of the enemy are overrun, while the enemy himself is reorganizing some miles away, or already moving into a position to ambush the troops on their triumphant way home after their "victory." The troops feel that they have proved their mettle, and demonstrated conclusively that the guerrilla is a cowardly chap who cannot resist them. Too often, if the unit is not ambushed on its way home, it reports that the "situation is under control," implying that they have deprived the enemy of the initiative. They do not realize, although Clausewitz did, that an enemy who has successfully disengaged may still maintain both tactical and strategic initiative.

Even this is not the worst way to fight the guerrilla. The worst is to assume that, because his initial volume of fire is great, the guerrilla is in overwhelming strength and offers a major threat to the troop unit. Withdrawal under such circumstances *might* be justified when facing a conventional enemy; withdrawal from frontal contact except as a preliminary to a flanking or encircling movement is intolerable in counterguerrilla warfare, unless it can be conclusively proved that the guerrilla is both overwhelming in strength *and* determined to attack.

An excellent SOP was formulated as follows:

"When a patrol makes contact with guerrilla, the automatic-weapons man (or men) immediately take the guerrilla under fire. He (they) should move back and forth along a line parallel to the observed front of the guerrilla, firing short bursts in his general direction. The rest of the force that has encountered the guerrilla should immediately divide into two parties. Each party should move to a flank, then seek to achieve a position behind the guerrilla, and drive him to the front, into the fire of the automatic weapons."

This was the standard tactic of some units of the Armed Forces of the Philippines for engaging the guerrilla in a surprise encounter or a meeting engagement. Its advantages are obvious; it subjects the troops to the least danger from the fire of the guerrilla, while at the same time forcing him either to fight to a finish or to withdraw immediately to prevent encirclement.

The military disadvantage is equally obvious. The guerrilla, unless sure that he possesses great superiority, will withdraw immediately he learns of the flanking effort, usually along a route that permits withdrawal faster than the advance of the flanking parties. An immediate all-out assault may overtake the guerrilla before he can withdraw, especially if he is in a camp or bivouac, whereas the time required for the encircling effort may multiply his safety margin two or three times. Nevertheless, the tactic described above is probably the best that can be achieved as a standard for counterguerrilla actions.

This standard can be achieved only if the troops are imbued with an aggressive spirit and with the self-confidence on which sustained combat aggressiveness so often rests. The soldier must know that man for man, his outfit for their outfit, he is better than the guerrilla in actual combat. This knowledge is based initially on training and indoctrination; it is reinforced by combat experience.

The conventionally trained and armed soldier, if properly led and oriented, can outdo the active guerrilla. He is a better fighter because he is in better physical condition, is better trained, maintained, and equipped; he is better prepared to destroy a designated target by force and violence. Other things being equal, the conventional soldier can move faster, react more intelligently, and obey orders better than his guerrilla enemy.

For maximum effectiveness as a counterguerrilla, the conventionally trained soldier needs additional training. This must emphasize and develop in the soldier his basic military assets and a high degree of self-confidence, so that he is prepared to fight, alone if need be, against the guerrilla on his own ground. "Offensive-mindedness" must be inculcated to the greatest degree possible, so that the soldier, conscious of his superior discipline, training, and armament, is prepared to take the initiative against a hidden enemy of unknown size, and under the most adverse conditions.

Tactical training for counterguerrillas may profitably start by pairing off soldiers, the establishment of "buddy teams." Two-man teams, made up of two rugged individuals accustomed to working together and trusting one another, form the basic building block for combat against guerrillas. In combat they advance by leapfrogging each other in short bounds, each sure from his training and experience that the other will be covering him. As long as he has his buddy, the soldier knows that he has someone who will support him and whom he must support, whether it be in attack or defense, sentry-go or patrol.

The smallest regular patrol formation taught to line troops for counterguerrilla operations normally will consist of a pair of buddy teams. This is the smallest patrol capable of holding ground or attacking by fire and maneuver. It enables the use of leapfrog tactics in either forward or retrograde movements. While patrolling, the two teams may be so separated, by distance or by cover, that only one team is likely to be observed and engaged by the enemy. The other team is thus left free to take the action previously assigned to the unengaged team (usually a flanking movement, possibly the establishment of a base of fire that will permit disengagement by the other team).

The squad is the basic combat command and should be intensively trained in operating as a self-sufficient team. When approaching possible enemy contact, it should adopt a formation that will enable it to force the enemy to fight. As practiced in the Philippines with an eight-man squad, this was usually a formation that placed the assistant squad leader and his buddy in the lead, on the trail or other route of approach. Flanking the lead team and slightly to the rear, concealed if possible from probable enemy observation points, was a team of two riflemen on either side. Bringing up the rear, and determining the rate of advance, were the squad leader and his buddy, usually an automatic rifleman. Since this formation may be extremely fatiguing for the flanking parties, the squad leader and his assistant may alternate in the lead, with the rifle teams alternating in the rear position.

If enemy were met, the team making contact would immediately establish a base of fire, and each flanking team would automatically seek to pass the enemy's flanks, in order to achieve a position from which it could advance on the enemy from his rear quarter. (All movements were normally executed in short swift bounds, one team member covering the other.) The rear element was left free to act in accordance with the directions of the squad leader. Closing with the enemy was mandatory. When possible, this was done on the signal of the commander, but if no signal was heard (often the case in a fight of this nature), each element would close in when it believed the others were in position to do so.

Uncontrolled flanking movements, especially double envelopments, are often frowned on because of the possibility of men being hit by friendly fire. This danger can be reduced by several means, the most effective being rigorous insistence on identifying a target before firing at it. The adoption of distinctive fire patterns or rhythms—*rat-a-tat-tat*—the habitual employment of slogans or passwords (one commander who survived many such engagements insisted that his men all sing the "Battle Hymn of the Republic" while advancing), and distinctive markings (e.g., use of hunter's headgear, bright side out in combat) are all effective in reducing unfortunate incidents.

"Talking it up" is useful in many ways. One very successful commander insisted that all commands be loudly and clearly addressed to a unit higher than the one actually addressed. Private Flores, signaling his buddy, Juan, to move up, would sound off: "Juan, move your team up." The squad leader, addressing Flores and Juan, would shout: "Flores, get forward with that squad!" By the time he was ready to move in with his "platoon," the enemy was likely to be feeling heavily outnumbered. One Huk unit, bluffed this way, actually surrendered to an army squad without a shot being fired.

It is almost impossible to overestimate the capabilities of aggressive, well-trained small units in combat against guerrillas. Encouragement of aggressive action against superior numbers may result in occasional disheartening losses, but it will result in more effective, sometimes even spectacular, damage to the enemy. One such incident is told by the commander who would have half-killed the officer responsible when he caught him, had that officer not been then in the process of being warmly congratulated by Secretary Magsaysay:

At midday, 9 May 1951, Lieutenant Delfín S. Castro, in command of a 15-man reconnaissance patrol, was approaching his objective, believed to be some 4,000 yards to the northeast. The mission of his patrol was to scout the Mount

Tacbuhan area, to verify the location of the headquarters of Hukbalahap Field Command No. 32.

The patrol rested on the side of a mountain trail, with an advance party of 4 men in front, a right-flank security party of 2 men situated 150 yards from the trail at an elevation of perhaps 75 feet above it, and a rear party of 3 men some 50 yards to the rear. Castro resumed the march at 1430 hours, reaching the general vicinity of his objective area at 1700. Due to the many peaks and military crests affording observation of his further route of advance, Castro decided to halt for the day, establishing bivouac about 500 yards from the trail under heavy vegetational cover.

Leaving his NCO second-in-command in charge, Castro with 3 men pushed forward on reconnaissance to take advantage of the remaining hour and a half of daylight. He discovered that had he continued the advance of his patrol for another 20 minutes he would have run against what proved to be the first Huk outpost guarding the only trail leading into the Huk base that was his patrol objective. Castro bypassed this outpost and penetrated the area another 500 yards, discovering a shack that could easily have accommodated 30 men, apparently the barracks of a second security post supporting the first one found. Noting a trail to the right of the shack, Castro advanced parallel to it for some 30 yards of uphill going. He found himself on the edge of the main Huk camp, which contained 17 shacks of various sizes, a clearing about 40 yards in diameter, and another large shack. Remaining in observation for about 15 minutes, Castro and his men estimated that no less than 200 Huk, men, women, and children were in the area. They counted 67 armed men, and noted a machine gun emplaced on a promontory on the southwest edge of the camp, guarding the trail they had avoided.

Deciding to circle the outside periphery of the camp, Castro studied the surrounding terrain carefully. He found that the camp was actually situated in a bowl formed by elevations on the east, northwest, and north sides, and skirted by a deep ravine on its western and southern edges. In this ravine ran a mountain stream, where the camp inmates were seen washing and drawing water. Castro withdrew from the camp at dark, and rejoined his patrol at 2030 hours.

Knowing that it would take 4 days to receive reinforcements, and fearing that his presence might be discovered before then, Castro decided to attack the Huk camp. He felt confident that a surprise attack from an unexpected direction would make up for the Huk superiority in armed men. The patrol was allowed to rest until midnight.

The attack formation consisted of 4 parties, each guided by a member of the evening patrol. Castro's own group was to approach the camp directly and attack the machine-gun post, his attack being the signal for the other groups to open fire. The second group was ordered to seek and occupy ambush positions to the northeast of the camp, covering any exit routes that might be found. The 2 remaining groups were to approach the camp from the west, cross the stream, negotiate the ravine, establish firing positions from which they could enfilade the camp, and await the signal for the general attack.

The parties attacked almost simultaneously about 053D hours 10 May, with Castro signaling the attack by blowing up the machine-gun post with hand grenades. The groups assigned to cover the northwest (ravine) and the high ground had arrived in ample time to organize their attacks.

During the height of the action, the personnel manning the by-passed first outpost and the security post retreated up the trail in the belief that a large government force was approaching from their front. These guerrillas were wiped out almost to the last man when they encountered the elements of Castro's force that had already entered the camp.

Huk losses were some 22 killed, 13 wounded (all captured), plus 9 men, 21 women, and 7 children captured. The patrol destroyed all the buildings and several "production patches" that were found in the vicinity, and captured several sacks full of Huk documents and propaganda material. Castro did not lose even 1 of his 15 men.

Few small-unit actions will be as successful or as lucky as this one. However, when a counterguerrilla campaign is successfully concluded, it will be found that most enemy casualties will have been inflicted in actions provoked or started by small units, and that such actions have been the immediate cause for many guerrillas' resigning from the war.

It cannot be repeated too often that the competent guerrilla will not stand and fight unless he is sure that he will win, or has no other alternative. It follows that, unless he can be attacked by surprise, the only ways in which he may be brought to combat to his disadvantage are through offering him "bait," cutting off his route of withdrawal, or making him lose his head. All these can best be accomplished by a multiplicity of small, mutually reinforcing patrols.

In the Philippines, large operations were most successful when they were essentially of this nature in their execution. When they were not, they seldom killed many Huk, or resulted in any casualties among the attackers. They did cause the abandonment of bases, of rations, sometimes of ammunition, and sometimes they resulted in the capture of significant documents. They effectively put the Huk on the run for a time, usually short, and did have some effect in reducing his will to fight. Sometimes, as in the operations against Mrs. Quezon's ambushers, they did result in substantial casualties among the Huk. The cost, in terms of effort, matériel, and troop time, of that operation makes it seem scarcely worthwhile in terms of damage inflicted on the enemy. It should have been successful, as a psychological operation, in convincing the people and the Huk that when the armed forces got mad they could and would succeed.

Unfortunately the people, by the end of that operation, were too absorbed in politics, and too busy worrying about alleged plans to use the armed forces against them in the coming election. Key Communist Party leaders similarly ignored the lesson, and decided to open an offensive against the army.

A form of meeting engagement very common in counterguerrilla warfare is that singularly unpleasant surprise to one side which is called an ambush. Who ambushes whom is largely determined by the aggressiveness and the intelligence support of the protagonists. Initially, as was the experience in the Philippines, most of the ambushing will probably be done by the guerrillas.

Ambushes by the Huk were generally placed in one of three general classifications: ambushes of foot troops, ambushes of military personnel riding in vehicles, and holdup ambushes. Of the three, the last was by far the most common. It was a standard method of replenishing supplies, especially of money, without the necessity of begging or the obloquy which attached to theft or robbery of homes. The Huk had a quite elaborate SOP for stopping buses, and occasionally private cars, in isolated spots, holding them under the guns of men stationed along the road, and rather politely relieving the passengers of most of their possessions. They made it a point to explain that they regretted the necessity for securing contributions in this manner, explaining that their actions were made necessary by the failure of government to promote properly the interests and welfare of its citizens.

The armed forces at times used decoy buses, seeking in effect to counterambush the ambushers. This practice was rather frowned upon, because of the danger it raised that Huk might no longer stop genuine civilian buses politely, but might stop them with a hail of bullets and ensuing heavy civilian casualties.

Many tactics for preventing ambush of vehicles were developed by aggressive commanders. Often these involved elaborate plans for the classification of roads according to the degree of anticipated danger of ambush, and traffic-control systems based on the classification and the terrain. Dangerous routes, if not closed to traffic other than military vehicles looking for trouble, were often placed under convoy restrictions. These required vehicles to stop at designated points and wait for enough other vehicles to make up a convoy, which would be escorted by armored cars.

Patrols were especially effective. Sometimes these were made by armored civilian vehicles carrying troops, sometimes by military vehicles. Frequently the patrols were made on foot, flanking the road, with supporting road elements linked to the footsloggers by radio. This type of patrol was particularly useful in discouraging holdup ambushes by small Huk parties.

One counterambush tactic sometimes taught was firmly prohibited by Magsaysay. This was the so-called reconnaissance by fire—firing into areas where guerrilla *might* be, without concern for the civilians who might equally well be there. This tactic may be permissible in regions where there is known to be no one except acknowledged enemy; it is seldom, if ever, permissible in counterguerrilla operations.

The only consensus on tactics to be adopted when vehicles are ambushed is that the occupants must do something. The accepted practice in the Philippines was for the occupants of the vehicles fired on to detruck immediately and establish a base of fire from the side of the road opposite the enemy. Vehicles not fired on were expected to advance or retreat, out of the area of fire, and their occupants to seek to attack the flank of the ambush party.

Some commanders insist that the only effective counteraction when vehicles are ambushed is for all passengers, in all vehicles that are halted or likely to be halted, to leap immediately to the attack, charging the ambush party. This tactic seems sound. It is the only effective action when both lead and rear vehicles of a convoy are stopped, as they are by a well-executed ambush. Whether the attack is frontal, as in this method, or flanking, as in the more conservative tactic, attack is the only acceptable response. It is also the only way of discouraging future ambushes.

There is no sure and generally applicable way of preventing the ambush of foot troops when the guerrilla is aggressive. Under the terrain conditions frequently found in this type of warfare, the habitual use of flanking parties will often intolerably delay the main body, and may result in the loss of these parties.

The best safeguard against ambush, of course, is sufficient knowledge of the enemy situation to be sure that there are no enemy in the area who are bold enough, and strong enough, to try an ambush. Next to this is the practice, already described, of sending units or small patrols on parallel routes within reinforcing distance of one another. So long as the guerrilla is aware of the possibility that there may be more troops just over the hill, or just around the bend in the trail, he is quite unlikely to attack. Needless to say, ordinary precautions, investigating likely ambush spots in advance of the arrival of the main party, using flank guards, and so on, should always be taken if the possibility of ambush exists, and the mission of the troop unit permits time to be taken.

The appropriate immediate action for foot troops when ambushed has never been satisfactorily decided. Some commanders strongly advocate immediate assault; head hell-for-leather into the fire. Others feel that a party caught in an ambush should seek to squeeze out of the ends, to get out of the killing zone and then execute an enveloping movement. The one point upon which all agree is that when caught in an ambush, troops must do something, must get out of the killing zone by advancing, retreating, charging, or autolevitation. They must have a prearranged plan that is known to every man, and that allots to every man, according to his position when the trap is sprung, a specific immediate action.

Ambushing guerrillas successfully usually requires much patient preparation, much painstaking gathering of information. Sometimes, prisoners will supply the needed data, more often it will be necessary for stay-behind parties to watch for days. Penetration agents among the guerrilla, or their civilian supporters, often can be of assistance. So can the casual chatter of civilians to other civilians of their acquaintance; details thus gleaned may be combined with other information to point the probable path of small guerrilla parties. Sometimes the information needed can be gained from spot observation and deduction, as in the ambush of the rice carriers conducted by Sergeant Oblenida.

Ambushes of single individuals or very small groups are rather common in counterguerrilla operations. Guerrillas visit their families or their girl friends. The information gets around, and another guerrilla disappears, or he may be left—as he was in some cases—showing one or more knife wounds, a mystery for his companions possibly to investigate, and fall into the trap. A tactic insufficiently exploited during the Huk campaign was the long-range sniping ambush, in which small parties deep in guerrilla territory pick off individuals in the vicinity of a base that cannot be approached, without discovery, by forces large enough to deal with it. Had suitable weapons for this, meaning silenced rifles, been available, the tactic could probably have contributed much to the campaign.

One constant problem in operating against individuals or small groups is the difficulty of positive identification of enemy. Huk on visits to their families or friends would often conceal their weapons and appear to be innocent farmers. Troops who claim to be the friends and benefactors of the civilian population cannot afford to make too many mistakes in identification. The simple tactic of knocking on the front door and running around to see who comes out the back is not sufficiently sophisticated to be a safe way of distinguishing between a guerrilla visitor and a casual Lothario. It was found, however, that knocking, so to speak, on the doors of a dozen houses in an isolated *barrio* by firing off flares or shooting a clip of M-1 ammunition into the air was sufficient to justify immediate action if a half-dozen men came bolting out of the houses in the middle of the night. These usually were Huk, and not a few died or were captured in this way.

The Armed Forces of the Philippines did not have occasion to develop and test effective defensive tactics against the Huk. There were few occasions on which the Huk actually attacked an armed forces position. When they did, it was usually a complete surprise executed against unsuspecting forces, or else was a probing attack that developed such stiff initial response that a full attack never materialized. Had it not been for the Huk strategy of avoiding attack during the first years of the campaign, it would have been much easier for the counterguer-rillas. Ordinarily, well-trained, well-motivated troops in a rationally sited and reasonably well-prepared position can ask nothing better than for the guerrilla to attack their position. It will eliminate many, and thoroughly discourage the survivors.

No consideration of ways of fighting guerrillas is complete without a discussion of weaponry. The AFP, in their campaign against the Huk, used substantially the armament normal during that period to an infantry battalion of the U.S. Army. The weapons for the individual soldier were about 60 per cent Garands (U.S. rifle, .30 caliber, M-1), approximately 25 per cent carbines (U.S., .30 caliber), perhaps 12 per cent Browning automatic rifles and .45-caliber submachine guns, supplemented with pistols and a very few unconventional weapons. In addition, they were well equipped with light and heavy .30-caliber machine guns, and with 60-mm. and 81-mm. mortars. There were also .50-caliber machine guns, and a number of batteries of 75-mm. or 105-mm. howitzers. These weapons were more than adequate. Actually, they were too heavy, and so was their ammunition.

For practical purposes, 80 per cent of the troops engaged in counterguerrilla operations might be satisfactorily armed with commercial .22-caliber sporting rifles. Possibly 10 per cent should be armed with M-1 or '03 rifles, or a comparable weapon, for the occasional long-range encounter. For the rest, a mix of noisy, fast-firing automatic weapons with a range of 20 yards or so, and a few unconventional, that is, silenced, rifles and pistols could do the job. Hand grenades are useful for their moral effect, as are shotguns. So are rifle grenades and light mortars or recoilless rifles, again primarily for their moral effect.

This is really the key consideration in weaponry for counterguerrilla operations—the moral and morale effects of the weapons. Troops with conventional training simply cannot be convinced, without long indoctrination, that weapons lighter than those in the standard military mix are effective. This goes from top to bottom of the military hierarchy. Some officers insist, in conventional as well as in unconventional warfare, that all officers, or at least themselves, should be armed with rifles. Actually an officer needs only a pistol with which to defend himself against a chance short-range encounter. The average soldier, given a choice between a carbine with 30 rounds of ammunition, weighing in all perhaps 7 pounds, and an automatic rifle with enough ammunition to keep it in action, weighing perhaps 40 pounds, is very likely to choose the heavier weapon if he believes there is a chance that he may have to shoot.

The principal problems in fighting guerrillas are finding them and getting into a position to fire at them. This means walking. Weighty weapons and ammunition cut down troops' ability to walk. Even so, unless the troops are so well trained in practical combat realities that they can overcome the years of conventional training, and the even more years of indoctrination by movies, comic books, and now by television, they will unhesitatingly reduce their effectiveness by picking the heavy weapon. If they are not permitted to pick it, their morale, and consequently their fighting effectiveness, is likely to suffer even more than had they been overloaded.

Warfare is a favorite realm of the gadgeteer. The campaign against the Huk was no exception, although it was prior to popular interest in "counterinsurgency." Several very effective unorthodox weapons were developed, but no one has yet come up with a really satisfactory general purpose weapon for guerrilla and counterguerrilla operations. It is needed.

Today there is an infinite range of speculation about gadgets for fighting guerrillas. Many of these may afford some help, but their principal value, or deficiency, will be their effect on the morale of the troops who use them, and on that of their opponents. Few weapons have quite the same effect on guerrilla morale as a pair of ice picks lashed together, used to puncture a guerrilla jugular, if the guerrilla is left for his companions to pick up. Next in effectiveness is a well-presented bayonet.

The guerrilla believes that he possesses moral superiority over his enemy. He feels that he is demonstrating it by being a guerrilla, by daring to stay in the field even though his enemy is better equipped and supported. If that enemy seizes every possible opportunity to assail him by violence, with little or no regard for numbers or position, the guerrilla will soon become discouraged, or dead. Persuade him that his enemy is more determined, more fearless than he, and as long as he remains persuaded, the guerrilla is not a threat.

Chapter 12

TARGET—THE CIVILIAN

THERE IS a more certain way of eliminating the guerrilla than seeking to hunt him down among the civilians; it is to turn the civilians against him. To return to Mao's analogy, it is to make the civilian "sea" no longer hospitable to the guerrilla "fish." The Communists call this sea the "mass base," including in that term all those not actively hostile to their guerrillas. As they well appreciate, without this mass base no guerrilla movement can long survive. Neither can an indigenous government.

When this is realized, the attitudes of the people, heretofore taken for granted, become suddenly as important to the government as they have been all along to the guerrilla. The guerrilla has been working on this target, using tactics designed to build doubts and bitterness, grievances and unrest wherever they might be aroused. He has been changing and modifying the attitudes of the civilian about his government, seeking to develop a suitable climate for guerrilla growth. Now the government must win it back, must make the sea of people unfriendly to the guerrilla, must reinforce and build new faith and loyalty in the nation, must persuade the mass base of people to back their own government against its would-be destroyers.

To accomplish this, the government must do many things. First, it must act effectively to seek and destroy the guerrilla, in order to prove its own military ability and capacity to protect the governed. Second, the government must understand, accept, and announce a mission that will warrant support. Third, the words and deeds of all representatives of the government must be compatible with the mission, or the representatives must be summarily and publicly disavowed. Fourth (and to this end every effort should be made), the words and actions of the government must be presented in terms readily understood and readily believed by the people.

In other words, a soldier who steals a chicken from a farmer cannot claim to be the farmer's protector. And a squad leader, a company commander, or a government that does not take action to punish the chicken thief weakens the credibility of the claim that the soldier is protecting the people.

A government official accused of enriching himself by malfeasance in office is *ipso facto* evidence that government officials do not regard public service as a public trust. Unless action is taken against such an officeholder, the credibility of the government's claim to seek the welfare of the people is grievously weakened.

Guerrilla warfare, far more than any other form of conflict, blends all normal government functions with combat to serve essentially political purposes. Every action taken has some effect on the nation, on the attitudes of the governed toward government, and toward the guerrilla.

In seeking to build favorable attitudes, the guerrilla conducts psychological-warfare operations. If the government is to succeed, if it is to build popular support, it must respond, not only with counterguerrilla psychological operations, but with operations designed to influence popular attitudes in its favor. For a representative government that functions by the consent of the governed, and encourages freedom of speech, thought, and action, to acknowledge the use of measures designed to influence the attitudes of the governed is not only difficult, but extremely sensitive.

True, seeking to influence the attitudes of people is an extremely popular pastime, especially under democratic governments. The practitioners of the art most often call themselves educators, statesmen, preachers, or advertising men. Even the teacher and preacher are likely to arouse hostility when they admit they are seeking to change attitudes; so, to a much greater degree, do the politician and the man in the gray-flannel suit, when they admit what they are trying to do. Call this effort "psychological warfare," and the immediate reaction is to picture a sinister individual, half Machiavelli, half mountebank. The mere mention of efforts to influence popular attitudes on behalf of a government generates reactions so strong that descriptive terms become emotionally charged, and definitions unduly limiting.

For this reason, the counterguerrilla, well aware that he must succeed in hitting the civilian target if he is to eliminate the guerrilla, must give careful consideration to what title he gives his efforts to influence popular thinking, and what the opponents of government may name them. Essentially, they are psychological operations, but because of the possible political repercussions, great caution is necessary in formulating their public definition and in stating the mission of the agency responsible for them. The definition should appear not merely innocuous, it should describe an indubitably desirable purpose. The assigned mission should not restrict operations, yet it should provide safeguards against obviously undesirable activities. Much greater latitude is required by the operator in a counterinsurgency situation than in so-called conventional war, yet it is precisely in the former that danger of improper political use (or, at least, accusations thereof) is greatest.

Possibly an appropriate definition of psychological operations in a counterinsurgency situation would be: "actions planned and conducted primarily to create emotions, attitudes, and behavior favorable to the accomplishment of the national objectives, including elimination of the guerrilla." Now change the term defined to "national revival operations" (instead of "psychological operations"), and the whole becomes as easy to defend as a campaign platform based on home, mother, and opposition to sin. Perhaps more important, if the national objectives are clearly defined and agreed upon, improper use of the mechanism can be detected and exposed.

Such a definition was in effect applicable to the psychological operations undertaken in the Philippines under the direction of Magsaysay. A mission directive formulated on the basis of this definition will give great freedom in the choice of means. It permits actions of countless sorts, as long as their purpose is influencing attitudes or behavior on behalf of the government. In practice, such actions will range from those undertaken to inform the target to those intended to terrify it. They will range from press handouts to using a "Voice of God" loudspeaker to tell guerrilla Tarlac Tommy and his friends that intelligence he supplied (in fact, he has not supplied it) has led to the death of Huk Commander Keling. On-the-spot promotions for soldiers who have killed guerrillas and the provision of an army band for a village celebration may both be useful psychological operations.

Most important, this definition and the mission based on it neither describe nor delimit the target of these operations. The reason and the necessity for this are obvious, in light of popular distrust of any activities designed to influence attitudes and behavior. In guerrilla and counterguerrilla operations alike, the target is, and must be, *everyone*—friends, enemies, innocent bystanders, foreign diplomats, international correspondents. The target is the sea, and the fish who swim in it, the birds who fly overhead, the pseudogang shark, and the porpoise playboy whose antics may be grist to the enemies' propaganda mill.

The definitions and missions commonly stated and primarily applicable to conventional war are not at all suitable for counterguerrilla warfare. Consider the latest available official United States definition of psychological operations:

> This term includes psychological activities and psychological warfare, and encompasses those political, military, economic and ideological actions planned and conducted to create in enemy, hostile, neutral or friendly foreign groups the

emotions, attitudes, or behavior favorable to thé accomplishment of U.S. policies and objectives.[1]

This is a fine, carefully worded definition, in some ways broad, in others carefully limiting, which is almost totally inapplicable to operations against guerrillas by the government they threaten.

If the civilian population in the area of operations (the mass base, the sea) is regarded as an enemy, or even as "friendly foreign groups," then the armed forces and the government have no legitimate claim on their support. If they are not regarded as enemies—and of course, the object of the exercise is to convince them that they are not—then they are not legitimate targets for psychological operations.

Take another definition, this one a statement of the mission of the Psychological Warfare Branch of the Armed Forces of the Philippines, adopted in July, 1953:

> to hasten military victory of the Armed Forces of the Philippines in time of war by reducing the enemy's will to resist military and civilian authority through the use of propaganda and such other operational measures of military nature as may be required.

It seems a strange definition indeed, coming from an armed force victorious over a guerrilla force—particularly since that victory was due, in large measure, to successful psychological warfare; psychological warfare targeted at everyone, from their own troops through the entire civilian spectrum to the die-hard Communist leaders of the guerrillas.

The reasons these definitions are so limiting may be summed up in one word: politics. Whenever a representative of government speaks to a potential voter, he may be accused of playing politics. Nowhere is this more true than in a counter-guerrilla effort. The use of government agencies to influence popular opinion is not uncommon, but to admit that use is to invite the harshest political attacks.

This reaction is not entirely unwarranted. The use of government publicity agents, the mounting, at government expense, of massive psychological operations to benefit the incumbent of high government office has all too long a history, all too many precedents. It has been the favorite device of dictators from the Pharaohs to Castro.

Success in counterguerrilla operations requires outstanding leadership at all echelons, especially at the top.

The leader of a successful indigenous counterguerrilla effort is almost certain to become a symbol of good government. He will appear as the spokesman for the good intentions of government, he will appear as the man who made them effective. Actions undertaken to build support for the government will almost inevitably build political support for the leader who, by his words and actions, exemplifies the intentions of government and the aspirations of the governed.

Politicians who see in the counterguerrilla leader a potential political rival will seek to destroy the leader, or at least to curtail or destroy the operations that, seeking support for the government, create support for him.

The very restricted mission given to the Psychological Warfare Branch of the Armed Forces of the Philippines arose from just such a situation: The immense success of psychological operations designed to win popular support for government had won corresponding support for the symbol of good government—Ramón Magsaysay. At the time the quoted mission was written, in mid-1953, Magsaysay was a candidate for the Presidency, obviously running far ahead of his opponent, the incumbent President, Elpidio Quirino.

Magsaysay, when he took office as Secretary of National Defense, was little concerned about definitions, organizations, or theories. He had, in fact, a strong aversion to all of them, and would have insisted that he had no theories. He would have said only that he "knew" some things. He did.

He "knew" that the government must win the support of the civilians if the soldiers were to defeat the guerrilla. He "knew" that in the operational area the soldier is by far the most significant element of government in contact with the civilians. He "knew" how every action of the soldier reflected on government.

Accordingly, he set out on a high run to make the actions of the soldiers reflect and emphasize their mission as friends and protectors of the people. One of the first things he changed was the manner in which troops entered a town or village.

In 1947, after President Manuel Roxas had proclaimed his "mailed fist" policy, the troops went on combat-alert status. By late 1950, under the prodding of the high command to be "truly military," they adopted the practice of entering every inhabited area in Huklandia in an exaggerated combat posture. Troops would move in by truck, obviously battle-ready, weapons pointing out in all directions as though they expected immediate assault. From their demeanor, it was to be assumed that they felt they were among enemies, that they anticipated momentary attack.

The psychological effect of this was deplorable. The people saw that these representatives of their government regarded them as enemies. The obvious effect on the troops themselves was to feel that the people were indeed their enemies. Soon, in small villages, the people simply disappeared when the troops came in. In larger towns and cities, soldiers were ignored or treated as a bad smell. The very insecurity that the guerrilla feeds on was heightened both in the protector and the protected.

Magsaysay issued orders that troops entering towns and *barrios* were to make no threatening display of weapons, adopt no threatening attitude unless there was clear and present danger. He instructed troops entering an inhabited area to conduct themselves as though they were coming among friends who, like themselves, might be subject to surprise attack by a common enemy.

These orders he enforced by most thorough checking of troop behavior himself and by reports from trusted members of his staff.

Magsaysay's next action was based on his recollections of the reactions of civilians, particularly children, to American troops who seemed always to have candy for children. He begged, he borrowed, he scrounged, perhaps he even stole, but he procured candy and chewing gum to issue to troops on the move; candy they, in turn, were to distribute to children whenever they halted in a village.

The results were prompt and far-reaching. As soon as soldiers came in friendliness, the *barrio* people at least stayed to see the next move. As soon as it became known among children that these soldiers, their own soldiers, gave candy to the kids, a patrol or a truckload could not enter the village without being surrounded by children coming to greet "Santa Claus."

This meant many things. First of all, the children quickly began to regard soldiers as their friends no matter how much the elders in the family disapproved of soldiers in general or sympathized with the Huk. It was hard to persuade the children that the Santa Claus with the candy was an enemy. Eventually, this rubbed off on the older folks; it is hard to dislike those who respond to children. Troops surrounded by children are not likely to be attacked by a guerrilla whose support depends on people to whom the children belong. Thus, the children formed the best possible shield for troops while they were in the village. And if the children did not appear when soldiers came in, it was reasonable to assume that the enemy might be nearby. The effect of the friendship-candy approach went even deeper, since friendships started by the children could lead to information for the soldiers.

About the same time that the wholesome effects of the "candy for kids" program became apparent, Magsaysay issued a statement to the armed forces declaring that every soldier had two duties: first, to act as an ambassador of good will from the government to the people; second, to kill or capture Huk. Nothing else, he said, really counted as far as he was concerned. Certainly nothing would qualify a man for promotion except to be an effective ambassador and an effective fighter. This policy would govern all actions, and he and his staff would be checking on it. He went further. He proclaimed it the duty and responsibility of everyone—civilian and soldier alike—to submit suggestions as to how these two objectives could better be accomplished.

Needless to say, his statements were received with considerable skepticism. But skeptics soon found out that Magsaysay and his staff were checking constantly and by every conceivable means to ensure compliance with his policies.

No commander, even in the most isolated outpost, could go to bed at night sure that he would not be awakened before dawn by an irate Secretary of National Defense. The Secretary only seemed irate by habit, irate to find anyone sleeping when he needed to talk to them. He would want to know how much the commander, be he sergeant or colonel, knew about the situation in his area; about the state of his command; when the troops had last been paid; what they ate for supper last night; how many Huk they had killed in the last week; why they hadn't killed more; what was the state of motor transport; what were the needs of the civilians in the area; what was the attitude of the civilians. And the commander could also be sure of a personally administered "shampoo," a sort of verbal but violent Dutch rub, if he didn't know the answers; it would be twice as severe if he tried to bluff.

(Of course, Magsaysay was not always an avenger. Had he been, he would undoubtedly have "happened to an accident" on one of his visits to the field. Just as he could be thoroughly unpleasant when someone fell short of his duty, he could be thoroughly warm and attractive, a real pleasure to have as a visitor. The senior author well remembers one morning when he was awakened by the duty officer, saying that "the man" was paying a visit to the camp. Fearing that he was due for a "shampoo," the author made his way to the officers' mess to find the Secretary of National Defense there ahead of him, busy preparing breakfast as a token of his esteem. The effect can readily be imagined. It was not a very good breakfast, but it may well be understood how much one appreciated the sort of chief who, finding breakfast not ready because we were all bushed, was considerate enough to fix it for us.)

Another source of irritation between soldier and civilian—and one of the most common difficulties in counterguerrilla operations—was the inadequacy of ration supplies for troops in the field. The problem of getting supplies, and of getting them distributed, frequently left troops with no alternative but the age-old one of foraging. And troops forced to appropriate rations are not inclined to be gracious to the farmer who supplies them. The Armed Forces of the Philippines were no exception. Troops often ate only what they could forage—and had no money to pay for it. Secretary Magsaysay recognized that by this practice alone the troops were placing themselves in an unfavorable position in comparison to the Huk. True, the guerrillas depended almost entirely for their sustenance on what they could extract from the farmers, but they always sought to make their extractions as painless as possible. The actual pickup of the food was often done for them by the Huk "tax collectors" on behalf of the cause. If the food was procured by the guerrillas themselves, it was customarily begged. The farmer was asked, politely and humbly, if he could spare some food for the men who were fighting "for his cause, on his behalf, and to establish the new peoples' democracy." Thus guerrilla foraging was actually made to contribute to their propaganda campaign.

Magsaysay took several steps to rectify this situation. The procurement and distribution of field rations was given emergency status. A new policy was established: Troops, especially patrols to remote areas, were required to carry more food than they needed for themselves. If this was not possible, emergency resupply was effected, often by air drop. Where this was impractical, troops were supplied with cash with which to pay for food purchased from civilians. The fact that the troops were able to depend on military resources, were self-sufficient, heightened their own morale and increased the respect of the civilians for the army.

There was another effect, a psychological reaction of perhaps greater importance than that induced by the self-sufficiency of the troops, by the demonstration that they were law-abiding citizens whose presence was not a burden on civilians. This resulted from the extra food carried by the patrols, food they could give to those in need, especially those in need because of the depredations of the Huk, the common enemy. In the past, the farmer who gave food to the Huk, however unwillingly, had been treated as clearly a sympathizer and supporter of the enemy. Now the assumption was that if he was actually in need because of taxes levied on him by the Huk, he was clearly a person entitled to help from his government. The troops made common cause with him against the common enemy, they said, thus tacitly imposing on him an obligation. It was clear that if the soldier gave a man food to replace what the Huk had taken, the man had an obligation to help the soldier find and eliminate the Huk.

Needless to say, there were many who could see no reason for these unusual practices, many who considered all this as tantamount to giving aid and comfort to the enemy. These people, if they were military, learned almost immediately that whether or not they approved of such practices, they would be most unhappy if they did not conform to them. It took some time, considerable organization, and a few thoroughly unpleasant experiences to get this across to everyone. Most soon perceived the value of these practices in terms of military accomplishment through achievements based on information received from civilians who now cooperated with them, instead of with the enemy.

Magsaysay realized that he could not singlehandedly implement his "Attraction Program," as he called his campaign to win acceptance of the soldier as a worthy supporter of a government that deserved the support of the governed. At first, he may have thought that the program was so obviously necessary and useful that, once started, it would be carried forward automatically. He did not make the mistake of thinking that simply issuing an order would be enough.

At no time was Magsaysay a victim of the popular misconception about armies, the idea that if an order is fed in at the top it will inevitably come out, obeyed, at the bottom. Probably this misconception of how an army functions is due to the equally fallacious concept of the "military mind." Many who should know better often expound at great length on this so-called military mind, implying, at the least, that it is a peculiarly rigid strait-jacketed response mechanism, probably incapable of thought, but one to be conceded the virtue—or the vice—of complying implicitly with orders received from superiors. Such a mind may be the ideal of some theorists, as it is the epitome of evil to others. Seldom can such a mind be found; certainly the robot condition it would create does not exist.

This is due to many factors, primarily the fact that an army is composed of human beings who must understand an order before they can carry it out; human beings characterized by the phrase commonly circulating in many armies that "if an order can be misunderstood, it will be misunderstood." More than this, men of responsibility, as soldiers commonly are, must appreciate the purpose of an order before they can execute it effectively. Finally, effective execution of an order presupposes not only understanding the order and its purpose, but having the knowledge to carry it out.

Thus, whenever new or special fields of endeavor arise, when new missions are given to an army, there must be officers especially trained in understanding the meaning, the purpose, and the execution of orders in this field. Desirably these officers will be especially motivated to secure the best possible accomplishment of the mission in their field, even though the execution of that mission is the responsibility of a commander whom they only advise.

The Attraction Program was, in practice, an enlargement of the mission of the armed forces—although certainly the principle was inherent in their basic mission. Effective accomplishment of this enlarged mission required officers especially trained and motivated to assist, advise, and, not infrequently, do the work, in the accomplishment of this new mission given to commanders.

An organization was created that became known as the Civil Affairs Office of the Secretary of National Defense. Although under the direct control of, and personally responsible to, the Secretary of National Defense, this organization functioned in much the same way as any technical service, such as the Chemical Corps, functions in conventional (pre-1962) U.S. military organization. Civil Affairs Officers were assigned to each echelon of command down to battalion level, and at each echelon functioned both as special staff officers (advisers to the commander) and as operational officers, responsible for duties in their specialty. In addition, there were special operational units directly under the Civil Affairs Office, which could be attached to tactical or administrative commands, and special sections (press, radio, etc.), which served the entire Armed Forces.

This rather unorthodox arrangement worked well for several reasons. First, the Joint Staff, as the General Headquarters of the Armed Forces of the Philippines would be called in contemporary U.S. terminology, was actually a functional one. There was no army headquarters, and the auxiliary services (air force and navy) bore the same relationship to GHQ as did the army military-area commands. Second, the Secretary of National Defense, by temperament, inclination, and in his own opinion, necessity, was in effect his own Chief of Staff. As far as he was concerned, every officer, every soldier, certainly every member of the general and special staff, was responsible to him personally, on exactly the same terms as any member of his own office. Most important, Magsaysay was not interested in organization or theory; he wanted, and got, results.

The mission of the Civil Affairs Office was never set forth fully and explicitly. Various written directives made the CAO responsible for advising and assisting commanders in establishing the best possible relations with civilians, a mission somewhat broader than that ordinarily given a public-relations officer. It was generally understood that any matter that might be expected to come within the purview of troop information and education, psychological operations, or military government came within the cognizance of the CAO. Finally, the CAO at higher echelons functioned as something similar to a publicity-minded Inspector General. The lack of clarity in the statement of mission of the CAO aroused much criticism from organization-minded members of the military, who could not see why these missions should not be spelled out, or why they should not be given the more commonly used military designations.

The reasons were very simple. Magsaysay realized the public criticism that any accurate statement of mission would arouse; he also realized the necessity for not imposing arbitrary or formal limitations on activities designed to win popular support for the armed forces. To his way of thinking, the duties of a Civil Affairs Office should be sufficiently implicit in the name, and anyone who could not understand the meaning of the words should go away and figure it out, not take up the valuable time of people trying to win a war. As for its position in his office rather than in GHQ, he felt, with justification, that without maximum command backing, his backing, the CAO could never accomplish its mission.

At its greatest strength, the CAO never totaled more than 200 officers, enlisted men, and civilians. This is comparable to one company of psychological-warfare troops in the U.S. Army. With little actual equipment of their own, they had to rely heavily on their own good judgment, the cooperation of their commanders, and a sensitive knowledge and understanding of their people and of the enemy.

Since the CAO headquarters was in the office of the Secretary of National Defense, and was responsible for advising and assisting the Secretary in maintaining the best possible relations with the civilians, it functioned as his public-relations office. Reporters scouting for news about the armed forces came to the Civil Affairs Officers for information. If it were for a follow-up on a report casting discredit upon the armed forces, they were coming to the officer who was not only authorized to give information about the incident, but also responsible for seeing that if such an incident had occurred, it was made to redound to the credit of the armed forces, if possible.

Suppose, for example, that a reporter came to the CAO asking information about a reported chicken theft by soldiers of the Second Squad, Third Platoon, Company B, Umpteenth Battalion Combat Team. The CAO was authorized to require, on behalf of the Secretary of National Defense, an immediate investigation of the incident and appropriate corrective action. It was further charged with following up the report to ensure that the appropriate action taken was so reported to the press as to convey the idea that an unfortunate and exceptional incident had received sudden and condign punishment.

A major mission of the CAO was to secure the widest publicity for all laudable accomplishments of the armed forces. Information was constantly fed to eager newspaper reporters and radio commentators. However, they were never forced to use any items nor to withhold any. The achievements of the armed forces and the developments on all fronts made headline news regularly and deservedly on their own merits. The few newshounds who remained hostile searched freely for subjects on which to base scathing remarks, while CAO Officers scurried to make these remarks boomerang on their makers. Public opinion about the actions of the government and of the armed forces was constantly monitored. Every effort was made to keep abreast of the attitudes of the Huk toward new developments. This monitoring kept the Civil Affairs Office constantly in touch with the impact of the various approaches tried, and gave excellent leads for further propaganda campaigns.

Wide publicity meant more than handing out news releases. It meant spreading the information to the people in the country, people who did not see the newspapers or hear the radio. One of the better devices for widespread dissemination of information about the helpful actions and good intentions of the troops was the publication of journals and newspapers ostensibly for the troops. These papers included general news, gave instructions on troop behavior with civilians, and reported commendable military activities, citing them as actions to be emulated. These publications were issued to the troops in large quantities, so that they might see in print what they were supposed to be doing, and what their rewards might be. More important, the soldiers were encouraged to give copies to the civilians, especially in the area of operations against the guerrilla. What form of propaganda could better carry conviction on the desires of government for proper troop behavior than official publications intended for consumption within the armed forces, and directed to the attention of every member of those forces?

In the Philippines, as in most countries where literacy is not (or has not long been) virtually universal, plays, skits, and recitations are traditional entertainment, and are exceptionally useful vehicles for transmitting information. This national practice was utilized in a number of ways. Movies were made, contrasting the laudable accomplishments of the armed forces with the deplorable actions of the enemy, who was shown acting in ways contrary to the customs and culture values of the country. Mobile projection units showed these movies widely in the remote areas. The Civil Affairs Officer of each BCT had a jeep, a projector, and a projectionist for just this purpose. Audiences came from far and wide to enjoy the entertainment.

Radio and movies were occasionally used ostensibly, sometimes actually, for tactical psychological operations. The mother of Luis Taruc, the most respected of the Huk field commanders, made a tape-recorded appeal for him to surrender. This was broadcast over the radio repeatedly, primarily to show that this "hero" was actually a person who would not heed his mother. Taruc did surrender shortly afterward, and claimed that this appeal, which he had heard repeatedly, did have an effect on his actions.

It was decided that a movie short of the mother making this appeal might be useful, but lack of suitable lighting made it impossible to film it "live." True to the spirit of improvisation that marked the operations against the Huk, and especially the operations of the CAO, the movie was made from the still portrait taken of the mother while she was appealing to her son. This was projected on a sheet billowing in the wind, which was photographed by the movie camera, and the sound dubbed in. The effect was so realistic that the old lady said that she did not know that a movie had been made while she was talking.

"Live" shows obviously offered more effective personal appeal than movies, so a number of traveling road shows were organized. Designed to improve relations between the military and the civilians by demonstrating the interest taken by the armed forces in the welfare of the people, they were good entertainment and extremely effective propaganda vehicles. In one area of Huklandia where transportation was largely by water, a "Show Boat" was rigged up and proved a tremendous success. Its programs, in the local language, featured news, songs, skits, and true-life stories. Ex-Huk, often former recruiters in the same area, were featured performers. When these men revisited the community to explain why they were no longer rebels, and made eloquent and obviously sincere pleas for support of the government as the protector of the people, the means by which the aspirations of the people could best be achieved, the effect was that of an old-fashioned revival preacher. There were few occasions when one or more Huk or Huk supporters in the audience failed to come forward to the "mourners' bench."

No effort was spared to get the word to the people. The army distributed pamphlets on topics from rice-growing to baby care. Comic books showing Huk crimes and army punishment of them (and army punishment of erring soldiers, as well) were passed out by patrols. Posters spread the word of the new policies. They showed Magsaysay offering "my left hand in friendship, my right hand in force," which was soon shortened to an offer of "All-Out Friendship or All-Out Force." Surrenders became more frequent as more opportunities and more persuasion were provided.

The Civil Affairs Office, by informing civilians and military of the actions and intentions of both the government and the armed forces, was actually conducting the most effective kind of strategic psychological operations against the guerrilla. Civilians, in contact with the Huk, either directly or indirectly, naturally passed along to them what they knew, or thought they knew, about the activities and intentions of the government. Inevitably, this carried greater credibility, greater conviction, than the same statements made directly by government officials.

Further, if what a civilian saw and heard about the government was good, was contrary to the Huk charges that the government was tyrannical, abusive, corrupt, it aroused in the mind of the civilian some doubt about the justification of further depriving himself in order to support the Huk. This doubt was transmitted to the Huk, at least by indirection, and a gulf began to open between him and his civilian friend. The loss of mutual confidence inevitably presaged a loss of voluntary support for the guerrilla.

Publicity, entertainment, and direct propaganda were only part of the mission of the CAO. The basic mission was the implementation, at all echelons, of the Attraction Program. Partly this was a matter of troop indoctrination, and of checking on the effectiveness of the indoctrination. Partly it was a matter of developing and securing implementation of programs by which the army could actively and concretely demonstrate its helpfulness to the people.

Magsaysay insisted on direct action by the troops to help the little people. Protecting them, pursuing their enemy—the guerrilla—came first, but whenever possible, the soldiers were to do more. They should actually improve the conditions of life. Out of this belief grew the activities called "civic action."

This has now become a well-recognized field of military endeavor, described in a U.S. Army News Service release dated February 9, 1962, as:

> The use of military forces on projects useful to populace at all levels in such fields as training, public works, agriculture, transportation, communications, health, sanitation, and others helpful to economic development.

This is a subtle and useful definition, for it camouflages the real purpose, which is to influence the thinking and behavior of all concerned, from the troops who build the schoolhouse to the guerrilla whose son is given a chance to go to school—by courtesy of the army. As a means for proving to all participants and observers the desire of government to be of service to the governed, an effective civic-action program cannot be excelled. It is also an effective way of accomplishing worthwhile projects with available labor. Practically speaking, however, it is doubtful if any civic-action projects can be afforded, in a counterguerrilla situation, which do not clearly contribute to the operational purpose of influencing the emotions, attitudes, and behavior of the people toward support of the government.

Too much emphasis cannot be placed on the importance, and often the difficulty, of impressing the troops with the true purposes of civic-action programs. In one Southeast Asian country—not the Philippines—a military commander was given detailed instructions on building and dedicating a bridge urgently needed by the local inhabitants. Without it, they were forced to climb down a precipitous slope, wade a river, and struggle up another steep incline, to go from their homes to the market. The commander built the bridge efficiently, dedicated it with due pomp and ceremony, which included civilian representatives, and then posted sentries at each end of the bridge with signs announcing "For Military Use Only"!

In practice, effective counterguerrilla action—especially that of troops—so intermingles concrete useful actions, protective actions (combat against guerrilla), and psychological operations that it is difficult to tell where one action leaves off and the other begins. Properly performed, they blend in a spiral, moving more and more rapidly from one success to another, from one field to another, until the desired objective is achieved, until the fish is driven out of the sea in which he can no longer live.

This was especially effective in the Philippines, where many ways were devised for the soldier to demonstrate his helpfulness and his good will to civilians. Medical-aid men were trained to accompany patrols and were provided with medicines and instructions for treating simple sicknesses and injuries of the civilians. Troop units were encouraged to assist in solving local problems—to evacuate persons seriously injured or threatened by Huk activities, to repair roads and bridges. This was civic action of the most basic sort. These were also psychological operations of the most effective type.

Developing national programs, like furnishing material to the national mass-communications media, was largely accomplished by the CAO in the office of the Secretary of National Defense. Actual accomplishments in the Attraction Program came primarily from the lower echelons.

The next command echelon under the General Headquarters of the Armed Forces of the Philippines was formed by the four military area headquarters, each with its Civil Affairs Officer and his teams. These military area headquarters conducted civic-action programs within their own resources. They repaired and built roads and schools, dug wells, moved houses, did all the thousand and one useful things that can be accomplished by troops not urgently required to be deployed to the field.

Under the area headquarters were sometimes sector headquarters which had much the same functions in smaller areas, and then the battalion combat teams, the basic building blocks of the Philippine Army. In each BCT headquarters there was a Civil Affairs Officer with a small group of enlisted men to assist him.

One of the most successful BCT commanders started the practice of calling the CAO the civilian representative on his staff. The CAO was required to know, and to maintain constant liaison with, all civilian officials in the BCT area of responsibility. All officers were, as a matter of course, supposed to know as many as possible of these civilian officials, but maintenance of continuing liaison with them was the primary responsibility of the CAO.

The CAO was made an integral and essential part of the battalion staff. He suggested operations based on information received from civilians. More important, proposed operations were coordinated with him in order to minimize their possible adverse effects on civilian activities. To the civilians, he was their representative, not the government's. He did conduct propaganda activities, but with his left hand, so to speak. Operations of an obvious propaganda nature were usually made to seem the responsibility of someone else, so that the role of the CAO as the "honest broker" between civilians and soldiers was not compromised.

One of the most important duties of the CAO on the BCT level was to ensure the creation and maintenance of the "image" of the troops as friends and benefactors of the people. This was not easy. It meant first of all indoctrinating the troops themselves with the concept, making them realize what it implied in terms of their actions and behavior, and making them understand the consequences of actions that harmed this "image." Part of his staff duty was checking on implementation of the policy that enlisted men or officers who committed offenses against civilians were to be tried on the spot, if possible, by a military court-martial or by civilian courts. He was further responsible for making certain that the results of such trials were immediately publicized in terms which made clear that crimes against the people were also crimes against the army and against the government. The CAO who could accomplish all this, without being tagged as a "spy" of higher headquarters or a tattletale, was a diplomat, teacher, and disciplinarian of high order.

In addition to seeking to indoctrinate the troops (and their leaders, and the civilians), the CAO suggested ways in which to implement the Attraction Program, and where appropriate and possible made the means available. It was his duty to secure leaflets, magazines, newspapers, extra supplies of medicine-all the things the patrols could take out with them and distribute to civilians in need either of help or of education about the purposes of government. The real payoff came in getting the soldiers, the patrols, to understand the importance and value to them of establishing good relations with the civilians in their areas of operations. How well this was eventually understood and how thoroughly this goal was pursued is aptly described in the following anonymous article in the *Philippine Armed Forces journal* for October, 1953:

EVERY SOLDIER A PSY-WAR MAN

To the successful prosecution of psychological warfare, it is essential for units down to the squad to win the people in their areas psychologically. Since, under the "Three-in-One Plan,"[2] each unit has a more or less permanent sector, the first step is for members of the outfit in any area to get acquainted with the people in their sector.

The approach should be friendly and informal. Every member of the team should maintain an attitude of cordiality. He should not pretend that he is more intelligent or more prosperous than the civilians; he should not assume an air of superiority; he must refrain from making the civilians give information by constraint. On the contrary, he should treat the civilians as his equals and friends, thereby adroitly making the civilian both an ally and an active, willing helper.

Never forgetting that he is a psy-war man, every member of the unit should perceive the manner in which the patrol is received by the people it comes in contact with. He should note whether the soldiers are welcomed spontaneously or received with cold indifference. Are the people reluctant to talk? Are they afraid of the man in uniform? Are they helpful or sympathetic to the army? Are they antagonistic? What is their general feeling toward the conflict between Communism and democracy? Are the people pessimistic of the country's future?

The attitude of the people toward the Armed Forces as well as toward the Huk is gauged in the process. The patrol, however, should be careful to make his observations without arousing suspicion among the civilians that they (the civilians) are under observation. He should record in his mind what he sees and hears and put them down on paper later. He should not start any argument.

As a psy-war agent, the patrol should distribute psy-war materials in its sector. Since it is not possible to furnish every inhabitant with psy-war materials, it is important for the patrol to make a wise distribution. The Huk allies and the fence-sitters (those who are indifferent) should get the patrol's first attention. In issuing the leaflets or posters or comic books he has at his disposal, the patrol observes the reaction of the people to such material. Are they eager to receive the leaflets, posters, etc.? Do they read these? What do they say? What is their reaction? Do facial expressions tally with what they say?

With the knowledge he has acquired of the people and the circumstances obtaining in his sector as his guide, the patrol should proceed, on its second or third visit, to take positive measures to correct the attitudes of the people toward Democracy, and toward the AFP and its efforts to bring the peace and order campaign to an early conclusion. The BCT public-relations officer, who is also the BCT's psy-war officer, may be consulted on the measures to be taken and how they should be implemented. It is essential, however, for the commanding officers, as well as the platoon, squad, and patrol leaders, to make every member of their unit acknowledge the fact that the present campaign cannot be won by bullets alone and at the same time make every man in the outfit realize that he cannot be an effective psy-war agent unless he enjoys the confidence of the people of his sector. To win that confidence, the soldier has to conduct himself properly and must take sincere interest in the people and their problems.

Under the "Three-in-One Plan" the soldier has three missions: operations, intelligence, and psy-war and public relations. It is a big job. It is important that the soldiers are thoroughly briefed by their leaders. The briefing should be done not once but as frequently as possible and before any patrol is sent out.

This was a radical departure from contemporary doctrine on patrol missions, but had ample (and almost forgotten) precedent in Philippine history. Routine patrols of the Philippine Constabulary in the first thirty years of this century had virtually identical missions, differently stated. If led by an officer into remote areas, they often served as mobile Justice of the Peace courts, sanitary inspectors, first-aid teams, educational inspectors, registrars of marriages, births, and deaths, tax collectors—were, in other words, an embodiment of the services of government, of good and concerned government.

So must it be in areas of counterguerrilla operations. Whether his commanders like it or not, the soldier symbolizes government to many of the governed. He must be made the best and most useful symbol possible, he must clearly demonstrate the moral justification for the existence of the government, and thus he will impose an obligation for the support of that government. This is a command responsibility. Civil Affairs Officers, military-government officers, psychological warriors, and a host of others may assist the commander in the execution of his duties, but the responsibility is his. This was recognized in the Philippines as it must be everywhere.

Most of the major projects of civic action were not carried on by the CAO. It was the function of the CAO to advise on such projects, to see that they were conducted in a manner likely to have the greatest impact on the emotions, attitudes, and behavior of the people, and to seek for them the most effective publicity. A plausible case could be, and was, made out that the CAO functioned only as a publicity agent for those operations. This was useful, since it helped take away the taint of "propaganda" from activities whose real utility was as a basis for propaganda.

The most significant and the best known of these major operations was that known as EDCOR. This was executed by the Corps of Engineers, under the guidance of the CAO and in the glare of publicity the CAO provided at the national level.

EDCOR (the term is an acronym for Economic Development Corps) was originally intended to be a program for ensuring food for the armed forces by providing homesteads for drafted and discharged soldiers. Magsaysay saw in this program, which had been approved by the Philippine Congress, an opportunity to demolish a major Huk campaign slogan: "Land for the Landless." Magsaysay proclaimed that if they really wanted land for the landless, if they were sincere in their claims, the way for them to achieve this objective was to surrender to the armed forces. If they did this, if they demonstrated a sincere desire to be loyal citizens working their own farms, they would be given farms of their own, and helped to get a start on them.

Captured or surrendered Huk who gave evidence of their sincerity were placed in specially established EDCOR resettlement projects, leavened with a number of settlers who were retired soldiers or ex-USAFFE guerrillas. Personnel selected for these projects were transported to the site, with their families, and given assistance in building houses and clearing land. Each was assigned about fifteen acres of land, to which he received title after he had done a certain amount of work on it. Until his own crops were harvested, each received a ration allowance and, if needed, clothing, medicine, seed, and tools. All was to be paid for when the harvest made payment possible. The effect of the two initial projects was extraordinary and far-reaching.

The Huk, necessarily and naturally, scoffed. They distributed propaganda leaflets showing ex-Huk in chains, slaving at bayonet point in the fastnesses of tropical jungles. This propaganda effort had been anticipated and desired. As soon as it was sufficiently well developed to commit the Huk leaders to the sponsorship of this line, the counterpropaganda began.

Letters from ex-Huk, pictures of them at home and at work, were dropped as leaflets, spread by hand, tacked up on walls and trees. News correspondents from all over the country, in fact from all over the world, were invited to visit the projects and see for themselves the truth about the conditions to be found in them. The only requirement was that the visitors report on what they had seen.

Huk commanders were invited to come in, under safe-conduct passes, to visit these projects and see for themselves the conditions under which their former comrades were now living. The only stipulation was that they must return to their units and tell them what they had seen. Some were reluctant to comply with this stipulation and wanted to stay in the project they visited. The reason for forcing them to return to their units was twofold: If they told the truth, it would seriously reduce their comrades' will to resist. Fanatic Huk, seeing this, might cause even more serious morale problems by actions against the converts. Either result would have the effect of alienating more Huk from their cause, strengthening their growing desire to give up the fight.

The direct effect on the Huk movement, in terms of government propaganda directly causing surrenders, was strong. The indirect effects were much stronger. The publicity given the EDCOR program, and the credibility it achieved, made a tremendous impression on people who had been supporting, or tolerating, the Huk. As long as the guerrilla could say that he was fighting for something worthwhile, something that could not be achieved without fight-ing, he had a moral claim to support, especially if he were a relative or a friend. When it became apparent that he could achieve this objective without fighting, that his avowed purpose for fighting had disappeared, any moral obligation to support him disappeared also. More, if he continued to fight, his motivation became suspect.

After the fact of EDCOR became accepted in the countryside, a Huk tax collector, or beggar, who came asking for rice was very likely to be told: "Look, if what you are fighting for is, as you claim, the chance to have land of your own, why don't you go surrender to the armed forces? We can't afford to feed you any longer. Can it be that you don't really want to work the land for a living the way we do?" Of course, EDCOR was not the only reason the civilian had for adopting this attitude. There were the other actions of the army and the government: the five-cent telegrams for stating complaints or asking for help, the legal aid given by army lawyers, the services rendered by the troops, reasons they saw themselves and reasons they heard about, all of which deflated specific Huk claims. They all added up to one answer: The civilian could no longer see any justification for helping the Huk, but he could see ample reason why he should support his government.

EDCOR became a fairly large operation, with three projects in Mindanao, and a fourth in Northern Luzon, on the fringe of Huklandia. The reason for concentrating the projects far from the Huk area was obvious, and bitter opposition was encountered when the one in Luzon was proposed. It was decided that the risk of setting up a safe haven for unsurrendered Huk was outweighed by the advantages of having a project that these same Huk might visit surreptitiously to see for themselves the advantages of surrender.

Even before the Luzon project was started, it gave striking evidence of the importance the Huk themselves gave to the program. Three officers and two enlisted men, passing through Huklandia en route to help lay out the new project, stopped in a peaceful town for lunch and were incautious enough to discuss their mission. Word of it went out through Huk intelligence channels, and that afternoon their jeep was ambushed and all five were killed. Needless to say, this murder drove several more spikes into the Huk coffin. If the Huk were fighting only for land reform, what possible justification could there be for the assassination of these men whose mission was to establish a settlement where the landless could receive land, where the Huk dream could be fulfilled?

In addition to the resettlement projects, EDCOR undertook two other major operations. One of these was a rehabilitation center right in army headquarters outside Manila. In a warehouse, a vocational school and carpentry shop were set up where captured or surrendered Huk who had given material assistance to the armed forces could learn and practice a trade. Not only did they learn, they produced, and they earned money. Several of them were able to set up profitable businesses after their release from custody, businesses built on the knowledge and funds garnered while they were prisoners.

Perhaps the most spectacular operation of EDCOR was one in which a whole village was transplanted. A *barrio* of the municipality of San Luis, in Pampanga Province, the home town of the Huk leader, was in dire straits. The land the residents were supposed to farm was not their own; worse, cultivation of much of this had been impossible for several years because of the activities of Huk and government forces in the area. The future seemed hopeless. A battalion of army engineers moved in to a piece of public domain not far from the *barrio* and cleared it of the tough cogon grass, which forms a root mat almost impenetrable to the plow. They cleaned it, they ditched and drained it; they built paddy-field dikes and elevated roadways. They finished by picking up the houses of the *barrio* dwellers and transferring them intact to a new location near the fields, to which the residents received title after a short period of work on them.

This project was expensive. It was a project that could not be justified in terms of its helpfulness to the nation, for it could not be repeated in the hundreds, perhaps thousands, of areas where similar help was needed. As a psychological operation, it was a tremendous success. Every member of that *barrio* had many relatives in the field with the Huk, men who now, by Philippine custom, were made to feel a sense of obligation to the government which had so dramatically helped their relatives. Magsaysay estimated the value of this operation as greater than that of another battalion combat team in the field.

The large EDCOR projects were valuable in convincing the people that the government was their friend, that the government would help them achieve their legitimate aspirations, asking only that they give in return the loyal support which any citizen owes his government. The projects did not in themselves make a significant contribution to the economic or social welfare of the country. They helped a few people, perhaps all told a thousand families were benefited directly by their assistance. Probably two or three thousand more were benefited indirectly and unintentionally by the establishment of these new communities which brought new business and new security to relatively untapped areas.

Their real value—and it was tremendous—was as dramatic proof of the intentions and desires of government, proof that lent itself to publicity, to propaganda. They could be called advertising stunts, but their value in selling the good intentions of government to the governed was tremendous.

There do not seem to be any reliable figures on how many counterguerrillas are necessary to eliminate 1 guerrilla. Estimates in published works, and computations of relative forces actually employed, suggest that from 10 to 50 government personnel are needed for each guerrilla active in the field. Assuming that a ratio of 20 to 1 is fair (it is an average between the Malayan and Philippine experiences) and assuming further that only 1,500 Huk left the field, either surrendering or quitting the business, as a result of the EDCOR program (a figure that is probably too low), EDCOR could be credited with accomplishing the same effect as 30,000 soldiers. This seems an extravagant figure, and it may be, but using the figures derived from other counterguerrilla operations would make it far larger. Scarcely more than 30,000 personnel were ever deployed against the Huk.

The strategic psychological warfare quite properly placed major emphasis on the Attraction Program, on offering and demonstrating justification for supporting the government rather than its enemies. Other approaches were not neglected. These ranged from "one-shotters" designed to destroy the credibility of a notorious opponent (such as the politician who received a commendatory cable ostensibly from a foreign Communist source, which would have been publicized had it not scared him into cooperation) to sustained operations designed to create distrust or enmity between the Huk and the mass base.

Often these operations served several purposes, as did the program of rewards for capturing or killing Huk leaders. Tens of thousands of posters were distributed, listing individuals wanted for crimes of murder, kidnapping, banditry, rape and offering rewards for these criminals. Emphasis was placed on the crimes, but the fact that they were committed by Huk, and were a part of their rebellious activity, was also mentioned. These posters deliberately sought to tear away the glamour of political motivation, of heroic guerrilla action, and to expose the Huk leaders as common criminals. This was most effective in reducing sympathy for them.

The liberal rewards offered brought the death, capture, or surrender of many Huk leaders. Sometimes these were effected by civilians, sometimes by other Huk. Whenever possible, these incidents were publicized, always in such a way as to protect the individual responsible while conveying the impression that it was someone the Huk had trusted. Rumors of Huk being killed or betrayed by their comrades were assiduously propagated, always with care lest government credibility be impaired if the rumors were proved false. (Surrenders to claim the rewards were not officially countenanced, since the government could not be a party to bribing criminals to surrender, but in practice "arranged" surrenders were not discouraged.)

The principal value of the reward program was in widening the gulf between civilians and guerrillas, and increasing the suspicion and hostility of the guerrilla toward civilians and toward his own comrades. The effect of the program was to commit an ever-increasing number of civilians to the fight against the Huk, and to make eventual success seem less likely to the Huk.

Not all the efforts to portray the Huk as criminals were wholly successful. Some of the posters depicting outrages, such as the massacre of hospital patients and nurses at Camp Makabulos and the wholesale slaughter of women and children in the vengeance raid on Aglao, proved too frightening and backfired. The men who committed these outrages were certainly despicable criminals, but they were also seen to be very dangerous men. Not a few who saw these posters took them as warnings that they had better cooperate with any Huk who came along.

In his efforts to convince the people of the sincere concern of government for their welfare, Magsaysay did not neglect the possibilities offered by agencies of government other than the armed forces. He was able to secure control of the "Peace Fund," a partially governmental, partially civilian, fund originated to help the victims of the fighting, but generally considered a political "slush" fund. This he used for on-the-spot relief, as well as for rewards to civilians who had made significant contributions to restoring peace, such as causing the surrender or death of notorious Huk "bandits."

The Social Welfare Administration, often derided as an ineffectual dilettante charity, although actually a part of government and ranking as a Cabinet department, was swept into the action. When Magsaysay saw a chance for it to make a contribution, he called the matter forcefully to the attention of Social Welfare personnel, usually by sending transportation and an officer who obviously expected immediate acceptance of the invitation. The SWA became a familiar concomitant of operations designed to lessen suffering caused by Huk actions and a useful exponent of government concern for the general welfare.

The success of the campaign to win popular support for the government through the actions of the military derived essentially from three sources: leadership and command emphasis; a military organization, that is, an element within the military establishment to plan and supervise implementation; and, finally, an effective program tailored to the attitudes and needs of the people at whom it was targeted. All three elements are necessary to the success of such a campaign.

Success, it must be understood, is not to be measured in terms of actual concrete accomplishments, of numbers of people resettled, or wells dug, or schoolhouses built. Success is not susceptible to measurement; it is qualitative rather than quantitative. When the words of government are believed, when the statements of the chief executive or of Private Blanco of the rear rank are accepted as evidence of the intentions of government, success has been achieved. It is manifested by actions of the people which show that to them the government and the armed forces seem to be their friends and benefactors, to whom they owe allegiance and support.

In retrospect, it is clear that the most effective psychological operations were those targeted against everybody, for those were the operations that tended to bring everybody into the fight, consciously or unconsciously. They built a political base on which the government could rest with stability; a base with an inherent capacity for resisting attack. The smaller psychological operations were useful, and often entertaining to the operators; but the development of confidence in government was the cement that bound the elements of the community together, and rendered the Huk effort futile. Effective action to win the civilian guaranteed, as it facilitated, success against the guerrilla.

NOTES

1. Joint Chiefs of Staff, *Dictionary of United States Military Terms for Joint Usage* (February, 1962), p. 173.

2. A coordinated intelligence, psychological warfare, and combat operations program developed by Lightning Sector, II MA.

Chapter 13

TARGET—THE NATION

A GUERRILLA movement may well be likened to an infection, a malignancy attacking the body politic. It is an infection that must be directly counterattacked before it reaches a vital spot. At the same time, it must be recognized that the infection became dangerous only because it attacked a weak point in the body, a point which reflects, perhaps is the focus of, a weakness of the whole body politic. Had the body been thoroughly healthy, the guerrilla infection would never have become serious. If the body politic becomes healthy, the infection will inevitably shrink and ultimately perish.

The chief concern of the physician—the government, the counterguerrilla—is the health (mental and physical) of the nation as a whole. It must necessarily be his first concern because it is upon the health of a nation that his own health, if not his continued physical existence, depends.

All actions must contribute to the health of the patient—must be consonant with the announced and understood mission of government. These actions fall into three categories: surgical action to excise or convert the guerrilla to stop its debilitating or toxic effects on the body politic; topical applications to the affected portion of the body to help it resist, if not expel, the guerrilla; and finally, psychiatric and systemic treatment of the body politic, to assist it to stop the spread of the infection, and to counter its effects. All, it must be emphasized, have one ultimate objective which they promote: the health of the nation.

The guerrilla malignancy and its relation to the body politic is of a type that is only beginning to be understood in medicine. The conditions which give rise to it are partly specific physical conditions, but to a large extent, they are psychosomatic. Unsatisfactory conditions of land tenure, employment, or the administration of justice or a wide disparity in the distribution of wealth, these or other conditions may predispose the body politic to the guerrilla infection, and their alleviation may predispose the same body to the elimination of the guerrilla.

The essential requirement for the existence of a guerrilla movement, however, is psychological. The weakness that enables the guerrilla malignancy to gain lodgment and to proliferate is the result of the attitudes, the "thinking" or "feeling," of people who make up the nation. The guerrilla malignancy feeds on (and often seeks to modify) their beliefs concerning the role, the actions, desirable and undesirable, of government, and their own reactions to the words and deeds of government. It thrives on hostile or indifferent attitudes of members of the government toward the governed. It spreads most rapidly when popular attitudes favor the guerrilla rather than the government.

The successful physician, the successful counterguerrilla, is the one who can recognize this psychological condition, and the physical factors that predispose to it, and can effectively allay the fears and encourage the aspirations of the body politic. Physical conditions are important, but the attitudes of the people are the key to the elimination of the guerrilla movement.

The history of the Philippines since 1895 affords the most striking proof of the importance of attitudes toward government, and of government toward the governed. In 1896, a few thousand Filipinos, mostly of the *ilustrado* class, desired independence from their Spanish rulers. The majority of Filipinos probably wanted only to be left alone. A revolution was launched by the few thousand desirous of independence, a revolution quickly ended by payment to, and exiling of, the leaders of the movement. Two years later, as an incident of the United States war with Spain, American troops landed in the Philippines, accompanied by Philippine leaders of the independence movement. The leaders claimed they had been promised immediate independence. U.S. leaders denied this, but Filipino leaders rapidly organized forces throughout the country, first to oppose the Spanish, and then the Americans. Early in 1899, these Philippine forces attacked the Americans, who had accepted the surrender of the Spanish in Manila and were systematically assuming the responsibilities of government for the Islands.

Some Filipino leaders and some Spanish adherents made common cause against the Americans. They preached far and wide a creed that the Americans were literally fiends incarnate, heretics come to make the Filipinos slaves. Throughout the Islands, an effort was made to form forces to fight the Americans. The success they met is well illustrated by this letter from a principal commander of these forces, written fourteen months after the opening of hostilities against the Americans:

> Considering that a sufficient time has passed, and various means having been employed as benignant as humanity counsels, to inculcate in the minds of misguided Filipinos the idea of the country and to check in the beginning those unworthy acts which many of them commit and which not only redound to the

prejudice of the troops but also to the cause which they defend, and having observed that such action does not produce any favorable result on this date, in accordance with the powers vested in me I have seen proper to issue the following Proclamation,

First and last article. The following shall be tried at a most summary trial, and be sentenced to death:

1. All local *presidentes* and other civil authorities of the towns as well as of the *barrios, rancherías,* and *sitios* of the respective districts, who as soon as they find out any plan, direction of the movement, or number of the enemy shall not give notice thereof to the nearest camp;
2. Those who give information to the enemy of the location of the camp, stopping places, movements, and directions of the revolutionaries, whatever be the age or sex of the informer;
3. Those who voluntarily offer to serve the enemy as guides, excepting if it be with the purpose of misleading them from the right road; and
4. Those who of their own free will or otherwise capture revolutionary soldiers who are alone or who should intimidate them into surrendering to the enemy.[1]

The general who issued that proclamation was a patriot, sincere in his belief that he was fighting for the freedom and welfare of his people. Why did he feel it necessary to issue such a threat? Why did other leaders soon after find it necessary to issue even more savage threats against their own people?

Part of the answer is to be found in the proclamation issued in Manila on April 4, 1899, by the First Philippine Commission, entrusted by the United States with the government of the Islands. That proclamation is too long to reproduce here in its entirety, but certain portions are worthy of note:

The attention of the Philippine people is invited to certain regulative principles by which the United States will be guided in its relations with them. The following are deemed of cardinal importance: . . . The most ample liberty of self-government will be granted to the Philippine people which is reconcilable with the maintenance of a wise, just, stable, effective, and economical administration of public affairs. . . . The civil rights of the Philippine people will be guaranteed and protected to the fullest extent; religious freedom assured and all persons shall have an equal standing before the law. . . . A pure, speedy, and effective administration of justice will be established whereby the evils of delay, corruption, and exploitation will be effectually eradicated. . . . Effective provision will be made for the establishment of elementary schools in which the children of the people will be educated. Facilities will also be provided for higher education.[2]

The rest of the answer is to be found in the actions of the two forces engaged in the conflict; in their actions toward each other and toward the people. Militarily, the U.S. forces quickly seized and consistently maintained the initiative. Wherever they could find the Philippine forces, they sought to bring them to battle. The Philippine forces began to adopt guerrilla tactics by September of 1899, nine months after the conflict had started; by November, all their forces had done so. Some were capable guerrillas, some were not, but the relentless pursuit by their opponents, the lack of support from the people gave them no alternative except death, capture, or resignation from the struggle.

It was their actions toward the civilian population that made the difference. The Philippine leaders felt that they had a just, natural claim on the support of the people; by and large, they took what they needed as a matter of right; they punished brutally those who failed to assist them. They talked of "independence," of a "republic," but they acted like feudal lords.

The leaders of the U.S. forces realized that their only claim on the support of the people was on the ground of good intentions; they realized that only their actions could prove their intentions. Some of the ways they offered proof, and the success achieved, are illustrated in this story, often heard from one of the most distinguished senior lawyers of Manila today, told here, as nearly as memory will serve, in his own words:

One bright morning in 1899, there were several companies of the Philippine insurrectionary forces on the beach near my home in Iloilo. My father was the leader of one of the platoons drawn up in formal array to oppose the landing of the Americans. Back of the beach, where we could watch, were the families of our soldiers.

When the American landing started, the troops were in such strength that our forces saw resistance was useless, so they decided to take to the hills as fast as they could. We spectators ran too. The Americans pursued us. As a little boy seven years old, I couldn't run as fast as the rest, so I dropped down behind a log to hide. One of the giant devils in a blue shirt jumped over the log and saw me. Instead of eating me, as I had been told he would, he picked me up, set me on his shoulder and continued trotting up the hill, looking for my father and his soldiers. Whenever he paused for breath, he would take a piece of candy out of his pocket and put it in my mouth. After a time, the pursuit was called off and the soldiers were ordered to return to the beach. My mount returned with them and carefully brought me along, setting me down not far from my home and saying something that must have meant "Run along home, sonny."

Quietly, the Americans entered the town, accepted the allegiance of the local officials, and left a small garrison before sailing away. Three days later, the school opened and a proclamation was made that all children should attend school. I had been going to school, but I didn't like it very much because the Spaniard who was the instructor believed the rod was the only road to understanding. My father, who had come home from the hills, insisted that I go back to school. Much to my surprise, there was an American as the teacher, an American I knew. It was the same soldier who had given me candy all the time he was chasing my father. From the first day of school on, I knew, and so did my family, that the Americans were not baby-eating devils; they had indeed come to free us and to help us to have a good government of our own. I have never found reason to change my belief.

The best evidence of how effectively the American soldiers persuaded the Philippine people that the United States' presence was in their interest is found in an address to the Filipino people that Emilio Aguinaldo, chief architect and director of the struggle against the Americans, issued on April 19, 1901. One paragraph is especially significant:

> The Filipinos have never been dismayed by their weakness nor have they faltered in following the path pointed out by their fortitude and courage. The time has come, however, in which they find their advance along the path impeded by an irresistible force—a force which, while it restrains them, yet enlightens the mind and opens another course by presenting to them the cause of peace. This cause has been joyfully embraced by the majority of our countrymen, who have already united around the glorious and sovereign banner of the United States. In this banner, they repose their trust in the belief that under its protection our people will attain all the promised liberties which they are even now beginning to enjoy.

That Aguinaldo then understood who had appealed most successfully to the attitudes of the people, that he prophesied truly and spoke at last for the people of the Philippines, history has amply demonstrated. Less than seven years after his address, the first Philippine Assembly met. Twenty-eight years after that meeting, the Philippines became entirely self-governing in name as well as in fact. The war launched by Japan in 1941 resulted in proof sufficient to convince the most skeptical that Americans and Filipinos were as one in their interests and their loyalty to the Philippines. It proved, too, that the Filipinos had been so imbued with the belief in constitutional government, in government of the people, by the people, and for the people, that they could and would not tolerate any other form of government.

Why, then, were the Hukbalahap successful in launching, and maintaining for some twelve years, a Communist guerrilla movement? Many factors contributed to the initial successes of the Hukbalahap, but the principal ones are clear and unmistakable. First, although the Huk were organized by a group whose purpose was to replace democratic government by Communism, this purpose was concealed behind a claim that their purpose was to fight the Japanese. So long as their announced targets were the Japanese, and the Filipinos who collaborated with them, the common people thought the Huk deserved support. By this deception, the Huk built their strength while the Philippines were governed by a brutal invader who scarcely bothered to cloak his actions under the simulation of law proffered by a puppet Philippine Government.

Second was the priority of emphasis given immediately after liberation, in 1945 and 1946, by the restored national government and its American assistants to re-establishing the normal services of government. The gravity of the threat posed by the Communists' field army was overlooked. This grave error, for which Filipinos and Americans must share the blame, gave the Huk an opportunity to consolidate their position, to direct their appeals to the attitudes most deeply rooted in the people of the area of operations.

The Huk called loudly for honest and efficient government (meaning one that would sweep away the debris of the war). The landlords they had previously attacked as Japanese puppets were now called exploiters, and the banners of "agrarian reform" and "Land for the Landless" unfurled. While they talked, and rebuilt their organization, the government was necessarily trying to achieve concrete results. It did achieve much, enough to satisfy reasonable people, but not enough to satisfy those who would not be satisfied. The government was handicapped in its efforts by the fact that it was an elected, constitutional government, not a dictatorial one. It held office by consent of the governed. No matter how conscientious, how patriotic, how self-sacrificing a member of government might be, he must always think of the next election if he was to continue in the service of the people.

Gradually, action began to be taken against the Hukbalahap. The military action from 1946 through most of 1950 was not successful nor yet could it be called entirely a failure.

The civilian population of Huklandia was by no means ignored by the government during this time. Many actions were undertaken in an effort to attract their support. After the Presidential campaign, the first significant government action was the cropsharing act, which sought to ensure the tenants a fair share of the harvest. However, since the tenant farmers did not interpret it as effective proof of government concern for their interests because it did not effectively improve their conditions, it was of little value in winning support for the government. The amnesty offered to the Huk in 1948 and the Peace Fund established to help in the rehabilitation of those suffering from the guerrilla conflict were both proclaimed measures to prove government concern for the welfare of the governed. Both were understood as political ploys, neither aggressively implemented nor effective in achieving their announced purpose. The Social Welfare Administration with great publicity undertook direct relief activities on occasion and did render effective help in many instances. Finally, in an effort to rally the people against the Huk, a popular organization, the "Barangay," a name drawn from Philippine tradition, was activated.

Many other actions were undertaken, but all failed to hit the civilian target effectively, despite wide publicity. Almost daily statements by government officials of their concern for the people were recorded dutifully, if not convincingly, by the press. Many, perhaps most, of these statements were sincere, did in fact reflect concern for the popular welfare. Manuel Roxas, the first President to understand the true nature of the Huk and seek to act effectively against them, was a great statesman and patriot, but few in Manila or in Huklandia, other than his political partisans or personal friends, were willing to concede him the most elementary virtues. Somehow nothing convinced the majority of the people of Huklandia that they should support the government.

The failure to win support was not confined to the members of the political party in power. The legal opposition, the party out of office, had little better success in attracting support, except from the noisier elements of the press. The Huk were even less successful. They, too, failed to convince the majority of the people in Huklandia or anywhere else that they deserved support.

The majority, in Huklandia and in Manila, unquestionably opposed, mildly or violently, both the Communists and the people in government. There seemed a national consensus that elected members of government acted primarily to ensure their re-election, their continued enjoyment of the perquisites of office. The actions of the appointive members of government, especially the Armed Forces, were seen as motivated primarily by a desire to keep in power the incumbent elected officials or their political heirs. In other words, government failed to convince the governed that government was indeed primarily concerned with and effectively advancing the welfare of the people.

The people of the Philippines respected the form of their government; they believed that it was the best system yet devised, but they felt completely at a loss as to how to make it effective. The officials saw no practical solution to the problem of holding Huk prisoners legally. The people felt themselves faced with a similar impasse. They saw no way of obtaining action in their interest from those who held the symbols of power. Of the problems the government had to solve if it was to continue to exist, that posed by the attitude of the people was the most serious and seemed the least susceptible to satisfactory solution.

By mid-1950, the situation was critical. The loud screams of the losers in the 1949 elections had very nearly succeeded in convincing the people that they could not change the people who made up the government by the accepted practice of elections. The losers, and the Huk and their sympathizers and their dupes, all screamed night and day that honest elections were impossible to achieve.

It was in this atmosphere that Magsaysay took office as Secretary of National Defense. The target given him was the Hukbalahap. As the civilian chief of the Armed Forces, he was responsible for making them effective; he had to lead them in running down, capturing, killing, or discouraging the guerrilla in the field against the government. Magsaysay knew that the Armed Forces could not accomplish this so long as the guerrillas had the active support of at least a minority of the population in the area of operations, and the passive tolerance of the majority of the population. He knew, too, that the increasing support the Huk were receiving was a direct outcome of national dissatisfaction with the actions of government.

Magsaysay acted effectively against the two obvious targets. He made the Armed Forces an instrument for securing the support of the people for their government; he made them also an effective instrument for pursuing, capturing, killing, or permanently discouraging the guerrilla. He announced his intentions; he announced his dramatic policy of "All-Out Friendship or All-Out Force," and then he acted to make good his words.

He seemed to be everywhere, checking on the enforcement of his directives, checking on the actions of the troops, ensuring, in short, that what he said would be done was done. As he saw things that needed to be done, whether they were in the sphere normally assigned to the Armed Forces or not, he said that appropriate action would be taken and he ensured that action was taken, if necessary by the Armed Forces. He welcomed publicity for his statements; he sought maximum publicity for the actions taken in accordance with them. More, he did not object to publicity for actions that were not in accordance with the mission of the government or of the troops as he proclaimed it to be, because he well knew that such actions, appropriately punished or redressed, were the best means of ensuring credibility for the intentions of government, of the Armed Forces, of himself.

The publicity given to actions directed against the guerrilla, given to actions that demonstrated the concern and effectiveness of government for the welfare of the governed, was the best possible approach to the national target. This publicity, by word of mouth, by the commercial press, the radio, the movies, went far toward convincing the people that there were men in government who said what they meant, who meant what they said, and who could and would act effectively.

There remained, however, a major obstacle to popular support of the government. This obstacle was a doubt, a doubt engendered largely by the propaganda of the unsuccessful candidates in the past elections and by the propagandists of the Huk, a doubt that the people themselves would be permitted to elect the officials they wanted. Magsaysay was a phenomenon; Magsaysay was a man whom no one could doubt, but Magsaysay was an appointive official, not an elected one. Could they elect officials like him? That was the question.

As the time for the 1951 elections drew near, despairing voices, many of them inspired by the Huk, began to be heard. This election would prove the failure of democracy in the Philippines; this election would be a mockery, a farce. In their direct propaganda, the Huk advised the people to boycott the elections because their votes would not be honestly counted. Belief that the election would not be honest was so widespread that it is questionable if any action or any statement of government could have been accepted at face value.

It was at this point that ex-guerrillas, heroes of the struggle against the Japanese, made what was probably their greatest contribution to the welfare of the Philippines. They organized the National Movement for Free Elections (NAMFREL). This organization was endorsed by and received the support of virtually every civic and patriotic group in the Philippines, and especially that of the Philippines Veterans Legion. NAMFREL loudly proclaimed that there would be free elections; that they would act as a third force to ensure that elections were free and were honest; that they as impartial poll watchers would make known any infringements upon the honesty of the elections.

The President of the Philippines had, as a matter of course, proclaimed that elections would be free and honest, that the Armed Forces would ensure the freedom of the polls. Unfortunately, the statement, however sincere, received little credence, because most people believed that the Armed Forces had been the principal instrument of corruption in the 1949 elections. Even the popularity and credibility Magsaysay had achieved could not of themselves have overcome the doubt about the role the Armed Forces would play in the 1951 elections.

The guarantees, the implied threats of NAMFREL, gave the needed opportunity for Magsaysay to act with credibility. On behalf of the Administration, he announced that the Armed Forces would be employed to guard the polls, to ensure their freedom; that they would welcome the presence of NAMFREL watchers and would cooperate with them in every way. This was a startling announcement. Even more startling was the announcement that ROTC students (for the most part, high-school and junior-college students) throughout the Islands would be mobilized and blanketed into the army for the purpose of serving as guardians at the polls.

The results were phenomenal. The troops, including many ROTC students, did guard the polls from interference; NAMFREL watchers, mostly respected USAFFE guerrilla veterans, watched the official watchers and the Armed Forces guardians. Special communications systems were set up by which irregularities at the polls could be independently reported to the national capital, to the radio, to the watching newspaper world, immediately. The polls were free; everybody agreed. There were a few instances of violence at the polls; these were promptly reported and the offenders were promptly placed under arrest. When the vote was counted, not even the most skeptical could doubt that the election had been free, at least so far as government could make it, because most of those elected were opponents of the incumbent Administration.

To all intents and purposes, the 1951 election sounded the death knell of the Hukbalahap movement. Of all the actions before or after that were taken to convince the people that the government was indeed their government, responsive to their will, effective in their interest, the 1951 election was the most convincing. It convinced the people that they could indeed change the men in government by the legal and morally acceptable means of election. The national target had indeed been reached.

Many lessons can be learned from the operations that resulted in the elimination of the Philippine insurrection and the Hukbalahap insurrection. Both were nominally indigenous rebellions. Both owed ideological allegiance to systems of government strange to the majority of the people of the country. In the earlier struggle, the system of government advocated by the leaders appealed to the educated and the intellectuals; in the later, the system of government—not too clearly explained—appealed to some intellectuals and presented itself as new, modern, effective government by the people. In both rebellions, the leaders of the revolution believed that the people owed them loyalty and sought to impose their ideas by force on those who did not concur. In both, the people ultimately repudiated the actions of the rebels.

The most important lesson to be learned is that success in both counterguerrilla operations was primarily the result of one solid achievement: convincing the people of the country that the government, the counterguerrilla, was effectively promoting the welfare of the governed. The truth of this is strikingly emphasized by the fact that, in the earlier operation the counterguerrilla government was alien, imposed from outside, like the preceding Spanish government. (So, to many Filipinos, was the government the leaders of the Philippine revolution sought to impose.) The government that eliminated the Huk was indigenous, elected by the people under a constitution and legal system they respected and admired. It was a government which they were capable of changing, a government to which they gave unstinted support when they were assured they could change it by legal means.

The successful elimination of one rebellion took about as long as did the successful elimination of the other. Tactics successful in one were successful when applied in the other. The principles successful in one were successful in the other. The lesson is that a government—whether it be one imposed by force from outside or a freely elected indigenous one—which succeeds in convincing the governed that it is acting effectively in their interests can be successful in eliminating a guerrilla movement. It is necessary only for it to act intelligently and effectively for the people and against the guerrilla, always emphasizing, always demonstrating, its effective pursuit of the ultimate goal of government—the welfare of the governed. The nation is the target of the guerrilla; it must be the target of the counterguerrilla as well.

NOTES

1. Quoted in Dean C. Worcester, *Philippines Past and Present* (New York: The Macmillan Company, 1914).

2. Quoted in *ibid.*

APPENDIXES

Appendix I

PATROL SOP FOR COUNTER-GUERRILLA OPERATIONS

Introduction: The purpose of this SOP is to present briefly basic doctrine governing patrolling in counterguerrilla operations. It supplements but, except as it modifies, does not replace official doctrine and tactics for patrolling and small-unit operations.

I. *MISSIONS*

   A. *General:* All patrols have three missions:

     1. To capture, kill, or harass the enemy.

     2. To obtain and report information.

     3. To win the support of the people to the government and the armed forces, by demonstrating their concern for the people.

   B. *Specific:* Each patrol will have a specific mission that is primary. This specific mission will usually be in implementation of one or more of the three elements of the general mission. All elements of the general mission will be accomplished to the maximum extent possible without serious jeopardy to success in the specific mission.

   C. *Typical Patrol Missions:*

     1. *"Flag" Patrols:* To demonstrate presence and intention of government to assist and protect its citizens. Ordered to proceed to one or more designated places along generally designated routes, seeking, recording, and, as feasible, acting on information about the enemy, the local inhabitants, etc.

     2. *Combat Patrols:* To determine if enemy are in an area or at a designated place; attacking and destroying the enemy with violence. Aggressive leadership and a desire to close with the enemy are essential to success.

     3. *Reconnaissance Patrols:* To secure both specific and general information about the enemy, the physical environment, and the local inhabitants. Securing

and reporting the information desired is the primary duty of the patrol. Destruction or harassment of the enemy will be accomplished whenever possible without seriously jeopardizing the primary mission. Recon patrols may accomplish deep penetrations of enemy territory, in which case they may be directed to avoid any actions that would reveal their presence (Class D patrols).

4. *Security Patrols:* Often motorized, their specific mission is to deter, by showing military presence, enemy action on routes of communications or against friendly installations. Essentially a form of command life-insurance, these patrols are precautionary measures to supplement, not replace, aggressive patrol action.

5. *Miscellaneous Patrols:* Accomplish special purposes, including arrests, service of court orders, emergency aid to civilians, escorting visitors, etc. Patrols of this type may be especially successful in securing information and demonstrating both the concern and the effectiveness of government.

II. *PATROL CLASSES*

A. *Overt:* In uniform, welcoming contact with civilians along the route. "Flag" patrols and security patrols will usually be of this class. Other patrols may be overt or not, depending on instructions of headquarters ordering the patrol.

B. *Attack:* In uniform, but avoiding contact or identification by civilians or enemy until the objective area is reached and combat offered. Many combat patrols will be of this class.

C. *Covert:* In civilian (or enemy) clothing, with or without display of weapons. Identification as military or government personnel usually avoided, except in contacts with trusted informers or when the tactical situation requires.

D. *Surreptitious:* In uniform or civilian clothing, seeking to avoid any notice being taken of their presence. Deep-penetration patrols, stay-behind parties, and observation posts will often be of this class.

E. *General Notes:* Patrols may shift from one class to another depending on the situation. Patrol briefing will cover anticipated conditions requiring such shifts, but shifts may be made, if necessary, at discretion of the patrol leader.

III. *PATROL PREPARATION*

A. *Patrol Designation:* Commander of unit dispatching patrol will designate and alert leader of patrolling unit, if possible twenty-four hours in advance. This notification will include mission, class, composition, and any special factors affecting patrol, to the extent security considerations permit. Higher headquarters, up to BCT level, will ordinarily be notified at the same time. Smallest unit normally employed on patrol will be half-squad; will be no smaller than one "buddy team." Unit integrity will be maintained, to include approval of replacements by patrol leader. Specialists may be attached. Subject to above limitations, patrols will be of smallest size commensurate with the mission, situation, and duration of the patrol.

B. *Patrol Leader Actions:* Notifies members of the patrol, inspects their clothing and equipment, draws necessary additional equipment, rations, and munitions. (See Section I of Patrol Report, Attachment 1, for composition and equipment of typical two-day Class A patrol.) Draws patrol notebook (see Attachment 2), propaganda and welfare materials, etc.

C. *Patrol Briefing:* Patrols will be briefed before departure by appropriate commander or staff officer. (When possible, all except routine security patrols will be briefed by BCT S-2 and S-5.) Briefing will follow standard five-paragraph field-order form, emphasizing specific and general missions of the patrol and any authorized departures from general mission. It will include review of administrative details, including passwords, commo plan, possible or probable contacts with other friendly forces, emergency resupply or evacuation plans, signals, etc. Briefing officer accomplishes Section I of Patrol Report (Attachment 1).

D. *Inspection:* Patrols will be formally inspected in ranks by an officer, preferably a commander. He will satisfy himself that all personnel are physically fit, alert, properly equipped, familiar with their duties and the patrol SOP.

E. *Patrol Order:* Patrol leader issues his patrol order immediately prior to departure. An officer of the company or higher headquarters will be present.

IV. *CONDUCT OF PATROL*

A. *General:* Will follow procedures consonant with good troopleading, appropriate to the mission and class of the patrol, and suited to the situation and the terrain. All-around security and a formation that will prevent the entire patrol from offering a single target are mandatory. In terrain affording cover or concealment, rendezvous points will be designated hourly.

B. *Reporting:* Commo checks will be made as scheduled, the situation and the equipment permitting. Patrol leader's notes will be written up every three hours when traveling, and after every significant incident.

C. *In Case of Doubt:* Act! If enemy, attack; if unknown, identify; if civilians, seek to assist if in need.

V. *AFTER PATROL*

A. *Immediate Action:* Upon return to base, patrol is formed and formally presented to an officer of the unit. Immediate medical attention will be given to those requiring it. Patrol leader will submit an oral report, in presence of patrol, covering important points: current information of enemy, enemy encounters, and conduct of members of patrol. Patrol will then be given hot meal.

Subsequent Action: After patrol has eaten and been dismissed, patrol leader, using his notes, completes Patrol Report in triplicate, and submits it, with verbal additions, to briefing officer or intelligence officer.

Notebook is filed in company headquarters, triplicate copy of report in company Intelligence section. Original and duplicate go to BCT headquarters. Original, after approval by BCT CO, is filed by AG. Duplicate copy is collated by S-2, S-3, and S-5 sections, and forms back-up for Barrio File. (See Attachment 3.)

ATTACHMENT I

HEADQUARTERS —TH BATTALION COMBAT TEAM ARMED FORCES OF THE PHILIPPINES

PATROL LEADER'S REPORT
SECTION I

Patrol #: *C-026*   Class A:
Patrol Leader : CHAMALES, J.E.,
  S/Sgt.

Organization: __Plat __Co

Briefing Officer : *LT. CARRANZA*
Departure: *090340 Hrs* __19__
Scheduled Arrival : *101700 Hrs*
____19__

MISSION (S) :
To proceed to
Bo. MACAN STO
CRISTO, TERESA,
and verify EN
CONC reported
thereat.

Members:

1. Patrol Ldr.—CHAMALES, J.E.,
   S/Sgt ASN 218926

2. Asst Patrol Ldr.-de la PAZ,
   Bert, PFC ASN 523141

3. Rifleman-RUPERTO, A.,
   PFC ASN 478524

4. BAR Man-SEGUNDINO, Q.,
   PFC ASN 478524

5. Radio Man-CANONIGO, A.,
   PFC ASN 499873

6. Aidman-Cook-LUNA, B.,
   PFC ASN 499871

Weapons & Equipment :

4 rifles M-I
  w/48 rds/ea.
1 Carbine M-1
  w/60 rds
1 BAR w/120 rds
1 Radio SCR-300
1 rifle grenade
  launcher
6 rifle grenades
6 hand grenades
4 flares
4 bayonets
1 trench shovel
1 guy rope 15
  feet
1 camera
1 kit, first
  aid, special

SECTION II

DATE-TIME   *LOG*

091015	Arrived Sitio MALAKING BATO. Conferred with Bo. Lt. ANSELMO NAGAHAS. Conditions peaceful and normal.
091630	Bivouacked at Sitio PUTIK. Conferred with store owner PROCOPIO BITING. People afraid Huks will rob the sitio.
100630	Arrived at MATAAS NA LUPA (hill) and observed. Obj (Bo. MACAN) guided by ANDRES REYES of Sitio PUTIK. Observed for 1 hr. Nothing suspicious. Entered Obj at 100810 hrs. Conditions normal and peaceful.
101300	Departed for home station.

SECTION III

INFORMATION SOURCE	SIGNIFICANT INFORMATION	CLASSIFICATION
Bo. Lt. MALA–KING BATO	He says: "Huks u/d Nr passed thru night of 8–9 Sept going North but did not molest anyone."	A-2
JOSEFA VELEZ	She says : "Comdr. TAGLE and 3 men armed with pistol and rifles visited Bo. MACAN night of 2-3 Sept with promise to return in 15 days to pick up supplies ordered from Bo. Lt. PEDRO LAHING."	B-2
MARIANO REYES of Sitio PUTIK	He says: "Unless AFP will push patrols up to Lagundi, the Huks will continue foraging at Putik."	C-3

Note: See the sketch locations of Sitios BULOG and LAGUNDI.

SECTION IV

Route Sketch (prepare on separate sheet, indicating patrol leader name, number of patrol, date, and area covered; staple to this sheet).

SECTION V

S-2 _____ PATROL LEADER   *CHAMALES, J.E. (S/Sgt.)*
S-3 _____ PROCESSED BY   *M. B. CARRANZA (1st Lt.)*
EX 0 _____ DATE FILED   *102310 HRS.*

Instructions: Use additional pages as needed. Staple together securely.

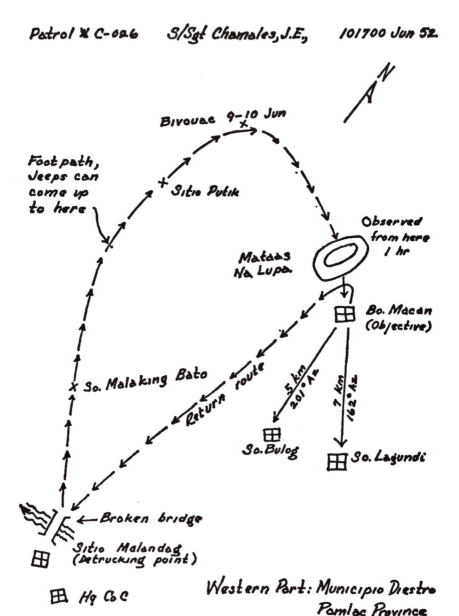

ATTACHMENT 2

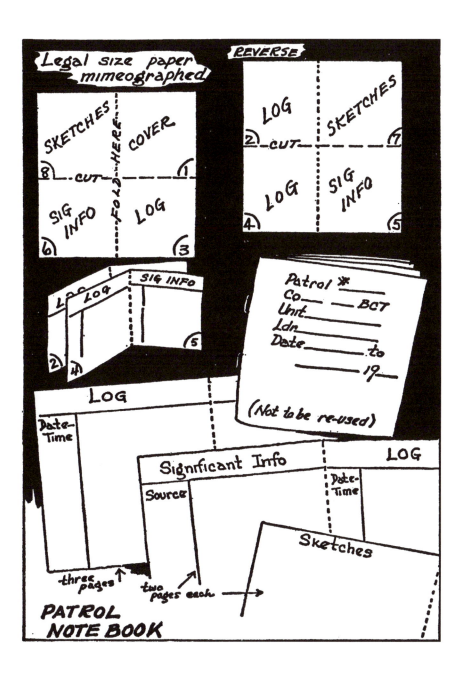

ATTACHMENT 3

THE BARRIO FILE (Maintained in company BCT headquarters):

a. This file will contain the following:

    (1) Name of barrio

    (2) Officials in the barrio

    (3) Sketch of the barrio and vicinity

    (4) Population and revenue

    (5) Geographical data

    (6) Economic data

    (7) Known enemy personalities originating from the barrio and their relatives

    (8) Names of suspects

    (9) Names of persons interrogated or investigated (detained or released)

    (10) Names of foreigners and their means of livelihood

    (11) List of licensed firearms and their holders

    (12) Political and social information

    (13) Religious organizations or sects and respective heads

    (14) Local defense

    (15) Names of government sympathizers

b. The Barrio File will be kept up to date and will be subjected to unannounced inspections. At BCT level, it is a joint undertaking of the S-2 and the CAO sections, the former being charged with the efficient maintenance of the file.

APPENDIX II

SUGGESTED SPECIAL
WARFARE BATTALION

Introduction: The Battalion Combat Team (BCT), as organized and employed by the AFP, well demonstrated the suitability of this type of organization for counterguerrilla operations. The British have successfully used battalions, grouped together in brigades to suit the occasion, for many years. Even the U.S. Army, in its "ROCID" divisions, recently sought to achieve the flexibility and economy of force offered by the separate battalion, with its "Battle Groups," as they were originally formed.

On the basis of the experience in the Philippines, and elsewhere, a battalion especially adapted to "special warfare" is suggested here. It is designed for area responsibility (its area may range from 200 to 2,000 square miles) and semi-independent action under conditions likely to be found in underdeveloped regions, where roads are few, cross-country trafficability (except by foot) is low, and resupply a problem for both antagonists. If its personnel are properly trained and motivated, the suggested Special Warfare Battalion is believed suitable for operations against numerically superior enemy, either guerrillas, who do not normally seek to hold terrain, or conventional forces, who use conventional tactics against it. By attaching a battery of artillery (or mortars, or rocketlaunchers) and issuing explosives (especially the Claymore type) to the combat elements, the SWB could well be employed in more conventional operations.

No attempt is here made to do more than suggest basic organization and purposes of the elements that compose it. The utilization, tactics, and justification for such an organization as the SWB have been covered, it is hoped, in the main text. Basically, the suggested organization (see Chart I) consists of a Headquarters and Service Company, to which is attached the battalion headquarters complement, an Air Support Detachment, a small Medical Detachment, and four Combat Companies.

Battalion Headquarters (Chart II): Follows conventional staff organization, but enlarged and adapted to meet special-warfare requirements. The Intelligence (S-2) section is strengthened, a Finance Officer added (in the S-1 section) to service the much larger "cash flow" requirements of successful special warfare, and an S-5 section established for civilian affairs and psychological operations. This S-5 section consists of one Civil Affairs Officer and four EM, with enough transportation and special equipment (projector, public-address system, mimeograph, portable power unit, etc.) to function effectively.

Headquarters and Service Company (Chart III): Services battalion headquarters, affords administrative and logistical support to the Combat Companies, accomplishes special operational missions for the battalion, and includes limited security forces. In addition to its company headquarters for internal administration and supply, it has two battalion support platoons: the Communications Platoon (Chart III-A) and the Transportation Platoon (Chart III-B); and two operational units: the Heavy Weapons Platoon (Chart III-C) and the Intelligence Platoon (Chart III-D).

The Communications Platoon is designed to provide normal communications services, including maintenance and repair. In addition, it is intended to have the capability of rehabilitating and supervising operation of civilian communications facilities, which, in operational areas, will often be found virtually abandoned. Further, it is designed to furnish communications support to clandestine operations conducted by intelligence or supporting units.

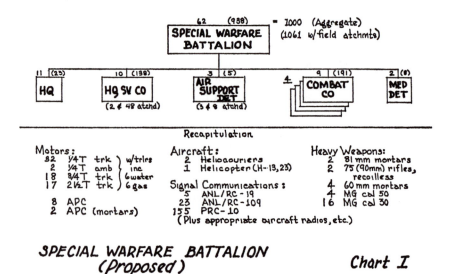

SPECIAL WARFARE BATTALION
(Proposed)   Chart I

The Transportation Platoon, which operates the battalion motor pool and performs third-echelon maintenance and repair for the battalion, has enough transport to move one-third of the battalion to any point in the operational area accessible to wheeled vehicles. In addition, it includes an APC (Armored Personnel Carrier) section to supply often needed armored track vehicles for road patrolling and for essential transport over routes under enemy fire. When operated for patrol or escort duties from Battalion Headquarters, they may be

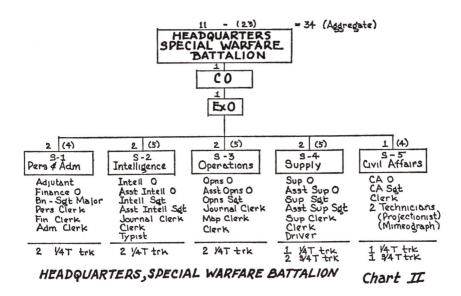

HEADQUARTERS, SPECIAL WARFARE BATTALION   Chart II

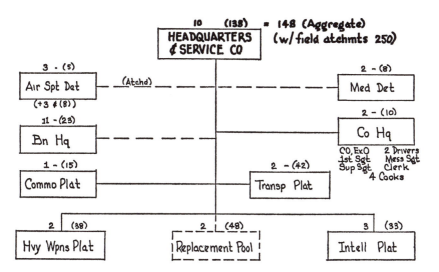

HEADQUARTERS & SERVICE CO (Special Warfare Bn) Chart III

manned by personnel of the Combat section, Heavy Weapons Platoon. Normally, under stabilized conditions, APCs will be attached to the Combat Companies and manned by their personnel.

The Heavy Weapons Platoon provides the support by high-explosive shells occasionally desirable in special-warfare actions. The Mortar section, armed with 81-mm. (or 4.1-inch) mortars, has vehicular mobility, since two of the ten

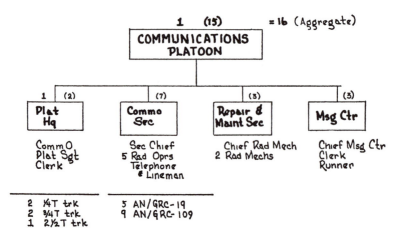

COMMUNICATIONS PLATOON
Hq & Svc Co (Spl Wfr Bn)

Chart III-A

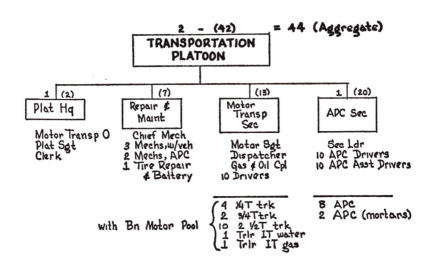

TRANSPORTATION PLATOON
Hq & Svc Co (Spl Wfr Bn)

Chart III-B

APCs are mortar carriers. The Rifle section is shown armed with 75-mm. recoilless rifles, which may be adapted for use either on quarter-ton trucks, or readily hand-carried. (Heavier rifles, either 90-mm. or 105-mm., may be desirable under some circumstances, but their greater weight, and especially the greater weight of the ammunition, render them less desirable for special warfare). The Combat section, in addition to its primary role in furnishing battalion road-patrol personnel and headquarters-area security, may be used to augment weapons crews, provide them local security, or act as ammunition bearers. All

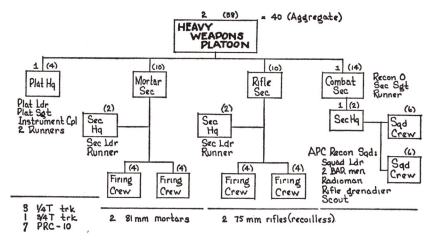

HEAVY WEAPONS PLATOON
Hq & Svc Co (Spl Wfr Bn)   Chart III-C

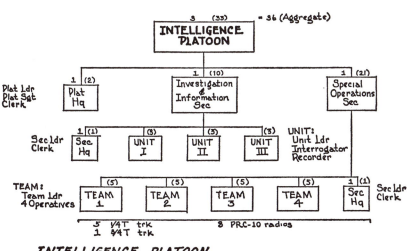

INTELLIGENCE PLATOON
Hq & Svc Co (Spl Wfr Bn)   Chart III-D

platoon personnel should be trained on other conventional infantry-support weapons, and the platoon should be furnished with an assortment of these, ranging from light machine guns and mortars to pyrotechnics and demolitions, all ready for immediate employment.

The Intelligence Platoon has two basic divisions, an Investigation and Information section and a Special Operations section. The former is responsible for supplying the Battalion Intelligence section with both overt and covert tactical, political, economic, and "societal" intelligence concerning the operational area. This section, which should operate in close liaison with any other intelligence organizations in the target area, will normally do the bulk of the work of organizing and servicing civilian-informant nets and of conducting "undercover" investigations among the civilian population. Its personnel should normally operate in civilian clothing and, in many cases, be kept physically away from the battalion area.

The Special Operations section, as its name implies, is the agency of the Battalion Intelligence Officer for special operational missions, ranging from penetration of enemy territory by surreptitious means to the capture of special prisoners. Each of its teams may be broken into smaller units, if the mission requires, or two or more teams may work together on major raids. Personnel of this section should be trained both for long-range patrol duties and in intelligence procedures.

In addition to the elements described, it is recommended that the Headquarters and Service Company be augmented by a non-TO replacement pool of approximately two officers and forty-eight enlisted men, when the battalion is assigned operational duties. This will not only permit keeping TO elements at strength, but also prevent the diversion of personnel from their assigned missions. If this is not done, it is recommended that one "patrol" (half-squad) of each Combat Platoon be deactivated, with half the personnel so made available placed in the company overhead to provide fillers for the squads, and half attached to the Headquarters and Service Company to be employed as auxiliaries.

Air Support Detachment (Chart IV): An organic Air Support Detachment, integral to the battalion, and normally attached to the Headquarters and Service Company, is deemed essential. For maximum economy in the employment of aircraft and trained personnel, the aircraft, with one pilot for each, and the enlisted service crews may be attached from higher echelons when the battalion is assigned operational duties. This will be acceptable only if the aircraft and personnel are then placed under the complete control of the battalion commander and made part of his own Air Support Detachment, whose permanently assigned personnel have trained with, and feel themselves an integral part of, the Special Warfare Battalion.

At operational strength, the Air Support Detachment is divided into a Headquarters section, a Flight section, and a Maintenance section. The Flight section

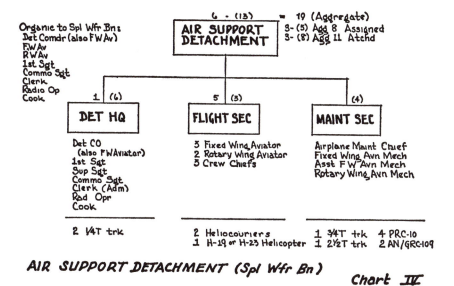

Organic to Spl Wfr Bn:
Det Comdr (also FWAv)
FWAv
RWAv
1st Sgt
Commo Sgt
Clerk
Radio Op
Cook

6 - (13) = 19 (Aggregate)
3- (5) Agg 8 Assigned
3- (8) Agg 11 Atchd

AIR SUPPORT DETACHMENT

DET HQ 1 (6)

Det CO
  (also FWAviator)
1st Sgt
Sup Sgt
Commo Sgt
Clerk (Adm)
Rad Opr
Cook

2 1/4T trk

FLIGHT SEC 5 (3)

3 Fixed Wing Aviator
2 Rotary Wing Aviator
5 Crew Chiefs

2 Heliocouriers
1 H-19 or H-23 Helicopter

MAINT SEC (4)

Airplane Maint Chief
Fixed Wing Avn Mech
Asst F W Avn Mech
Rotary Wing Avn Mech

1 3/4T trk   4 PRC-10
1 2 1/2T trk   2 AN/GRC-109

AIR SUPPORT DETACHMENT (Spl Wfr Bn)

Chart IV

is equipped with two light fixed-wing aircraft (preferably Heliocouriers), which should be fitted to carry light armament and supplied with radio relay equipment enabling linking PRC-10 and AN/GRC-109 radio nets. These aircraft are capable of furnishing airlift to small parties on special missions and of performing extensive aerial resupply and reconnaissance missions. In addition, the Flight section should have one light helicopter, to be used primarily for air evacuation of casualties or prisoners and for command, reconnaissance, and liaison missions.

Medical Detachment: Consisting of two officers and eight enlisted men, this detachment operates the battalion "hospital" and its ambulance service. A large portion of its duty will normally be the provision of medical service to civilians in the area of operations and "back-up" of the provision of services and supplies through the Combat Companies.

Combat Company (Chart V): There are four Combat Companies in the proposed Special Warfare Battalion, of which three may normally be assigned operational areas (ranging from 20 to 500 square miles) and one held as battalion reserve. Essentially an overstrength light-rifle company, the Combat Company is augmented by personnel for the special missions characteristic of special warfare. The company is divided into a Headquarters and Service Platoon and four Combat Platoons.

The Headquarters and Service Platoon performs for the Combat Platoons the services the Headquarters and Service Company performs for the Combat Companies. It includes Administrative, Intelligence, Communications, Transport, Medical, and Civil Affairs sections. The company commander should normally serve as his own intelligence and operations officer, while

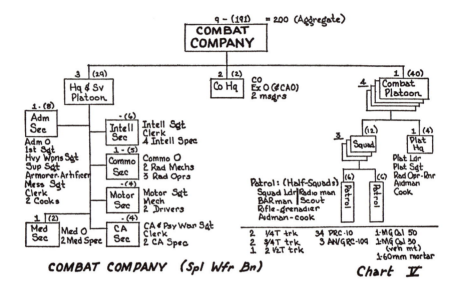

COMBAT COMPANY (Spl Wfr Bn)   Chart $\mathbb{V}$

the company executive officer assumes responsibility for civil affairs and for the supervision of the other staff sections. The heavy-weapons sergeant should organize and train crews, drawn from the platoon, for the heavy weapons assigned to the company. An all-around, self-contained platoon of this type will enable the company to accept responsibility for a relatively large sector and to operate effectively with its organic resources, organizing civilian-informant nets and civil-defense units, assisting the civilian population in relief and rehabilitation activities; in short, functioning as an effective representative of government. It may well be virtually the only representation that government has to its citizens in the area.

The Combat Platoon is the principal combat element of the SWB and may be expected to have much the same role as a company in conventional warfare according to contemporary doctrines. To this end, its headquarters includes a cook (who may serve in the company kitchen when the platoon is living with the company) and a well-trained aid man. It may undertake independent missions whose duration and range are limited only by the communications and logistic support given them. Each of the three squads in the platoon is divisible into two patrols, each with a radio and a rifleman with some knowledge of basic cooking and first aid. If buddy teams are, as is desirable, the basic training and maneuver elements, the "patrols" are the basic operational elements, and should be so trained and employed. Since in special warfare intensive, aggressive patrolling is the principal activity, the twenty-four half-squad "patrols," plus Headquarters and Service Platoon personnel, provide the capability for effective action from as many as five self-sufficient bases, and may be used either in uniform or "civvies" as the situation may dictate.

Comments: The flexibility of the proposed organization seems apparent. Two or more battalions can be grouped under a skeletal headquarters as a task force or brigade, or elements as small as a platoon may be detached for special missions.

Modifications in organization may be required for special situations. Most often, appropriate modification will consist of augmentation by personnel with special skills or elimination of vehicles.

Modifications in equipment, especially communications equipment, are greatly to be desired. Desirably, basic armament might consist of Armalite T-15 and T-7 rifles (with telescoping stocks). Individual equipment should be reduced to the minimum, with each soldier carrying barely more than poncho, warm underwear, and dehydrated rations.

Training, emphasizing initiative, self-reliance of buddy teams, aggressive action, and motivation, is second in importance only to good leadership.

Finally, the proposed organization is convertible. It can be employed in the field against guerrillas; or it may be infiltrated by increments into a denied area, and become an effective quasi-guerrilla force itself, one that may rapidly take on the desirable characteristics of a true guerrilla organization.

APPENDIX III

RECOMMENDED READING

A. SPECIAL WARFARE

Following is a somewhat arbitrary selection of publications pertinent to the subject of Special Warfare, especially as practiced in the Philippines. Inclusion of a title herein does not necessarily indicate that the bibliographer agrees with any, or all, of the ideas expressed, but it does indicate that the publication is judged significant. Works of special interest, but not readily available, are marked with an asterisk (*).

1. Basic Readings

*CALLWELL, MAJOR C. E. *Small Wars: Their Principles and Practice.* London: Intelligence Division, War Office, 1899.

> A museum piece of real value. Many of the tactics are as obsolete as the crossbow—yet, like the crossbow, are still effective, and may be required by tomorrow's wars.

Che Guevara on Guerrilla Warfare. With an Introduction by MAJOR HARRIES-CLICHY PETERSON. New York: Frederick A. Praeger, 1961.

> Possibly this manual has the greatest current significance (in view of Khrushchev's endorsement of the Cuban operation) of any readily available publication from the enemy camp.

CLAUSEWITZ, CARL VON. On *War.* Translated by O. S. MATTHIJS JOLLES. Washington, D. C.: Combat Forces Press, 1950.

———. *Living Thoughts of Clausewitz.* Washington, D.C.: Longmans, Green & Co., and *The Infantry Journal,* Fighting Forces Series (paper), 1943.

FORESTER, C. S. *Rifleman Dodd.* Little, Brown and Company, 1943.
    Fiction, but one of the best "worm's-eye" (or guerrilla's-eye) view books ever
    written. Should be mandatory reading. See also *The Gun* and *Ship of the Line,* by
    the same author.
GIAP, VO NGUYÊN. *People's War, People's Army: The Viet Công Insurrection Manual
    for Underdeveloped Countries.* With a Foreword by ROGER HILSMAN. New York:
    Frederick A. Praeger, 1962.
HEILBRUNN, OTTO. *Partisan Warfare.* New York: Frederick A. Praeger, 1962.
    This is the best of the readily available books on the theory of guerrilla war-
    fare, and its practice. Unfortunately, it tends to overemphasize Mao's doctrines,
    which are not in all respects basic to success in guerrilla operations.
*LANSDALE, EDWARD G. *Civic Activities of the Military in Southeast Asia.* Memoran-
    dum, Washington, D.C., 1959.
LINEBARGER, PAUL M. A. *Psychological Warfare.* Washington, D.C.: Combat Forces
    Press, 1954.
Mao Tse-tung on Guerrilla Warfare. Translated and with an Introduction by BRIGADIER
    GENERAL SAMUEL B. GRIFFITH. New York: Frederick A. Praeger, 1961.
MARSHALL, S. L. A. *Men Against Fire.* New York: William Morrow and Company,
    Apollo Edition, 1961 (paper).
*———. *Soldier's Load and the Mobility of a Nation.* Washington, D.C.: Combat
    Forces Press, 1950.
NEY, VIRGIL. *Notes on Guerrilla War.* Washington, D.C.: Command Publications, 1961.
    Should be read by everyone feeling a sense of personal concern for the defense
    of the U.S.
*U.S. MARINE CORPS. *Small Wars Manual.* Washington, D.C.: Government Printing
    Office, 1940.
    This is still by far the best official U.S. publication on the subject. Although a
    new version is reported to be in preparation, this, or an earlier edition, should be
    reprinted, for any new edition will probably omit the very realistic comments on
    desirable U.S. actions, as well as many valuable, seemingly obsolete but still useful,
    data on the use, selection, and care of animal transport, etc. The chapters on proper
    U.S. policies, supervision of elections, and relations with civilians are unexcelled.

2. The Philippine Experience

BACLAGON, ULDARICO S. *Lessons from the Huk Campaign in the Philippines.* Manila:
    M. Colcol & Co., 1960.
CHYNOWETH, B. G. "Lessons from the Fall of the Philippines," *Military Engineer,*
    Vol. XLVI (September, 1954).
DOROMAL, JOSÉ DEMANDANTE. *The War in Panay.* Manila: Diamond Historical Pub-
    lications, 1952.
ELARTH, H. S. *Khaki & Red* [n.p., n.d.].
FERTIG, WENDELL W., and KEATS, JOHN. *They Fought Alone: Fertig and the Mindanao
    Guerrillas.* Philadelphia: J. B. Lippincott Company, forthcoming.
    An account, by the commander, of the best-organized and most successful
    World War II guerrilla movement in the Philippines.

HOEKSEMA, RENZE L. *Philippine Communism.* Unpublished Ph.D. dissertation, Harvard University, Cambridge, Mass., 1956.

HOWZE, HAMILTON H. "The Rescue of Lt. Gillmore," *Army,* June, 1961.

*HURLEY, VIC. *Jungle Patrol.* New York: E. P. Dutton, 1938.

Possibly the finest book ever published on the achievements of men of two races fighting as one, it gives a vivid appreciation of the Filipino fighting man and his achievements in counterguerrilla warfare. It is highly readable although badly organized.

MOJICA, PROCULO L. *The Guerrilla Movement in Rizal Province.* Unpublished Master's thesis, Far Eastern University, Manila, 1955.

SCAFF, ALVIN H. *The Philippine Answer to Communism.* Stanford, Calif.: Stanford University Press, 1955.

This is a very good brief history of the Communist Party of the Philippines; rather goes overboard about EDCOR.

SHAW, HENRY J. *A Study of a Communist War of Liberation—The Huk Rebellion in the Philippines.* Unpublished Master's thesis, University of Virginia, 1962.

TARUC, LUIS. *Born of the People.* New York: International Publishers, 1953.

Written by Taruc and William Pomeroy and edited by Jesus Lava, this is a quasi-official Party-line history that fully satisfied none of those concerned, but gives much insight into the propaganda line of the Huk and the Communist Party of the Philippines, as expounded or accepted, perhaps not always too willingly, by these leaders.

*U.S. ARMY. *The Guerrilla Resistance Movement in the Philippines.* General Headquarters, U.S. Army Forces, Pacific: 1946.

Although incomplete, this is the best available general survey of the topic.

YAY, COLONEL [MARKING, YAY PANLILIO]. *The Crucible.* New York: The Macmillan Company, 1950.

3. Theory and Practice Elsewhere

"Atomic War and Partisans," reviewed in *Military Review* (June, 1957).

CHAPMAN, FREDERICK SPENCER. *The Jungle Is Neutral.* New York: W. W. Norton & Company, 1949.

DIXON, C. AUBREY, and HEILBRUNN, OTTO. *Communist Guerrilla Warfare.* New York: Frederick A. Praeger, 1954.

FRANCO ISAZA, EDUARDO. *Las Guerrillas de los Llanos.* Bogotá, Colombia: Librería Mondial, 1959.

HANRAHAN, GENE Z. *The Communist Struggle in Malaya.* Mimeographed. New York: Institute of Pacific Relations, 1954.

HENDERSON, IAN, and GOODHART, PHILIP. *Manhunt in Kenya.* Garden City, N.Y.: Doubleday & Company, 1958.

IND, ALLISON. *Allied Intelligence Bureau.* New York: David McKay Company, 1958.

Infantry. All 1962 issues of this magazine so far published contain useful material. See especially "Characteristics of Guerrilla Operations," in May–June issue.

KRUGER, RAYNE C. *Goodbye Dolly Gray.* Philadelphia: J. B. Lippincott Company, 1960.

The last chapters are a "how-to-do-it" guide for those who believe success in counterguerrilla operations can be achieved by physically isolating the guerrillas. A calculation of present-day costs would be useful.

MIERS, RICHARD C. H. *Shoot to Kill.* London: Faber & Faber, 1949.

OGBURN, CHARLTON. *The Marauders.* New York: Harper & Brothers, 1959.

OSANKA, FRANKLIN MARK (ed.). *Modern Guerrilla Warfare: Fighting Communist Guerrilla Movements, 1941–1961.* New York: The Free Press of Glencoe, 1961.
     This collection of articles includes the only readily available material on the Huk movement.

PEERS, W. R. "Guerrilla Operations in Northern Burma," *Military Review,* Vol. XXVIII (June, 1948).

SPECIAL OPERATIONS RESEARCH OFFICE. *Unconventional Warfare—An Interim Bibliography.* Washington, D.C.: The American University, 1961.

"The Three-in-One Plan," *Philippine Armed Forces Journal,* October, 1953.

U.S. ARMY, SPECIAL WARFARE CENTER. *Readings in Counter-Guerrilla Operations.* Fort Bragg, N.C.: 1961.

U.S. ARMY. *Special Warfare.* Washington, D.C.: 1962. See especially "Both Sides of the Guerrilla Hill," by R. C. H. Miers, and "Soldier of the Future," by Boyd T. Bashore.

"Ximenès," SOUYRIS, A., *et al.* "La Guerre Révolutionnaire," *Revue Militaire d'Information* (February–March, 1957).

ZAWODNY, J. K. (ed.). *Unconventional Warfare (The Annals of the American Academy of Political and Social Science,* Vol. CCCXLI), May, 1962.

B. THE PHILIPPINES

FORBES, W. CAMERON. *The Philippine Islands.* Boston: Houghton Mifflin Company, 1928.

SPECIAL TECHNICAL AND ECONOMIC MISSION. *Philippine Land Tenure Reform.* Mimeographed. Manila: U.S. Mutual Security Agency, 1952.
     One of the most opinionated and controversial official publications ever to come to the attention of the authors, this report is of value for its large body of data collected from many sources. These data form, in the report, the bases for value judgments which closely follow the old line, adopted by the Huk, of critical need for land reform in Central Luzon. These data can as readily be interpreted to show that Central Luzon probably should not receive priority in land reform or agricultural assistance.

TOLENTINO, ARTURO M. *The Government of the Philippines.* Manila: R. P. Garcia, 1950.

WORCESTER, DEAN C. *The Philippines Past and Present.* New York: The Macmillan Company, 1914.

INDEX

About the Authors

NAPOLEON D. VALERIANO was among the most highly regarded counter-insurgency experts in the Philippine army. During his career he was a key aide to President Ramón Magsaysay and the chief of police in Manila and of the Philippine Constabulary. Colonel Valeriano also was an advisor on security matters in Vietnam with his colleague Charles Bohannan. Subsequently, he was appointed a Philippine representative to the U.N. Security Council. He retired to the United States where he joined government-sponsored threat assessment teams in Guatemala and Colombia, and helped to train Cuban paramilitary forces.

CHARLES T. R. BOHANNAN was an American officer who survived the Bataan Death March and then became adept in irregular warfare while fighting the Japanese behind-the-lines. Trained as an anthropologist and geologist, he conducted operations after World War II against the communist guerrillas in the hinterland of the Philippines. Colonel Bohannan also served as an advisor in South Vietnam under Edward Lansdale, and later teamed with Valeriano to train anti-Castro forces in the Florida swamps.